HEALTHCARE
STRATEGIC
PLANNING

FIFTH
EDITION

HEALTHCARE STRATEGIC PLANNING

JOHN M. HARRIS AND
MEREDITH C. INNIGER, EDITORS

HAP

ACHE Management Series

Your board, staff, or clients may also benefit from this book's insight. For information on quantity discounts, contact the Health Administration Press Marketing Manager at (312) 424-9450.

This publication is intended to provide accurate and authoritative information in regard to the subject matter covered. It is sold, or otherwise provided, with the understanding that the publisher is not engaged in rendering professional services. If professional advice or other expert assistance is required, the services of a competent professional should be sought.

The statements and opinions contained in this book are strictly those of the author and do not represent the official positions of the American College of Healthcare Executives or the Foundation of the American College of Healthcare Executives.

28   27   26   25   24   5   4   3   2   1

Library of Congress Cataloging-in-Publication Data is on file at the Library of Congress, Washington, DC.

ISBN: 978-1-64055-438-2

The paper used in this publication meets the minimum requirements of American National Standard for Information Sciences—Permanence of Paper for Printed Library Materials, ANSI Z39.48-1984. ∞ ™

Manuscript editor: Deb Ring; Cover designer: Mark Oberkrom; Layout: PerfecType

Found an error or a typo? We want to know! Please e-mail it to hapbooks@ache.org, mentioning the book's title and putting "Book Error" in the subject line.

For photocopying and copyright information, please contact Copyright Clearance Center at www.copyright.com or at (978) 750-8400.

Health Administration Press
A division of the Foundation of the American
   College of Healthcare Executives
300 S. Riverside Plaza, Suite 1900
Chicago, IL 60606–6698
(312) 424–2800

Contents

Preface

Since the fourth edition of this book was published, healthcare organizations have faced the most extreme challenges in decades. A global pandemic, financial stress, workforce shortages, disruptive competition, and payment models shifting from volume to value have all forced healthcare organizations to make profound changes to survive and effectively serve their communities.

To be sure, many of these changes were emergency adjustments to operations needed to address the COVID-19 pandemic and its aftermath. But even when quick action was required, organizations that had a strong strategic plan in place were able to decide which strategies they would delay and which they would add or prioritize to address changing circumstances. Organizations with a strong strategic planning history were able to build on a culture of effective decision-making, prioritization, and teamwork—all critical skills required to succeed in these tumultuous times.

As healthcare leaders wrestle with rapid and profound changes, they must help their organizations develop and implement effective strategies to thrive. This fifth edition of *Healthcare Strategic Planning* provides a how-to guide for healthcare organizations to undertake strategic planning in this dynamic environment.

In the seven years since the previous edition was published, the strategic planning process that we outline in this book has evolved based on the insights of our Veralon consulting colleagues who apply this process as well as feedback from the clients with whom it was used.

In this revised edition, we provide core insights into strategic planning practice and theory and illustrate how those insights can be applied to healthcare organizations. In addition to a step-by-step presentation of the strategic planning process, the book includes essential advice on critical aspects of successful planning, such as stimulating truly strategic thinking, executing implementation, and maximizing results through annual plan updates.

We also provide something completely new in this edition. As we worked with leaders of hospitals, health systems, and other healthcare organizations, they pointed to the need for clear information on key topics that often need to be addressed in the strategic plan. In chapters 13–19, we provide brief yet in-depth guides for thinking about key strategic topics. We are deeply appreciative of our "Brain Trust"—our colleagues at Veralon, a national healthcare management consulting firm—for contributing this material based on their areas of expertise.

The following individuals were key contributors to these new chapters:

Chapter 13: Strategic Financial Planning—Ross Shuster, Clare O'Mara
Chapter 14: Innovation—Mark Dubow, John M. Harris
Chapter 15: Intensifying Competition—Mark Dubow, Meredith Inniger
Chapter 16: Partnerships, Mergers, and Affiliations—Danielle Bangs, Daniel M. Grauman
Chapter 17: Value-Based Care—Molly Johnson, John M. Harris
Chapter 18: Physician Enterprise—Rudd Kierstead, Karin Chernoff Kaplan
Chapter 19: Governance—Keith Wysocki, Meredith Inniger

The tools provided in this new edition will help CEOs, planners, physicians, trustees, and other professionals understand key concepts and make the planning process a robust learning and growth experience for their organization.

The following is a chapter-by-chapter summary of the updates and additions to this text since the last edition:

- Chapter 1—The Value of Strategic Planning
  In this chapter, we have placed more emphasis on the value and benefits of strategic planning alignment among stakeholders, particularly between the board, executive team, and management, as well as how planning has evolved since the beginning of the COVID-19 pandemic.

- Chapter 2—The Benefits of Strategic Planning
  This chapter covers new issues that planners should consider, such as the impact of social media on hospitals, the new focus on physician alignment, how the pandemic has fundamentally changed access to care, patient expectations for telehealth, workforce implications, and the national focus on health equity.

- Chapter 3—Organizing for Success
  We have added an emphasis on stakeholder engagement by category and applying learnings and takeaways from prior planning processes.

- Chapter 4—Major Planning Process Considerations
  This chapter includes updated tools with a new focus on engaging stakeholders virtually and new facilitation considerations.

- Chapter 5—Encouraging Strategic Thinking
  In this chapter, we have updated the discussion of using strategic thinking in management.

- Chapter 6—Phase 1: Analyzing the Environment
  This chapter includes an expanded framework for internal and external analyses.

- Chapter 7—Phase 2: Organizational Direction
  We have updated and added new examples (from organizations in healthcare and other industries) and reconceptualized the chapter for more organized reading.

- Chapter 8—Phase 3: Strategy Formulation
  This chapter has been entirely updated to provide a more direct approach to strategy development, consistent with how our practices with clients have become more streamlined.

- Chapter 9—Phase 4: Transition to Implementation
  We have added new research and expanded ideas for developing annual implementation plans to help keep the strategic plan alive.

- Chapter 10—Annual Review and Update
  This chapter includes updated ideas on how to make strategic planning stick based on lessons learned in the field.

- Chapter 11—Enabling More Effective Execution
  An important piece of any strategic planning process, lessons learned outside of healthcare and new strategies for effective implementation have been added to this chapter.

- Chapter 12—Future Challenges for Strategic Planners
  We have summarized research and recommendations for the future for healthcare strategic planners and strategists including special skills and knowledge required.

- Chapter 13—Strategic Financial Planning
  This new chapter focuses on key issues related to strategic financial planning, how financial planning connects to the overall strategic planning process,

prioritizing initiatives that require investment, and other
financial planning considerations.

- Chapter 14—Innovation
  This new chapter addresses key clinical and
  technological innovations in healthcare and how they can
  affect the strategic planning process, outcomes, and overall
  competitive advantage.

- Chapter 15—Intensifying Competition
  This new chapter addresses the variety of new
  competitors that are emerging in healthcare, highlights
  key elements of these new competitors' strategies, and
  identifies strategic responses that healthcare organizations
  can use to address these new competitive challenges.

- Chapter 16—Partnerships, Mergers, and Affiliations
  This new chapter focuses on the key types of
  partnerships, mergers, and affiliations and provides
  considerations for healthcare leaders when evaluating
  different relationship types and addressing this complex
  issue in the context of the strategic planning process.

- Chapter 17—Value-Based Care
  This new chapter provides an overview of the current
  state of value-based care and population health, explores
  why many organizations are including value-based care
  as a core strategy, and discusses how to address it in the
  strategic plan.

- Chapter 18—Physician Enterprise
  This new chapter focuses on the key features of the
  physician enterprise (e.g., quality, culture, alignment,
  financial performance) and how to address the physician
  enterprise as part of the strategic plan.

- Chapter 19—Governance
  This new chapter highlights governance best practices, discusses how governance practices intersect with strategic planning, and explains how to address the evolving complexity of governance as healthcare organizations grow.

We hope that you enjoy the fifth edition of *Healthcare Strategic Planning*. Seven years of interaction with clients and presenting to audiences and colleagues have offered much grist for the mill in updating this book. We express our sincere gratitude to all clients of Veralon. By responding to your questions and needs, we have been able to customize and refine our approaches, and we have gained insights that we have the privilege of sharing throughout this book.

John M. Harris
Philadelphia, Pennsylvania
Meredith C. Inniger
Bentonville, Arkansas

March 2024

Making the Case for Strategic Planning

- Identify the organization's current position, including present mission, long-term objectives, strategies, and policies.
- Analyze the environment.
- Conduct an organizational audit.
- Identify the various alternative strategies based on relevant data.
- Select the best alternative.
- Gain acceptance.
- Prepare long-range and short-range plans to support and carry out the strategy.
- Implement the plan and conduct an ongoing evaluation.

The first edition of this book synthesized steps from these two approaches, as illustrated in exhibit 1.1. Since then, this process has been used by the authors for a variety of healthcare organizations.

The first stage is the strategic assessment, which focuses on the question, *where are we now?* It has three primary outputs:

1. Evaluation of competitive position, including advantages and disadvantages
2. Assumptions about the future environment
3. Distillation of key strategic issues to address

The goal of the strategic assessment is to determine how an organization may fare in the future given its current position and likely future conditions and to pinpoint the factors most critical to generating future competitive advantage.

The second stage of the planning process is organizational direction, followed by the third stage, strategy formulation. Stages 2 and 3 address the question, *where should we be going?* The main activity of the organizational direction stage is to define a desired future state by examining possible future external realities, mission, vision, and values.

Strategy formulation establishes goals, objectives, and major initiatives for the organization. The purpose of stages 2 and 3 of

Exhibit 1.1: The Strategic Planning Approach

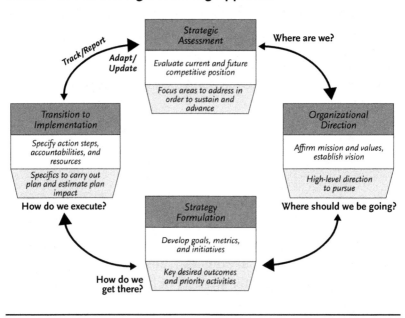

© 2024 Veralon Partners Inc.

the planning process is to determine what broad future direction is possible and desirable and what future scope of services and position the organization will strive to achieve.

The fourth stage is implementation planning—*how do we get there?* This stage involves identifying the actions needed to implement the plan. Key activities include mapping out the tasks to accomplish the goals and objectives, setting a schedule, determining priorities, and allocating resources to ensure implementation. Implementation should begin as soon as possible after completion of the plan, if not during the final stage. Teams should ensure that commitment to ongoing monitoring of plan implementation and completion of periodic updates and revisions, as needed, are in place prior to finalizing the plan. Each stage of the planning process is discussed in detail in the following chapters.

BUT WHY STRATEGIC PLANNING?

Understanding Primary Criticisms

As referenced in the opening of this chapter, not everyone agrees that strategic planning is an effective way to set good strategy. Several criticisms and possible pitfalls commonly arise (the next section comprises a list of the latter), but three primary criticisms of strategic planning prevail:

1. It relies on past or current conditions and performance as relevant predictors of the future.
2. It yields a static output that is unable to account for dynamic realities.
3. The formality and prescriptiveness of the process may actually hinder the thoughtful reflection and forward-looking creative thinking that is critical to good strategy.

Note that none of the primary criticisms of strategic planning actually preclude it from being a useful means to good strategy. Criticisms assume that certain attributes of planning are inherent or immutable, and that potential problems with some planning processes can be generalized to discredit the whole of strategic planning. As evinced in part in the following chapter and elaborated in later chapters, these assumptions are not necessarily valid.

For example, consider the first of the primary criticisms noted earlier—reliance on the past to predict the future. Yes, the practice of scanning the environment and the organization's performance and position requires using historical data. However, in a well-conceived strategic planning process, findings from analysis are not intended to be used as a basis to project forward. Rather, as described in chapter 6, historical data are just one input that must be contextualized based on assumptions about the future environment. This criticism falsely assumes that because planning *could* rely solely on past information to make decisions about the future, then it must necessarily do so, or that it could not be otherwise balanced by incorporation of future-oriented thinking.

The second criticism implies that strategic plans are not effective guides once the environment shifts or the organization undergoes change. This inference would be logical if the planning process ended after strategy formulation and development of initial action plans; however, as described in chapters 9 and 10, an effective planning process establishes and activates a continuous implementation and plan management approach that ensures ongoing review and updates. These activities are typically sufficient to minimize the risk of plans becoming gradually less relevant and thus less useful over time.

The third criticism is more philosophical. It suggests that formal structures impede originality and therefore undermine strategic thinking. However, every artist works in a particular medium or media. Artists are constrained in some ways by the guidelines and tools of their chosen medium, but they nonetheless express inspiration and imagination. A well-structured strategic planning process, as described in the remainder of this book, functions much like these guidelines and tools. It provides a framework to gather information, input, and insight supporting the development and implementation of effective strategy. Absent such a structure, an organization could theoretically get lucky, creating and executing great strategies, but it would be following a far riskier path that could more easily lead it astray.

Despite these criticisms, organizational leaders should focus on getting the strategic planning process right for their organization, not skipping it. While modifications to the comprehensive strategic planning process that outlined in this chapter can be made, the fundamental logic behind and core steps of the planning approach should remain. While there is an ongoing debate over the efficacy and methods of strategic planning, it remains the most relevant means to develop strategy. Too often, leaders who avoid strategic planning also bypass strategic thinking.

Even so, linking strategic planning to good strategy and specific organizational success is difficult (Ginter, Duncan, and Swayne

2018; Kaissi and Begun 2008). However, because strategic planning requires examining functionality and sustainability, it improves awareness of an organization's relative strengths and weaknesses. This enhanced awareness generates focus, which alone can have a positive impact on organizational performance and thus improve chances of long-term survival. Nonetheless, pinpointing specific effects of strategic planning is challenging, and success will depend on and vary with managerial, environmental, and organizational factors (Taiwo and Idunnu 2010).

The authors of this book fully acknowledge that strategic planning has limitations, and it is not a foolproof way to create effective strategy. Further, we reiterate the merit in understanding and purposefully addressing key criticisms. In fact, subsequent chapters dedicated to each of the four stages of the strategic planning approach specifically identify how planning can go wrong and how to recognize and proactively correct for such challenges.

Understanding Common Pitfalls

The previously mentioned primary criticisms are the basis of many common problems faced in strategic planning, but several others are worth noting, as they often leave leaders jaded about the value of such planning.

Failing to Involve the Appropriate People
Sometimes too many stakeholders are involved; sometimes too few. Sometimes the number of participants is fine, but those involved are not necessarily the "right" people. Thoughtful involvement of the right type and mix of internal and external stakeholders is essential to both strategy development and successful implementation.

Conducting Strategic Planning Independent of Financial Planning
If financial considerations are excluded from the strategic plan, strategies may never become a reality. Sound strategic planning explicitly

incorporates financial realities and tests the financial reasonableness of executing an identified strategic approach.

Falling Prey to Analysis Paralysis

The fast-paced healthcare market demands that provider organizations respond to opportunities and threats without extensive delays. Therefore, squandering time by endlessly analyzing and reanalyzing data in the hopes of more accurate baselines or forecasts works against the intent of planning: to prepare for and effectively respond to change.

Not Addressing the Critical Issues

Planning teams may avoid the most pressing issues because they are too difficult to discuss or address. In addition, planning teams may identify a litany of issues but fail to narrow the list to those that are most critical. If leadership is not prepared to address key issues or to actively ensure a sense of focus, strategic planning can ignore or overlook the most threatening challenges and potentially powerful opportunities.

Failing to Align Board, Executive Team, and Management

Even an objectively great strategic plan cannot succeed unless it is strongly supported by those responsible for its execution. Leadership and strategic plan facilitators must purposefully build this support and cannot ignore disagreements or even a lack of strong, visible consensus on key plan components. The board should receive commitment from management on the goals and initiatives that have been agreed upon. Similarly, management receives authority delegated by the board to implement these initiatives and the commitment of resources to achieve success.

Ignoring Resistance to Change

Like the inability to tackle what is truly critical or to build appropriate consensus, ignoring resistance to change will have detrimental long-term consequences. The types and degree of change proposed in a plan must be seen by all involved as necessary to future organizational success. Organizational leaders must swiftly and directly address persistent opposition to change to avoid devastating effects, including significant delays, wasting of time and resources, and even complete derailment of progress.

Ineffectively Transitioning from Planning to Execution
Failure to execute is both common and highly detrimental. An organization cannot simply identify goals and objectives and assume that identification will result in implementation. Rather, a purposeful and thorough transition from planning to execution must occur that clearly establishes accountabilities and the action steps that create a path forward. Without such care, the day-to-day operational crises that inevitably arise will consume staff and leaders, leaving execution of strategy an afterthought. Further, goals and objectives must be precise and measurable enough to create individual accountability and make success or failure obvious.

Understanding Key Benefits

Chapter 2 is dedicated to realizing the benefits of strategic planning, but a high-level summary of the advantages of strategic planning is helpful as well. C. Davis Fogg (2010) suggests the following benefits of strategic planning:

- It secures the future for the organization and its leaders by crafting a viable future business.
- It provides a road map, direction, and focus for the organization's future—where it wants to go and the routes to get there. It lets each part of the organization align its activities with the direction of the corporation in a continuous process.
- It sets priorities for crucial strategic tasks, including complex, pressing issues such as lack of direction

and growth, lack of profitability, and organizational ineffectiveness—issues that everybody talks and knows about yet remain unaddressed.

- It allocates resources available for growth and change to the programs and activities with the highest potential payoff.
- It establishes measures of success so that the progress of the organization and individuals can be gauged. Knowing where one stands is a fundamental business and human need.
- It gathers input and ideas from all parts of the organization on what can be done to ensure future success and eliminate barriers to that success, following the old adage that two (or ten, or a hundred, or a thousand) heads are better than one.
- It generates commitment to implementing the plan by involving all parts of the organization in the plan's development.
- It coordinates the actions of diverse and separate parts of the organization into unified programs to accomplish objectives.

Fogg (2010, 76) further notes that "when all is said and done, employees also recognize what's in it for them personally: the resources to do what they want if they plan; a more secure future if the organization plans well and does well; financial rewards if they make themselves heroes as a result of the process; recognition by their peers and superiors if they succeed; and, of course, the inverse of all the above if they fail."

Ginter, Duncan, and Swayne (2018) believe that the three stages of strategic management—strategic thinking, strategic planning, and strategic momentum—provide many benefits, including

- tying the organization together with a common sense of purpose and shared values;
- improving financial performance in many cases;

- providing the organization with a clear self-concept, specific goals, and guidance and consistency in decision-making;
- helping managers understand the present, think about the future, and recognize the signals that suggest change;
- requiring managers to communicate both vertically and horizontally;
- improving overall coordination in the organization; and
- encouraging innovation and change in the organization to meet the needs of dynamic situations.

For many organizations, the true value of strategic planning lies in the process more than the plan document. However, as David A. Nadler (1994) points out, most plans have a fast rate of depreciation, and they must be refreshed to maintain their currency. Furthermore, much of the value of planning isn't the actual plan, but rather the shared learning, shared frame of reference, and shared context for ongoing decision-making.

Indeed, changes that influence a strategic plan may occur daily, and new ideas may surface once the plan is complete. A successful strategic plan enables providers to establish a consistent, well-articulated direction for the future. However, it is also a living document that teams must monitor and revise to meet the anticipated and unanticipated needs of the organization and the market, whether changes occur in clinical services, managed care, integrated delivery, payment models, healthcare reform, systems development, technological advances, or other arenas.

STRATEGIC PLANNING IN HEALTHCARE

Compared to organizations in other major sectors of the economy, healthcare provider organizations historically survived using less formalized planning approaches. Prior to the 1970s, healthcare provider organizations were predominately independent and not-for-profit, and healthcare planning was usually conducted on a local or regional basis by state, county, or municipal governments. Though strategic planning was formally introduced in the early 1970s, healthcare organizations used it only sporadically, and their focus remained on better identifying and meeting community needs rather than more modern competitive objectives.

As illustrated in exhibit 1.2, government regulation became more prominent in healthcare in the late 1970s. Healthcare organizations undertook planning efforts in part to address new regulatory barriers, but the fee-for-service system continued to ensure a steady revenue stream. Therefore, when healthcare organizations engaged in strategic planning, the effort often focused on creating physical capacity to accommodate more and more volume—the prevailing notion being that "if you build it, they will come." The 1980s brought privatization and corporatization to the healthcare sector. Hospitals were consolidated into systems, and healthcare corporations began to enter and organize other healthcare-related fields. The 1990s and the first decade of the 2000s were characterized by the chaos of managed care and competition among providers that had previously been collegial. Strategic planning conducted at this time heavily emphasized maximizing reimbursement.

As the central principles of broader healthcare reform took shape in the 2010s, it started to become clear that healthcare organizations would have to do more with less. This continued into the 2020s amid the COVID-19 pandemic and the financial difficulties that health systems subsequently experienced. These issues remain true today and will likely hold, regardless of future political changes, because some certainties are clear: Healthcare costs have grown at rates above general inflation, increasing the burdens on employers, governments, and individuals. The population will continue to age. Patient care that is coordinated and that produces objectively higher-quality outcomes will be rewarded. The shortage of physicians, nurses, and other care professionals will not go away. As a result, providers across the country are examining their current and future role in an era when quality, consumer orientation, cost competitiveness, scale and scope, and integration will move to the forefront of strategic priorities. Many will need a strategic overhaul to orient the organization to the realities of a new era in healthcare delivery, financing, and competition. Providers will be challenged to innovate across all domains, and differentiation will require proactive development of an array of new competencies for clinicians and business leaders. Transformational information technology and competition from entrepreneurs outside healthcare as well as both for-profit provider and financing entities will add additional complexity to the healthcare landscape. Healthcare provider organizations with thoughtful, sound strategic plans will be best positioned to adapt with contingency plans as change takes place.

Evolution of Healthcare Strategic Planning

The first-generation healthcare strategic planning approach that was developed in the 1970s is clearly much less relevant in today's complex environment. As a result, the application of strategic planning in healthcare organizations today differs from that of the past in five critical ways:

1. Healthcare is changing at an unprecedented pace. This pace presses organizational leaders to conduct strategic planning in a more dynamic fashion. Historically, strategic plans were completed on a ten-year time horizon. Now, that timeline is often three years, and rarely longer than five years.

2. The competitive environment is much more intense than at any time in the past. The number of competitors, the increasing for-profit influence in healthcare delivery, the decline of geographic barriers to competition as a result of the internet, and other less significant factors raise the competitive stakes and force strategic planning to be more externally focused and fluid.

Exhibit 1.2: A History of Healthcare Strategic Planning

	1960s	1970s	1980s	1990s	2000s	2010s	2020s
Environment	Medicare and Medicaid established Fee-for-service (FFS) Cost-plus reimbursement	FFS Federal regulation Growing hospital expenses and profits	Hospital system formation Diagnosis-related groups (DRGs) Capitation	Growing competition Expansion of managed care First-generation federal health reform proposed	Pay for performance (P4P) State-based health reform Major pharma and technology advancements	Emergence of value-based payment Reduced hospital-centricity Affordable Care Act (ACA)	COVID-19 pandemic Investor-backed disruption
Strategic Planning Focus	Little need; not widely used Meeting community needs	Adding capacity; building hospitals	Consolidating hospitals Containing costs	Maximizing reimbursement Protecting territory and margins	Optimizing payer mix Maximizing P4P incentives Appealing directly to consumers	Creating scale Integrating care delivery Demonstrating quality and cost performance	Reestablishing financial sustainability Achieving efficiencies through consolidation Stronger competitive stance

3. Healthcare organizations have grown into vast multi-entity systems. The emergence of such systems, especially in the past five to ten years, has ratcheted up the complexity of strategic planning.
4. Intense competition and the COVID-19 pandemic have destabilized the financial underpinning of healthcare delivery. When organizations are operating in an environment of increasing financial risk and uncertainty, strategic planning needs to be linked more clearly to financial planning and contribute more directly to financial performance.
5. The time frame in which to act and generate results is tightening. Strategic planning must address near-term pressures while still directing organizations toward long-term targets.

However, even if healthcare strategic planning has become much more sophisticated, planning approaches must continue to evolve to address emerging and dynamic challenges affecting all aspects of healthcare delivery and financing.

Ensuring Applicability of Strategic Planning in Healthcare

Much strategic planning and strategy for healthcare organizations has emphasized operational effectiveness—doing the same things as peers and competitors but doing it better (that is, with higher quality or more efficiently) as opposed to true competitive differentiation. However, some strategy experts (Porter 1996) assert that operational effectiveness is not strategy, largely because operational effectiveness does not satisfy several of the criteria for effective strategy: sustainability, competitive advantages, and direction. Organizational leaders often express a similar sentiment when they say, "Achieving operational effectiveness is a given."

Although typical business practices in the for-profit and private sectors have been advocated as applicable to healthcare, there are legitimate questions about the validity of assuming that business paradigms are appropriate in healthcare (Ginter, Duncan, and Swayne 2018). In addition to, and in some ways as a result of being a primarily not-for-profit and mission-driven field, healthcare is different from other fields in key ways that may mitigate the applicability of standard business practices, including the following:

- Healthcare services are not a typical product and cannot be standardized.
- It is difficult for users to predict when they will need healthcare or how much they might need.
- Unpredictable needs result in unpredictable costs and little price transparency, making it hard for consumers to make decisions based on value.
- The user is not the payer for most of the cost, though high-deductible health plans are reducing this dynamic.
- Information asymmetry persists, as the provider of services has knowledge and expertise that the user would not reasonably have, even with access to online medical information.
- Physicians are key decision makers but may not be part of the healthcare organization or subject to the same set of incentives.
- Providers routinely address serious health issues (some are life and death) that elevate individual and societal expectations beyond those in a simple commercial transaction.
- Healthcare organizations are subject to a unique set of regulations:
  - They may not be able to divest from a service even if it is not profitable.

- They can only "choose" customers to a limited degree.
- They are subject to significant governmental and other regulatory bodies, mandates, and compliance requirements.

Ginter, Duncan, and Swayne (2018) summarize the implications of these unique traits on healthcare providers with regard to strategic planning and strategy:

- Some strategic alternatives available to nonhealthcare organizations may not be realistic for many healthcare organizations.
- Healthcare organizations have unique cultures that influence the style of and participation in strategic planning.
- Healthcare has always been subject to considerable outside control.
- Society and its values place special demands on healthcare organizations.

These factors clearly call for healthcare providers to develop a customized approach to strategic planning that accounts for the industry's distinctive qualities—a process that, to an extent, has begun to occur and will continue to evolve with time. The sector's uniqueness does not, however, discredit the relevance of strategy-related business practices in general. In fact, the type of healthcare sector changes underway, as well as the fast pace and amplitude of changes, suggests that strategic business practices from other industries may be more relevant to healthcare in the future. In any case, healthcare sector transformation necessitates healthcare organizations' adoption of sophisticated strategic planning and management practices to adapt and thrive in the future.

REFERENCES

Beckham, J. D. 2016. *Beckham on What Good Strategy Is.* Southeastern Institute for Health Care Strategy and Innovation. Published July 29. www.hcstrategyinnovation.com/assets/WhatGoodStrategyIs .pdf.

———. 2000. "Strategy: What It Is, How It Works, Why It Fails." *Health Forum Journal* 43 (6): 55–59.

Campbell, A. B. 1993. "Strategic Planning in Health Care: Methods and Applications." *Quality Management in Health Care* 1 (4): 12–23.

Eisenhardt, K. M. 1999. "Strategy as Strategic Decision Making." *Sloan Management Review* 40 (3): 65–72.

Evashwick, C. J., and W. T. Evashwick. 1988. "The Fine Art of Strategic Planning." *Provider* 14 (4): 4–6.

Fogg, C. D. 2010. *Team-Based Strategic Planning: A Complete Guide to Structuring, Facilitating, and Implementing the Process.* Scotts Valley, CA: CreateSpace Independent Publishing Platform.

Ginter, P. M., W. J. Duncan, and L. E. Swayne. 2018. *Strategic Management of Health Care Organizations*, 8th ed. Hoboken, NJ: John Wiley & Sons.

Hamel, G., and C. K. Prahalad. 1989. "Strategic Intent." *Harvard Business Review*, May–June, 63–76.

Kaissi, A. A., and J. W. Begun. 2008. "Strategic Planning Processes and Hospital Financial Performance." *Journal of Healthcare Management* 53 (3): 197–208.

Martin, R. L. 2014. "The Big Lie of Strategic Planning." *Harvard Business Review*, January–February, 3–8.

Mintzberg, H. 1994. "The Fall and Rise of Strategic Planning." *Harvard Business Review*, January–February, 107–13.

Nadler, D. A. 1994. "Collaborative Strategic Thinking." *Planning Review* 22 (5): 30–44.

Porter, M. E. 1996. "What Is Strategy?" *Harvard Business Review*, November–December, 61–78.

Rumelt, R. 2011a. *Good Strategy, Bad Strategy: The Difference and Why It Matters*. New York: Crown Business.

———. 2011b. "The Perils of Bad Strategy." *McKinsey Quarterly*, June, 30–39.

Simyar, F., J. Lloyd-Jones, and J. Caro. 1988. "Strategic Management: A Proposed Framework for the Health Care Industry." In *Strategic Management in the Health Care Sector: Toward the Year 2000*, edited by F. Simyar and J. Lloyd-Jones, 6–17. Englewood Cliffs, NJ: Prentice Hall.

Skinner, W. 1969. "Manufacturing—Missing Link in Corporate Strategy." *Harvard Business Review*, May, 136–45.

Sorkin, D. L., N. B. Ferris, and J. Hudak. 1984. *Strategies for Cities and Counties: A Strategic Planning Guide*. Washington, DC: Public Technology, Inc.

Taiwo, A. S., and F. O. Idunnu. 2010. "Impact of Strategic Planning on Organizational Performance and Survival." *Research Journal of Business Management* 4 (1): 73–82.

CHAPTER 2

The Benefits of Strategic Planning

Good fortune is what happens when opportunity meets with
planning.

—*Thomas Edison*

The true measure of your worth includes all the benefits
others have gained from your success.

—*Cullen Hightower*

Why should an organization carry out strategic planning? What
benefits can be expected from this effort? How can the strategic planning process be structured and managed to maximize the likelihood
that benefits will be realized? These and other important questions
are addressed in this chapter.

Unfortunately, while there may be a sound basis for conducting
strategic planning, strategic plans regularly do not achieve their full
promise. Survey results in the literature on healthcare and other
industries reveal that many organizations struggle to realize the benefits of strategic planning. Extensive surveys of the literature on this
subject yield decidedly mixed results depending on how strategic
planning is defined and what specific benefits are under consideration.

The authors of this book routinely survey healthcare provider
organizational leadership on this topic and find that leaders feel that
benefit realization does not match up to the quality of the plans

developed and the planning processes. Respondents indicate that despite very effective strategic planning processes, strong plans, and reasonably good implementation, the results achieved (i.e., benefits) did not meet expectations.

Though there are likely many reasons for these results, we attribute these findings primarily to a lack of clarity in and visibility of the benefits sought from the outset and throughout the planning process. Some organizations plunge into strategic planning without identifying what may be gained through the process (see chapter 3 on the organization of the preplanning process for recommendations on avoiding this particular pitfall). Some groups identify so many expected outcomes that it is difficult to interpret or remember the main purposes. Others provide only vague expectations, so stakeholders are not really sure of the purposes or the potential benefits. Still others get off to a clear, good start, but then veer off course during the process through inadequate, inconsistent, or contradictory communications about intended benefits.

This chapter provides guidance on identifying potential benefits as well as how to promote realization of these benefits.

IDENTIFYING STRATEGIC PLANNING BENEFITS

Substantive (i.e., non-process-related) strategic planning benefits can be identified at the outset and pursued throughout the planning process. These benefits should fall into one or more of four categories for potential improvement:

1. Product and market position
2. Financial benefit
3. Quality and operations
4. Addressing community needs

The following sections review each category of benefit and describe what is desirable and possible to achieve.

Product and Market Position

Historically, strategic planning has been oriented toward achieving product and market benefits. Larger service areas, higher market shares, more comprehensive products and services, and, recently, improved linkages among services have formed the core concerns of healthcare strategic planning (see exhibit 2.1). Relative to other areas of potential benefits, product and market improvement has been addressed fairly well by healthcare organizations. However, many organizations are reevaluating traditional product and market strategies and metrics as they move from a fee-for-service to a fee-for-value model and shift to bundled and risk-based payments and population health management.

Market or service area. Every healthcare organization's strategic plan is at least somewhat focused on protection, if not expansion, of its market or service area. Even in the most rural areas and certainly in all urban and suburban areas, the geographical area primarily served by the organization is of interest to competitors and is increasingly at risk. Because of the increasingly competitive nature of healthcare, offensive strategies that target new geographical markets are quite common. Despite the primacy of this topic, strategic planning efforts have achieved mixed results regarding growth and defense of service areas. Often, the populations in certain markets are shared among providers. Sharing populations is likely to become less common with the shift toward population health management and as taking responsibility (clinical and financial) for a clearly defined group of people becomes more prevalent.

Market share. Equally important are strategies to increase existing market shares. Most strategic plans conclude that market share increases are desirable and feasible, particularly as utilization rates (the number of units of service provided to a given population) are anticipated to decrease through better population health management. In the majority of cases, such conclusions and related initiatives do lead to increased shares, at least for some services if not overall.

Readers should also note that, in connection with the defined population concept, market share targets for some provider organizations may also include a share of covered lives in addition to the traditional market share for inpatient or outpatient services.

Product scope and extent. Most healthcare providers now recognize that the growth of products (i.e., programs, services) can no longer be managed on an ad hoc basis or exclusively in an opportunistic manner. Rather, leadership teams must explicitly formulate a focused and systematic approach to appropriately broaden and deepen service offerings and to better organize and integrate the overall product portfolio. Further, and as a result of changing sector norms and consumer expectations, the strategic plans of healthcare organizations increasingly feature recommendations for development and growth that extend beyond acute care and, in some instances, beyond healthcare services delivery (e.g., they may include a payer function). Exhibit 2.2 presents a framework for identifying and organizing the potential range of products and competencies offered by health systems today. The framework also illustrates how services and programs should interrelate and provides context on the relationships, functions, and expectations that shape a modern health system's product portfolio. As a result of the incorporation of relatively novel functions and the associated complexity of aggregating and managing a broader array of products, realization of strategic planning benefits in this domain is uneven across health systems to date.

Continuity of care. Related to the broadened and evolving definition of product scope and extent is the consideration of how services and programs in a health system's portfolio are coordinated and managed to ensure continuity of care. Continuity of care is basically a second-generation result of integrated care delivery, and many

Exhibit 2.1: What Product or Market Benefits Can and Should Be Achieved?

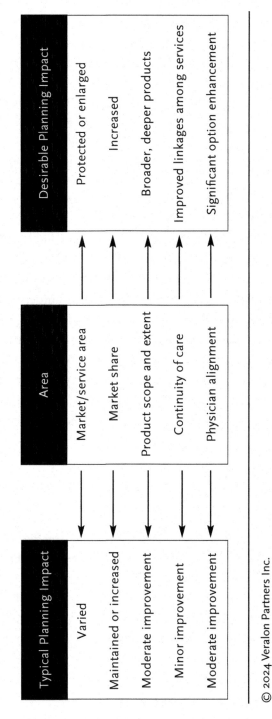

Typical Planning Impact	Area	Desirable Planning Impact
Varied	Market/service area	Protected or enlarged
Maintained or increased	Market share	Increased
Moderate improvement	Product scope and extent	Broader, deeper products
Minor improvement	Continuity of care	Improved linkages among services
Moderate improvement	Physician alignment	Significant option enhancement

healthcare organizations now attempt to address continuity and coordination of services across care settings and continua as part of the strategic planning process. Though care continuity is not novel for organizations with a historical commitment to vertical integration, or to early adopters of population health management principles, its benefits are nonetheless hard to achieve. Effective coordination of care depends on the ability to offer a broad range of services that are both owned and affiliated, as well as clear linkages among and seamless transitions across services. Healthcare leaders increasingly appreciate that developing capabilities and capitalizing on the potential benefits of integrated delivery take time, and thus continuity of care is an increasingly common and important modern strategic planning topic.

Physician alignment. In light of the greater competition that healthcare organizations face and the current and growing provider shortage, forward-looking organizations are rethinking their strategy around physician alignment. Offering a broad array of alignment options to fit the needs of individual physicians and groups will be a necessity in the future and a strategic advantage if done right. (This topic is explored further in chapter 18, "Physician Enterprise.")

Financial Benefit

This category of likely substantive benefit is probably the most obvious, and it is applicable to all healthcare organizations; however, realization of financial benefits has been mixed at best. Exhibit 2.3 identifies four general areas of financial benefit along with the historically most prevalent outcome versus the desired planning impact. Healthcare organizations can better achieve financial benefits if they effectively involve financial leadership and integrate financial planning into the process.

Exhibit 2.2: Modern Healthcare System Product Scope Framework

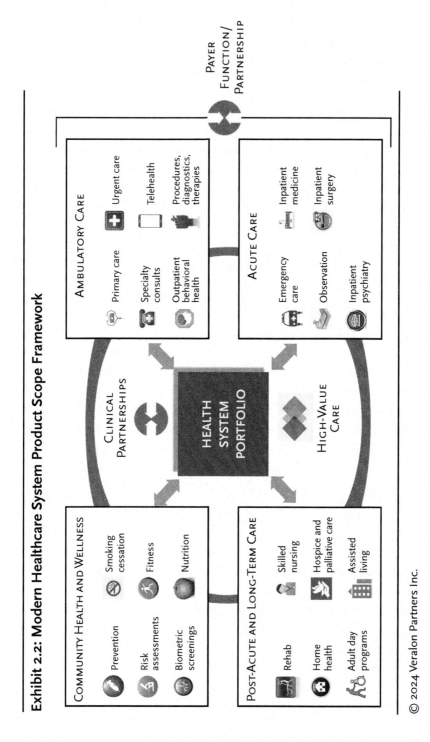

Operating margin. Few, if any, healthcare organizations have such a high operating margin that they can ignore the need to maintain or increase it. For many organizations today, increasing the operating margin is a primary goal of strategic planning. Unfortunately, strategic plans often identify initiatives that require significant operating resources to execute, which can cut into the margin. In addition, operating margins can suffer when healthcare organizations try to balance volume optimization under fee-for-service arrangements with population health management and reduced utilization in a value-based payment environment. Finally, some healthcare organizations generate strategic plans to satisfy internal constituents without appropriate regard for the impact on financial performance generally. As a result of all these factors, and consistent with the results of the literature on strategic planning, plans are just as likely to decrease operating margin as they are to increase it.

Non-operating income. This issue has not been a high priority for many healthcare organizations until fairly recently. However, the bull market of the 1990s and stock market volatility in the twenty-first century raised the profile of this issue considerably. In addition to sound investment management, an increasing number of healthcare organizations have targeted philanthropy as a high-priority strategy. Such organizations have developed sophisticated, comprehensive fundraising programs and have generated significant non-operating income to fund capital projects, as seed money for clinical program investment, and to build endowments. A growing number of organizations have developed large-scale clinical research enterprises, innovation centers, consulting practices, and other ventures unrelated to patient care to tap into additional non-operating income sources. Though considered commonplace today, diversification away from the core healthcare business can be difficult and should be approached cautiously.

Exhibit 2.3: What Financial Benefits Can and Should Be Achieved?

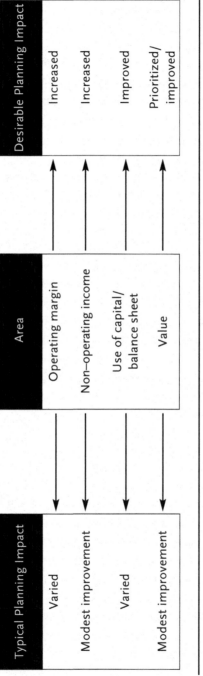

Typical Planning Impact	Area	Desirable Planning Impact
Varied	Operating margin	Increased
Modest improvement	Non–operating income	Increased
Varied	Use of capital/balance sheet	Improved
Modest improvement	Value	Prioritized/improved

© 2024 Veralon Partners Inc.

Access to capital; balance sheet indicators. Another typical reason for commencing strategic planning is to help support or rationalize capital-intensive facilities, technology, or other investments. In fact, strategic planning is commonly used outside healthcare for the purpose of making difficult choices among capital investment alternatives, and some healthcare organizations use strategic planning in a similar manner. Unfortunately, even today, some strategic plans lead to capital consumption without appropriate regard for the downstream financial impact.

Further, despite the increasingly difficult financial climate in healthcare, improvement of the balance sheet is only now becoming a commonly stated desired strategic planning outcome. Given the frequent failure to improve operating margin, it is understandable that the balance sheet can often deteriorate as a result of strategic planning. Nonetheless, few organizations can afford to see their balance sheets suffer, even as a result of important projects. Balance sheet management has not been a priority in the planning process among nonfinancially oriented healthcare executives and boards, but there is a positive and growing trend toward accurately estimating and accounting for the balance sheet impact of strategic planning.

Value. The high and rising cost of healthcare in the United States has brought the concept of value to the forefront in healthcare strategic planning. Value is created when the quality (e.g., clinical outcomes, consumer satisfaction) derived from healthcare delivery exceeds the cost (or price). Readers should note that many healthcare providers are broadening their scopes of interest from the value of a procedure, hospital stay, or visit to the value across an episode of care (e.g., bundled payments) or across all care received by a given patient population (e.g., accountable care organizations [ACOs], risk sharing). Value often tops the list of healthcare organizations' critical issues today and thus is becoming a standard strategic planning priority.

Case Example: Strategic Planning Facilitates Realization of Financial Benefit for a Large Integrated Health System in the Midwest

Amid financial and organizational uncertainty associated with a significant leadership transition, a billion-dollar integrated delivery system based in the Midwest—consisting of several acute care hospitals, a large employed medical group, an expansive network of ambulatory and extended care services, an ACO, and a health plan—embraced strategic planning as a means to structure organizational turnaround efforts and achieve financial results in all four areas described in exhibit 2.3.

Championed by a new and stabilized executive team, the strategic planning process yielded focused growth strategies aimed at restoring and securing financial health. The year after plan completion, the health system achieved an operating margin of approximately 5 percent. In addition, the plan called for extensive modernization of its philanthropy program, which boosted non-operating income. These improvements allowed the system to undertake its largest capital investment in nearly a decade the following year, setting in motion growth initiatives that should reap significant dividends in the years to come.

In addition to targeted efforts to bolster the operating margin and cultivate new sources of non-operating income, the strategic plan emphasized differentiating based on value. Value-driven strategies focused on maximizing the ACO to reduce costs and improve quality for a defined population and on partnering with a number of community health agencies to manage the costs of caring for residents in more rural, outlying service area regions.

Quality and Operations

In contrast with financial benefit, operational benefit tends to be an underrecognized and underappreciated category. In addition, some planners make the error of avoiding operational benefit because they believe operational concerns are not strategic. Yet operational benefit is of strategic importance to nearly all healthcare organizations, and many aspects of this category will increase in strategic importance over the next decade. Leaders can realize tremendous strategic improvement by including operational improvement in strategic planning. To effectively address operational improvement in strategic planning, the planning team must elevate the focus to high-level areas rather than get dragged into debates over minor operational issues.

Exhibit 2.4 identifies four general areas of operational improvement benefits, along with the historically most prevalent outcome versus the desired planning impact.

Patient satisfaction. In a service sector such as healthcare, few topics are as important to success as satisfied and engaged customers. Yet customer satisfaction was not a major concern of healthcare organizations until the competitive era emerged in the 1990s and early 2000s, brought on by the financial uncertainties of managed care and cemented by direct-to-consumer advertising. Now, with increased visibility and availability of comparative healthcare organization information, customer satisfaction has moved from the background to the foreground in competitive—and therefore strategic—importance. In this digital age, patients want the same access and convenience that they have via technology in other parts of their lives. Furthermore, healthcare providers are dealing with a new and more real-time level of accountability and visibility on social media as patients complain publicly about care or service issues.

The emergence of patient-centered care delivery models and consumer-oriented services design are evidence of provider organizations' recognition of this development. Whether the patient satisfaction metrics proposed by sector experts and used by healthcare organization leadership teams today truly reflect patient and family satisfaction with healthcare services is unclear, but the ubiquitous presence of these metrics on health system and hospital scorecards emphasizes the awareness and criticality of this area. Plans that do not acknowledge (or better yet comprehensively address) this area are likely to fall short of the mark in terms of the realization of key benefits.

Quality. Healthcare quality was in a position similar to that of customer satisfaction until the late 1990s—it was a major concern of the general public but not necessarily of healthcare organizations. Awareness and action were incited by the publication of the first Institute of Medicine (1999) report on medical errors, which highlighted significant safety and general quality-of-care issues. Efforts to measure consistently and to publicize healthcare quality data have taken hold, and competing on quality level is considered a strategic imperative.

Significant advances in measuring and improving healthcare quality have been made in the last decade, specifically on structure and process measures. Improving performance on outcomes measures has proven more challenging for healthcare organizations and will be even more crucial as a greater proportion of provider reimbursement is tied to demonstrating value. Tremendous gains in quality are likely to emerge over the next decade. Strategic plans need to emphasize improved performance on the more transformational measures of outcome that will almost certainly be key factors in differentiating healthcare organizations in the future.

Access. The majority of healthcare consumers access services in community settings, yet most health systems remain primarily oriented to the business of the hospital. The proven importance of a high-functioning primary care network to overall health system sustainability—and to managing population health—supports the notion that access to care should be a central strategic concern. Linked to the broader consumerism movement, convenience and all facets of accessibility, including virtual access, have become paramount concerns. Access was fast-tracked and quickly adopted by patients and providers (and paid for by insurers) over the course

Exhibit 2.4: What Operational Benefits Can and Should Be Achieved?

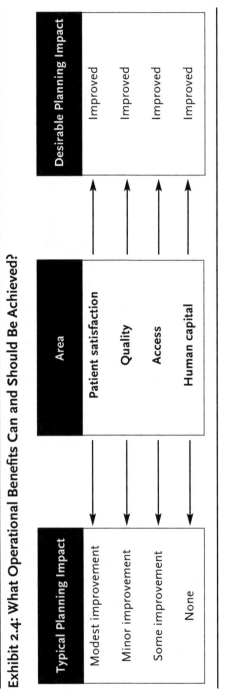

Typical Planning Impact		Area		Desirable Planning Impact
Modest improvement	→	Patient satisfaction	←	Improved
Minor improvement	→	Quality	←	Improved
Some improvement	→	Access	←	Improved
None	→	Human capital	←	Improved

© 2024 Veralon Partners Inc.

of the COVID-19 pandemic. Many providers have now pulled back on the unlimited virtual access model and have gone back to in-person care. However, patients continue to express the need for and importance of digital health services, particularly in behavioral health. As a result, many new companies have appeared in the market to fill this access void.

Nearly all organizations face challenges in organizing the right suite of coordinated outpatient and physician services in the right places. Because of the magnitude of problems in this area, its large and growing importance as a centerpiece of state and national reform initiatives, and the capital and incremental operating expenditures required to address these issues, this topic has been the priority of many strategic planners in the past few years, with modest success to date and much more needed in the future.

Human capital. The centrality of employees and physicians to the success of healthcare organizations has long been acknowledged, but effectively harnessing human capital still eludes even the best provider organizations. Fierce competition to recruit clinicians makes setting high expectations difficult, but problems with meaningful alignment and engagement represent the real hurdle. Further, the COVID-19 pandemic significantly worsened the workforce shortage for clinicians of all types—a situation that is expected to become the new norm. As a result, healthcare organizations will face increased competition for fewer members of the workforce, driving organizational spending higher than expected to address the issue over the near and medium term.

Despite the significance of this issue, it is on the big-picture strategic agenda of only a handful of organizations; most expect the human resources department and operations leaders to do the heavy lifting. As a result, it is often ignored in the strategic planning process, even though the magnitude of the challenge, its systemic nature, and its highest-order strategic implications suggest otherwise. An effective strategic planning process should highlight the potential competitive differentiation that a focus on human capital can yield by calling for initiatives to better align, engage, and leverage talent across the healthcare delivery enterprise.

Case Example: A Large Academic System's Focus on Realizing Operational Benefits

Like many first- and second-generation integrated delivery systems, University Health System (UHS) has done much to streamline operations and make them more patient-centric. UHS has largely achieved its primary goals of growth and financial health in the course of its strategic planning and execution over the last 15 years. In the most recent update of its strategic plan, while growth and financial health remained priorities, operational integration and improvement were of equal or possibly greater importance.

UHS consisted of a university hospital, a large multispecialty physician group, and a health plan. It operated primarily in the Midwest. The hospital and physician group were separate though related organizations, and as independent entities, they did not always work well together for the patients they jointly served. To make a great leap forward in providing value-based care, the highest priority in the strategic plan for the umbrella organization, UHS, was to make integration a reality. The initial result of this was the merger of the hospital and physician group.

This merger enabled the organization to undertake important strategic initiatives to improve quality and care delivery. The initial efforts in patient- and family-centered care, begun a few years earlier, were expanded to all parts of the organization, with a particular focus on the emergency department. Continuous quality improvement was formalized through physician and administrative leader dyads. A major push was made to standardize all primary care to meet the requirements of patient-centered medical homes. The goal to make UHS the best possible workplace and academic environment also received significant attention over the past few years through workforce planning, training and integration, formalized leadership training, and team-based care delivery models. As a result, quality and patient satisfaction scores rose significantly.

Addressing Community Needs

Not-for-profit healthcare organizations typically have focused on and attempted to demonstrate community benefits as part of their strategic plan. Often, however, and increasingly so, this area of benefit is "talked up" more than it is actually addressed, even though not-for-profits are required to prioritize and respond to the needs of the communities they serve. In fact, there have been challenges to the tax-exempt status of health systems based in part on their failure to demonstrate meaningful community benefit.

For many modern healthcare organizations, there is a growing disconnect between their community service mission and the actual attention and resources devoted to making it a reality. This gap is, at least in part, because healthcare organizations have become larger, more complex businesses serving broad areas. Thus, they are more distant and detached from the communities that originally spawned them. Though the ways in which healthcare organizations can generate community benefit and the types of community benefit sought have evolved, this area represents an instance in which recalling a more traditional, historically held mindset, particularly around addressing the social determinants of health, may actually help organizations succeed in the future. Social determinants of health are widely recognized as comprising five factors: economic stability, education access and quality, healthcare access and quality, neighborhood and built environment, and social and community context (DHHS 2023). Further, the extent to which a health provider can or should directly address these issues, rather than partner with other local or social service organizations, is often a key discussion point in planning processes.

Exhibit 2.5 identifies four general areas of community benefits, along with the historically most prevalent outcome versus the desired planning impact.

Needed services provided. Identifying community needs and ensuring that the needed care is provided were the primary concerns of healthcare strategic planning on inception and, appropriately, remain important today. Providing needed services is probably the community benefit that healthcare organizations most effectively realize, in part because healthcare provider competition has traditionally been focused on service breadth and depth, thus heightening the relevance of pursuing this benefit. Additionally, an Affordable Care Act mandate requires a community health needs assessment be completed every three years. These assessments are often a precursor to the strategic planning process and a key input for the strategic assessment.

Community health improvement. Many healthcare organizations have made community health improvement the centerpiece of their mission statements. Periodically, this area has been an important strategic concern. On a more frequent basis, it has been given lip service and addressed indirectly, if at all. Especially for not-for-profits, contributing to community health improvement should be a key element of community benefit. Difficulties in having a measurable, population-level impact and the inherent conflict of a field traditionally oriented to treating the sick in an episodic way hinder constructive efforts. However, health systems are well positioned to support these efforts through education, wellness, and outreach efforts, often for a relatively low cost. In addition, the importance of, and in many ways accountability for, community health improvement has been given a boost by the increasing emphasis on broader accountability for the care of a population (see the section titled "Population health management").

Partner of community. All not-for-profit healthcare organizations and some for-profit healthcare organizations collaborate with their communities. As healthcare has become a bigger and bigger business, many organizations have moved away from community partnering. Meaningfully carrying out the typical healthcare organization's mission of "effective caring" in an increasingly complex world would seem to require more and better interrelationships with the vast array of community agencies and groups that could contribute to this end. Greater sensitivity to the social determinants of health has raised the profile of community partnerships, and some health systems are delivering a more coordinated set of services that include coordination with community organizations. Other health systems have retreated primarily to doing what they can control through ownership and operation. Many health systems can improve their position and effectiveness through better community partnerships.

Population health management. The creation of ACOs and the emphasis on value- and risk-based payment have ushered in an era of population health management. In its simplest form, population health management is the notion of taking responsibility, both clinical and financial, for the care of a defined group of people. In more evolved forms of population health management, demonstrable community health status improvement (for some or all of a defined community) is an important goal and a key success metric. Most healthcare organizations are putting the building blocks in place to manage population health; becoming competent and eventually expert in this area is a critical strategy focus for many organizations.

Health equity. The increased focus on population health and the social determinants of health, coupled with the sociopolitical environment and increasing research highlighting health disparities, has made health equity a key issue in healthcare clinical practice and research. Groundbreaking research by Michael Marmot (2015), former president of the World Medical Association, has connected the social determinants of health to large differences in life expectancy among population groups and identified social injustice as the greatest threat to global health. The US Department of Health

Exhibit 2.5: What Community Benefits Can and Should Be Achieved?

Typical Planning Impact		Area		Desirable Planning Impact
Yes	→	Needed services provided	→	Yes
Little or none	→	Community health improvement	→	Some
Little or none	→	Partner of community	→	Some
Little or none	→	Population health management	→	Some
Little or none	→	Health equity	→	Some

© 2024 Veralon Partners Inc.

and Human Services defines health equity as "the attainment of the highest level of health for all people. Achieving health equity requires valuing everyone equally with focused and ongoing societal efforts to address avoidable inequalities, historical and contemporary injustices, and the elimination of health and health care disparities" (DHHS 2023). Many hospitals and health systems have recognized the importance of health equity as a critical strategic concern, incorporating initiatives or partnerships focused on decreasing health inequities as part of the strategic planning effort.

Case Example: Community Hospital Pioneers Wellness Care

Community Healthcare has been a leader in community-focused healthcare since its inception in the 1950s. From the outset, this medium-sized community hospital in a historically rural (but now suburban) part of an East Coast state drew national attention for its emphasis on wellness and primary care.

In its prior strategic plan, Community Healthcare continued its progressive history of service to the community. Its vision—"We are a national model for providing community-focused healthcare that is consumer-centered and driven by a passion for clinical excellence"—is not a slogan, but a guidepost for all that the organization does. Community Healthcare believes that building a healthier community is not an innovative program, but a grassroots effort to change people's behavior. The organization pursues this goal in part by giving patients the tools needed to make healthier choices in order to improve their well-being.

For five years in a row, Community Healthcare's county has been rated the healthiest in its state. This outcome is, at least in part, the result of Community Healthcare's increasingly geographically distributed primary care and ambulatory care service network (more than 80 percent of local residents claim to have a primary care physician, a very high percentage). These networks are supported by a diverse array of Community Healthcare wellness services, including nutrition, exercise, and other lifestyle-related programs. The organization has operated a program called Partnership for

Health with more than 40 organizations in its community for over 25 years to provide education, outreach resources, and programs that contribute to better prevention and, ultimately, better health. While many other organizations are just beginning to focus on population health, Community Healthcare has been a leader in this area for many years.

Going forward, Community Healthcare's strategy is to be an invaluable healthcare resource for the communities it serves, an approach that entails three key pillars: providing the best value, improving health, and simplifying healthcare. Being a "resource" means continuing to go above and beyond its role as a provider of healthcare services and truly contributing in a broad and meaningful way to population health.

CONCLUSION

Strategic planning must become more outcome oriented. Good process is important, and will remain so, but tangible benefits, not just a feel-good ending, need to be achieved. Deriving benefits starts, at the outset of the process, with identifying and communicating categories and types of benefits that could be realized through strategic planning.

This chapter has reviewed four categories of substantive benefit and 18 subcategories of possible benefits in these broad categories, which are summarized in exhibit 2.6. Leadership needs to agree on which benefits should be realized through the strategic planning effort, and the process needs to keep these potential benefits highly visible and to continually drive toward their realization. An orientation toward benefits realization will make future strategic planning more relevant and effective and help lead strategic planning into a new era of prominence as an important discipline in healthcare organizations.

Exhibit 2.6: Potential Strategic Planning Benefit Categories

Product and Market Position	Financial	Quality and Operations	Addressing Community Needs
Market/service area	Operating margin	Patient satisfaction	Needed services provided
Market share	Non-operating revenue	Quality	Community health improvement
Product scope and extent	Use of capital/balance sheet	Access	Partner of community
Continuity of care	Value	Human capital	Population health management
Physician alignment			Health equity

© 2024 Veralon Partners Inc.

REFERENCES

Institute of Medicine. 1999. *To Err Is Human: Building a Safer Health System*. Washington, DC: National Academies Press.

Marmot, M. 2015. *The Health Gap: The Challenge of an Unequal World*. London: Bloomsbury Press.

US Department of Health and Human Services (DHHS). 2023. *Healthy People 2030*. Accessed September 14. http://health.gov /healthypeople.

SUGGESTED READING

Office of Disease Prevention and Health Promotion. 2022. *Health Equity and Health Disparities Environmental Scan*. Published March. https://health.gov/sites/default/files/2022-04/HP2030 -HealthEquityEnvironmentalScan.pdf.

SECTION 2

Setting the Stage for Successful Strategic Planning

CHAPTER 3

Organizing for Success

There is in that act of preparation the moment you start caring.

—Winston Churchill

The only difference between a mob and a trained army is organization.

—Calvin Coolidge

Thoughtful and purposeful preparation is critical before beginning the actual work of strategic planning. Without the right prep work, even the most well-designed planning process with objectively sound outputs can fall flat. The following chapter discusses 12 steps representing four key categories of preparation: communication and expectations, management and leadership, context, and mindset. Leadership teams should complete these steps in advance of strategic planning to minimize avoidable challenges and maximize the chances of planning and plan success.

COMMUNICATION AND EXPECTATIONS

The concept of communication is integral to the first six steps of organizing for strategic planning; however, it remains critical to

Exhibit 3.1: Effective Planning Preparation Steps

Preparation Categories	Communication and Expectations	Management and Leadership	Context	Mindset
Preparation steps	Step 1: Identify and communicate desired strategic planning outcomes Step 2: Describe and communicate the planning process Step 3: Establish and communicate the strategic planning schedule	Step 4: Assert CEO leadership of strategic planning Step 5: Define and formalize the roles and responsibilities of other organizational leaders Step 6: Identify the strategic planning facilitator	Step 7: Conduct strategic planning orientation meetings Step 8: Review past strategies and identify successes and failures Step 9: Assemble relevant historical data	Step 10: Resolve not to overanalyze historical data Step 11: Prepare to stimulate new thinking Step 12: Reinforce a future orientation

success throughout planning and especially during the transition to implementation. To ensure a high level of organizational participation and engagement, emphasize communication of strategic planning objectives, the proposed planning process, and the schedule from the outset.

Step 1: Identify and Communicate Desired Strategic Planning Outcomes

The importance of clear outcomes to successful strategic planning cannot be overstated. Outcome-oriented statements such as "strategic planning will provide our organization with a road map for the future" or "strategic planning will allow our organization to allocate scarce resources in the most effective manner possible" are too general to warrant the time, resources, and focus that strategic planning requires.

In addition, at the outset of the process, collecting objectives from stakeholders promotes staying on track after planning begins. Various stakeholders or groups will have their own issues or wants from the planning process, and having these named is important. It allows stakeholders to view the plan as a vehicle to address important issues and motivates them to be involved. Objectives should be clear signposts that are periodically revisited as planning takes shape to demonstrate progress and encourage a sustained focus on the issues that matter most. Issues to address in the modern healthcare strategic planning process may include determining how to

- coordinate and integrate care across the care continuum;
- increase access to services, especially primary and other ambulatory care services;
- effectively align hospitals and physicians to manage the health of populations;
- respond to increased consumerism, including demands for more person-centric care delivery and transparency of information;

- prepare for and respond to provider and payer market consolidation;
- achieve the best clinical outcomes at the lowest cost;
- prioritize investment of organizational resources; and
- align management commitment and board support.

Step 2: Describe and Communicate the Planning Process

Too often, planning begins without an understanding of what the planning process entails. Without a clear sense of the sequencing of activities and the ideal progression, planning participants may have different expectations of what is to be done and in what order; as a result, key stakeholders may feel reluctant to participate in the planning process or removed from it entirely. Even if key stakeholders do engage, the lack of clarity in approach may yield planning efforts that are unfocused, inefficient, and even unproductive. Worse, it can lead to broader organizational confusion and skepticism about strategic planning and the strategy it generates.

To proactively avoid these challenges, prior to initiating strategic planning it is imperative to outline a stepwise planning process that is appropriately customized to meet your organization's specific needs. Whether or not your organization chooses to follow the strategic planning process delineated in this book, teams should clearly define and document the activities for and the outputs of each step. Then this information must be communicated effectively to leadership and all other key stakeholders.

Step 3: Establish and Communicate the Strategic Planning Schedule

Although strategic planning should be an ongoing activity and not simply a one-time event, development of a comprehensive strategic plan or a complete update of the current plan usually occurs every three years. Comprehensive plan development or updating requires a more detailed and structured timeline compared to routine updates and ongoing strategic planning activities, but both should have formally established schedules.

As with the previous two steps, and particularly for more comprehensive planning efforts, the planning team should determine the schedule of the strategic planning process before planning activities are initiated, and they should clearly communicate it to all relevant stakeholders. The schedule for comprehensive strategic plan development should align with the stages of the planning process developed in the previous step.

There is no consensus on the optimal duration of the full strategic planning process. Some believe the plan should be completed as quickly as possible to maintain a high degree of focus and to begin execution promptly. Others believe that an extended schedule allows for broader participation, more time to generate buy-in, more advanced critical thinking, and connection to important organizational processes like budgeting. The authors of this book often employ a timeline for a full planning process of approximately four to six months, generally allowing for broad participation but fully appreciating the value of focus and expediency.

MANAGEMENT AND LEADERSHIP

Step 4: Assert CEO Leadership of Strategic Planning

In nearly all organizations, including healthcare organizations, the CEO actively champions and leads the strategic planning process. Other leaders may also play important roles, and in a not-for-profit organization the board of directors is especially critical. However, the CEO should be the primary leader.

C. Davis Fogg (2010) suggests clarifying key roles and responsibilities of the CEO at the outset of the strategic planning process. Roles and responsibilities of the CEO are to

- demonstrate and continually reinforce the importance of planning in the organization;
- allocate time, money, staff support, and personal support to the planning process;
- set high standards for the planning process and results;
- encourage creativity and the search for the unlikely or not so obvious;
- lead the development of an inspired, comprehensive, and far-reaching vision for the organization;
- make, push, or affirm timely decisions;
- serve as the principal link between the planning process and important external constituencies;
- hold senior staff and others accountable for results and reward them accordingly;
- install an ongoing integrated planning process and infrastructure;
- visibly champion strategic planning; and
- encourage input from all participants and avoid dominating the discussion.

By asserting a strong presence at the start of the strategic planning process and then executing key elements of the leadership role throughout, the CEO can increase the probability of smoothly functioning processes and successful results.

Step 5: Define and Formalize the Roles and Responsibilities of Other Organizational Leaders

The Board

Strategic planning is a major responsibility of the board, particularly in many not-for-profit organizations wherein the board represents the community at large. As such, the board needs to play an especially significant role in setting and guarding the mission and values of the organization (phase 2 of the four planning phases outlined in chapter 1). The board members should also serve as key advisers to senior staff on other significant plan elements. Ultimately, it is the board that must approve or reject the strategic plan.

Who, How, and How Much

There is no right answer for every organization as to who should be involved, to what extent, and via what mechanisms. Some experts believe that the senior management team is principally responsible for planning and that other stakeholders' involvement should be limited by stakeholder group type or role played. Some believe that the best plans are developed when stakeholders from all levels of an organization have opportunities to contribute, or at least formally react. The perspective espoused in this book falls closer to the latter view, within reason and without excessively or detrimentally affecting planning efficiency. Chapter 4 discusses our perspective on this issue further.

Given that no "one best way" exists, the CEO and senior management team have to make choices about participation and roles (in conjunction with the board to the extent appropriate). Regardless of what is ultimately determined, these choices should be made and clearly communicated before the planning process begins. Modifications can be made if necessary once planning begins, but each major participant group must understand expectations regarding its participation and role at the outset of the process.

The general consensus among experts, including the authors, is that for healthcare organizations, strategic planning should actively engage aligned physician leaders in determining the organization's future direction and priorities. Depending on the nature of the organization, it may be important for other clinicians to also play a key role in strategic planning. Again, which specific physician leaders and other physician representatives and in what capacities are to be determined by executive leadership. A deeper discussion of stakeholder involvement can be found in chapter 4.

Oversight Bodies

A strategic planning steering committee is typically established to oversee the planning process. This group typically comprises senior leadership, including physician leaders, and key board members. At the outset of the process, the steering committee should aim to accomplish the following, though the group's role becomes more expansive once planning begins:

- Develop, affirm, and set a plan to communicate the desired strategic planning outcomes
- Affirm (or revise as necessary) the proposed strategic planning approach and timeline, including identification of key milestones
- Identify meaningful gaps in knowledge or information (internal or related to the market), peers, and sector, and propose a plan to close any gaps
- Identify internal and external stakeholders to be interviewed
- Identify the need for external advisers and procure this support as necessary
- Select planning facilitation and management leads and their roles, including the strategic planning facilitator (internal or external), and all types of logistical support, including scheduling, outreach, and coordination with involved stakeholders

Step 6: Identify the Strategic Planning Facilitator

While the CEO is the strategic planning leader, another individual typically manages day-to-day facilitation of the process. The team must resolve who will assume this responsibility and how facilitation will be carried out at the outset of the process. Once the selection is made and facilitation duties are delineated, this information should be communicated widely before strategic planning formally commences.

Fogg (2010, 31) suggests that "most CEOs depend upon a skilled, objective strategic planning facilitator to jump-start the organization into strategic planning and to shepherd the process during the early years of implementation. A good facilitator helps the organization design and install an effective planning and review process, trains the planning team and the organization in facilitation techniques, intervenes when key organizational or strategic blockages occur, and exits once the team is self-sustaining and self-facilitating." Nearly all healthcare provider organizations must choose between an internal leader, typically the director or vice president of planning, and an outside consultant for this role. In small healthcare provider organizations, the CEO or another C-suite representative may act as the strategic planning facilitator, though it can be difficult for the CEO to effectively encourage open discussion given his organizational position (see chapter 4).

CONTEXT

Step 7: Conduct Strategic Planning Orientation Meetings

Orientation meetings set the stage for the official launch of the planning process. Although meetings may be deferred until the strategic planning process formally commences, these meetings should be scheduled during the preplanning stage.

To become fully engaged at the outset of the process and to provide important context as backdrop for the plan, senior management and the strategic planning steering committee might embark on a planning retreat. Here leadership and other committee members explore important environmental trends and their potential implications and preliminarily identify key strategic issues for the organization. As described in more detail in the next section, such a planning retreat often also serves as a forum to review the organization's past planning initiatives, including successes and failures.

Holding strategic planning orientation sessions for other groups in the organization may be desirable at this point as well. Depending on the size and complexity of the organization and the breadth and depth of participation being sought in the strategic planning process, orientation sessions may be held with the entire board, other members of senior management, physicians, other professional staff, key external community leaders, or some combination of these. These sessions usually focus on a few of the areas outlined, such as objectives for strategic planning, the planning process and timeline, or the role of the affected constituencies in the planning process.

Step 8: Review Past Strategies and Identify Successes and Failures

A review of the organization's past strategies, successes, and failures is best completed before the strategic planning process formally starts. The review should include both process and content for ways to improve how the process was conducted and any planned outcomes that may have been unachieved. Doing this each planning cycle will allow the process to continually evolve and improve over time.

An objective review of past strategies can be enlightening. Often the actual strategies an organization used differed from those proposed in the strategic plan. Similarly, the actual strategies the organization employed may vary from those that leadership thought were being followed. A review of historical documents by someone outside the inner circle—a new senior staff member or a consultant—and a discussion of what was proposed, what was perceived, and what actually occurred over the previous three to five years can be a fascinating and important pre–planning process exercise. This review can also help identify shortcomings in the past process for implementing strategies and tracking results, thereby building support for better implementation approaches in the proposed planning effort.

As part of this process, the team should review what has worked, what has not, and why. Failure to pay adequate attention to unsuccessful strategies in formal planning can lead to recurring mistakes.

Step 9: Assemble Relevant Historical Data

Possessing accurate and relevant data is an asset to strategic planning. Conversely, having inaccurate and incomplete data, or the inability to assemble a comprehensive set of data, can be a major impediment to strategic planning. Therefore, it is never too early to begin assembling key data to support the strategic assessment phase of planning. Chapter 6 discusses the specific types of data required for successful strategic planning and analytical approaches. Generally, relevant historical data should profile the past three or so years of the organization's performance and position and the market in which it operates.

To get an early start on the time-consuming data collection process, organizations must be proactive in the identification and aggregation of necessary data. Further, taking a proactive stance is a critical element of a good data collection and organization timeline. While the amount and quality of data and analytic tools have certainly improved over time, the data are often from a third party, and collection timelines should be considered. Discovering at the middle or end of the process that essential data are missing or inaccurate is discouraging at a minimum and disabling at worst, especially if the problem is discovered in a public forum and undermines the credibility of the strategic planning process.

MINDSET

Step 10: Resolve Not to Overanalyze Historical Data

Historical data assembled to aid strategic planning can be a great asset, but data analysis can also trap the organization in a cycle of ineffectiveness and cause excessive delays. Planning teams should avoid analyzing every facet of historical performance or a few participants' overestimation of the impact that more, or more detailed, data will have on future strategy. Both challenges can derail the planning process and inappropriately bring into question the validity of data or analytic methods—they should be proactively mitigated.

To avoid wasteful and distracting overanalysis, the strategic planning facilitator and the CEO should make decisions about the data to be examined and the analytic methods used, in consultation with other senior leaders as appropriate, and communicate to all planning participants. In addition, the planning facilitator must consistently reinforce the notion that while historical data may help to define the problem, they are not the only—or even the most important—factor in determining key challenges, and they certainly are not the answer.

Although focusing on the past and dwelling on the familiar can be comforting, strategic planning should be oriented toward the future and driven from external factors. Organizations should resolve to use historical data for their intended purposes as defined, communicated, and reiterated by the planning facilitator and steering committee leaders.

Step 11: Prepare to Stimulate New Thinking

Meaningful Strategic Planning
As the strategic planning process gets underway, teams must resist the temptation to extrapolate from past performance and experience

to devise future strategy. In the more orderly and less frenetic world of past decades, passable and even good strategic planning may have resulted from this approach. But with nonlinear and fast-paced changes in the field, extrapolation would now likely lead to naive strategies at best and incorrect forecasts and flawed strategic direction at worst. Moreover, as highlighted in chapter 1, organizations must overcome the urge to focus primarily on operational effectiveness—doing the same things competitors do but more efficiently or with more favorable results—and engage in planning that yields more sustainable and meaningful competitive advantages.

Avoiding Mimicry

Another problematic strategic planning method that healthcare organizations frequently use is adopting or mimicking strategies used by other organizations in demographically similar but more advanced regional markets. This practice is seen most often when organizations in less advanced markets try to replicate a successful strategy implemented in California, Massachusetts, or a similarly advanced market. Although this approach may be appealing and may ultimately do no harm, it poses significant hazards, including the failure to truly understand one's market and develop strategies and plans that address more pertinent local market needs.

While potentially positive learning can occur in these situations, teams should emphasize creating a plan that effectively creates competitive advantages suited to an organization's strengths, opportunities, and unique market. As described in chapters 6, 7, and 8, healthcare planners must be thoughtful and intuitive in their characterization of the future environment, understanding implications of changing environmental conditions and considering strategies that might not make a large difference today but will be of potential critical importance tomorrow. Unfortunately, much strategic planning conducted by healthcare organizations assumes a static competitive environment, or at least underestimates the degree and pace of change that will occur. Such a mindset is even more dangerous than inappropriate mimicry given how dynamic the field has been in recent years (and will likely be in the future).

Promoting Creative Thinking

Preparation for the strategic planning process in each organization should include some review and summary of the enormous body of available strategic thinking literature, the incorporation of planning exercises designed to contemplate alternatives that may seem radical today, and the use of planning techniques that may help the organization leap rather than step forward in its strategic development (see chapters 5, 12, and 14 for more information on innovative thinking).

Step 12: Reinforce a Future Orientation

To successfully plan for the future, healthcare organizations must adopt a new perspective. This perspective must be broader, bolder, and more creative and dynamic than any required in the past. To counter the tendency to overemphasize past and present circumstances, leaders need to overcompensate actively and continually push their organizations to break with that past and consider alternative futures that differ vastly from what they know today. Injecting this kind of thinking into healthcare strategic planning invigorates the process and leads to thoughtful plans and strategies that will set the new standard by which successful planning and strategy development are measured in the decades to come.

CONCLUSION

Half a century after its emergence, healthcare strategic planning remains a relatively new practice, though there is evidence of growing sophistication. In this chapter alone, healthcare strategic planning has been characterized as historically focused rather than future oriented, limited in creativity, lacking necessary preparation, and applied in a hurried fashion. Part of the problem can be a lack of focus on clear, compelling results; another is minimal planning preparation by leaders, staff, and other key stakeholders. This chapter addresses both of these potential issues and, it is hoped, heightens awareness of the need to prepare for successful strategic planning.

REFERENCE

Fogg, C. D. 2010. *Team-Based Strategic Planning: A Complete Guide to Structuring, Facilitating, and Implementing the Process.* Scotts Valley, CA: CreateSpace Independent Publishing Platform.

CHAPTER 4

Major Planning Process Considerations

It is good to have an end to journey toward; but it is the journey that matters, in the end.

—*Ursula K. LeGuin*

The most important things a leader can bring to a changing organization are passion, conviction, and confidence in others. Too often executives announce a plan, launch a task force, and then simply hope that people find the answers— instead of offering a dream, stretching their horizons, and encouraging people to do the same. That is why we say, "Leaders go first . . ."

—*Rosabeth Moss Kanter*

Structuring and carrying out an effective strategic planning process is often more important to a healthcare organization, and to the success of strategic planning, than the plan itself. The increasing complexity of the healthcare environment and the growing vulnerability of provider organizations to myriad external threats have made it far more challenging to effectively carry out strategic planning and develop strategy.

At the same time, the increasing size, diversity, and complexity of healthcare organizations make for unwieldy entities to communicate in and manage. While it is possible to overdo the strategic planning process and derail or overwhelm the organization's capacities, in general, more process is better than less. As a rule, organizations should strive to maximize participation in the planning process within the limits of their budget and capabilities to manage the process. Further, participation should follow organizational norms, which have evolved over time. Historically, most meetings and events were held in person. The COVID-19 pandemic showed that teams can also be very effective in a remote setting; however, there are still instances in which gathering together in a room is preferable for discussion, team development, and consensus building. Exhibit 4.1 presents potential settings for strategic planning activities and meetings.

While this exhibit provides a guide, the process should address how your organization can maximize participation and efficiency. For example, in a large, geographically dispersed organization, virtual meetings may be preferable in most cases.

The key to an effective planning process is developing shared understanding—and ultimately consensus—about four important elements of the strategic plan:

1. Current, and especially future, environment
2. Critical issues the organization faces
3. Mission and vision to guide the organization to the future
4. Major plan outputs, including priority strategies and alternatives considered

An effective process builds acceptance, facilitates approval, and expedites the transition from planning to action.

The planning process needs to link effectively the many constituencies involved in healthcare organizations. If it does, it can facilitate better communication among staff and improved coherence in future operations. While the organization should certainly seek tangible outputs from strategic planning, the planning process presents important opportunities to improve communication across the organization and to forge new and stronger bonds among individuals and groups of stakeholders to help ensure the organization's future viability.

Exhibit 4.1: Potential Settings for Strategic Planning Activities and Meetings

Planning Meeting Type	In Person	Virtual	Either
Individual or group interviews		X	
Retreats	X		
Focus groups			X
Steering committee			X
Reactor panels			X

© 2024 Veralon Partners Inc.

This chapter addresses some of the critical elements of the planning process. While many of these elements have been mentioned in previous chapters, the importance of a strong planning process calls for more extended discussion.

FACILITATION

Facilitation is an extremely critical element of a successful strategic planning process. Someone needs to be primarily responsible for guiding the process throughout, ensuring that the important planning tasks are conducted and completed, assisting leadership and other key groups involved in the process in reaching decisions and achieving consensus, and then directing the transition from planning to successful implementation. While many individuals involved in the strategic planning process will have specific responsibility for facilitating one or two aspects of the diverse group work, one person typically takes the lead throughout, with overriding responsibilities for the entire process. What alternatives exist for effective facilitation of the strategic planning process? Many healthcare organizations have a planning staff or organizational development department (or occasionally other internal resources) that can facilitate the planning process. Some organizations retain consultants to fill this role. When evaluating possible consultants, organizations should look for individuals who are highly experienced, have experience in the healthcare field and comparable organizations, and possess a range of facilitation skills (described further in the following sections).

In some instances, the CEO may consider serving as the process facilitator. Most CEOs find this job extremely challenging. There is great risk of distraction and likely too little time available for the tasks to be performed well. In addition, a CEO facilitator makes productive group discussion and consensus development difficult. Most CEOs inhibit free discussion because of their power and authority, and they tend to dominate meetings when put in charge. Avoid this alternative if at all possible.

C. Davis Fogg (2010) suggests that the best facilitators have three types of skills (see exhibit 4.2):

1. Process: Putting the planning process together and making it work
2. Content: Giving specific solutions to business and strategic problems
3. Intervention: Breaking personal, organization, and business decision blockages

He adds that all three types of skills may not be, and often are not, possessed by any single individual. The more of these skills that are offered by one person or group, the more effective and efficient the strategic planning process will be. In nearly every strategic planning effort, the organization needs all three types of skills, and it must be prepared to provide them at appropriate points in the process. Fogg believes that the lead facilitator must have certain basic process skills, especially a keen understanding of all parts of the planning and implementation process, and know how to weave them together

Exhibit 4.2: The Facilitator's Job Description

What the Facilitator Does

Process

- Structure
  - Structures the process
  - Defines key analyses
  - Produces the manual
  - Handles documentation
- Training
  - Trains in planning and process
- Facilitation
  - Facilitates major meetings
  - Teaches others to facilitate
  - Gives private advice on process
  - Schedules meetings
- Resourcing
  - Identifies training
  - Identifies outside facilitators
  - Identifies content specialists

Content

- Solutions to specific strategic issues

Intervention

- Diagnostic interviewing
  - Initial
  - In process
- Private counsel,
- particularly CEO
- Team interventions
- Keeps process on time

What the Facilitator Does Not Do

- Develop the plan
- Write the plan
- Make decisions
- Become a power point
- Play politics
- Execute the plan

When the Boss Facilitates/ Is Part of the Team

- Be a member of the group
- Speak last
- Use good facilitator skills
- Be neutral
- Let the team come to consensus
- Do not dominate or be authoritarian
- You always have the deciding vote—use it sparingly

Source: Adapted from Fogg (2010).

successfully. She must also have knowledge of organizational behavior and the change process and strong leadership capabilities.

TEAMWORK

Much of the strategic planning process occurs through the efforts of informally or formally constituted, diverse groups. In the typical strategic planning process, important team work is performed by the strategic planning committee, board of trustees, senior management staff, and a variety of standing or ad hoc groups. How can the effectiveness of these many and varied groups be maximized?

Fogg (2010, 257) suggests that effective teams are "characterized by the following:

- Considerable discussion
- Open communication
- Debate, even conflict, on key issues
- Decision by consensus whenever possible
- Monitoring, measuring, and correcting of their own team behaviors"

Effective teams must also have a clear charge or objective to accomplish, good leadership by a chair who facilitates and directs but does not dominate, and accountability of the team and individual members for results. Among other qualities, individual team members must be good listeners, constructive participants, and willing to put aside their own self-interest for the sake of the group. All in all, this is a very tall order—but one that is essential to the smooth and successful flow of activities in the strategic planning process.

The interaction of the facilitator and team is a critical element of an effective strategic planning process. Fogg (2010) provides an extremely useful checklist (see exhibit 4.3) of facilitation tips to keep the teams on track and moving ahead.

Exhibit 4.3: Team Interventions

Process
- Facilitate team mission; roles/job description/process used
- Process checks during and at end of meetings—what is good and bad versus norms
- Redirect process when off track
- Point out dysfunctional team behavior

Meeting
- Off agenda/subject—get team back on track
- Summarize/crystallize key points; transitions
- Offer stand-up facilitation when team is bogged down
- Crystallize/facilitate/resolve conflicts
- Missing the point—suggest it

Content
- Wrong decision—point out correct options/process to define correct decision
- Suggest expert outsiders
- Give specific content solutions

Individual
- Point out dysfunctional behavior or interactions
- Offer individual/pair counseling

Source: Adapted from Fogg (2010).

PLANNING RETREATS

Almost every strategic planning process has at least one planning retreat. The retreat usually brings together board members, physicians, and other clinicians and members of management in an extended planning session. Some retreats are intended for board members exclusively, while others are for members of different leadership groups. Depending on the organization's style and preferences, as well as the particular focus of the retreat, the retreat may be held offsite and may even be carried out in a remote location combined with social and recreational activities. An offsite location may also be preferable to manage distractions and to enhance team building. The following section presents a review of the purposes of the different types of retreats that may be held.

Kickoff Retreat

Some organizations use a retreat at the beginning of strategic planning to jump-start the process and create enthusiasm and momentum. Thoughtful preparation—of both material and process during the retreat—is necessary to ensure success. The facilitator should build in some flexibility to adjust if the discussions are fruitful or take more time than originally allotted. Team building is often an additional goal of a strategic planning process; a kickoff retreat can help strengthen relationships. Team-building exercises can be unrelated to the planning topics, or they can focus on a specific relevant topic. Think carefully about your organization's culture when deciding what type of team-building exercises would be received well. The agenda for this type of retreat may include some or all of the following:

- Rationale for strategic planning (purpose, expected benefits)
- Strategic planning orientation (see chapter 3)
- Review of previous planning efforts, successes, and failures
- Review of the organization's recent performance
- Discussion of the organization's strengths, weaknesses, opportunities, and threats
- Review of current major strategic initiatives
- Identification on a preliminary basis of major planning issues

Often, one or more outside keynote speakers are used to discuss critical issues or environmental challenges. If external speakers present, they should be oriented to the organization's situation and their content previewed with the facilitator to ensure it is on topic and avoids statements that distract rather than enlighten. This type of retreat is a good vehicle for underscoring the importance of strategic planning and creating heightened interest in the planning process from the outset.

Midprocess Retreat

At any number of points in the middle of the strategic planning process, retreats can be held to do the following:

- Focus on a particular issue of concern
- Have extended discussion that is not possible in a regular planning committee session
- Obtain broad-based input, including input from the members of the planning committee and other important leaders not represented on the committee
- Brainstorm about approaches to issues facing the organization

External speakers may be used in midprocess retreats in a manner similar to kickoff retreats. The purposes of the midprocess retreat are information sharing, clarification, and direction. Sometimes this retreat is referred to as the "question" retreat—the attendees make sure the organization is focusing on the right strategic questions. These retreats are rarely used for decision-making or communicating "answers" to strategic planning issues.

Concluding Retreat

At or near the end of the strategic planning process, a retreat may be held for any of these purposes:

- Obtain additional, broad-based input before finalizing the recommendations
- Communicate the answers (i.e., the plan's key recommendations)
- Serve as a bridge to implementation, including strategizing about implementation opportunities and barriers
- Build a broader consensus on the plan and its recommendations than that offered by the planning committee alone

Often, this type of retreat is developed to expose all members of the board to a plan before it is brought to this group for formal consideration of its adoption. This type of retreat may also be used to signal to the organization that planning is (temporarily) over and implementation is about to begin.

Retreats may also be held in off years, when the organization is not undertaking a full strategic planning effort, to accomplish any of the purposes cited earlier and to keep the planning process going even as the organization's efforts are primarily devoted to implementation. Increasingly, healthcare organizations are using one or two planning retreats per year to review and revise the strategic plan, make important corrections to the direction and strategies, and obtain broad-based consensus on key initiatives to keep the organization moving forward. (See chapter 10 for more discussion of the annual strategic plan update and the potential role of retreats.) These retreats are an excellent vehicle for maintaining momentum and organizational commitment in the face of constant day-to-day pressures that consume management and have the potential to take the organization off course.

RESEARCH APPROACHES

Much of the success of the strategic planning process is dependent on information gathering and the involvement of key constituencies, which comes through various research efforts. The importance of constructive involvement of key constituencies in the strategic planning process cannot be overstated; implementation is dependent on a broad base of support for the plan's recommendations and actions. This support is only likely to occur if stakeholders believe they have been heard and had a true opportunity to shape the results. A brief review of the range of research approaches used in strategic planning follows. Most strategic planning processes employ more than one of these research approaches.

Interviews

Interviewing is typically part of every strategic planning process. Individual or group interviews usually occur early in the strategic planning process to gather information and demonstrate sensitivity to the perspectives of internal parties; they are also intended to accomplish one or both of these purposes with external parties. Sometimes, interviews may be carried out during the middle of the process to gather additional information on issues of concern or involve select parties in review of alternative approaches for addressing particular issues.

The facilitator may also use interviews to gently educate individuals such as board members with less knowledge of a complex topic. These interviews can be conducted in an individual or group setting.

Surveys

Surveys are the second most frequently employed technique, and they are often used for information gathering early in the strategic planning process. Many organizations participate in ongoing survey efforts that provide valuable input for strategic planning—patient satisfaction, quality and outcomes tracking, and consumer perception are among the most common. Surveys may be carried out internally to gather broad input in a less expensive way than possible through other research approaches. Internal surveys may also allow each member of an affected group to be involved in the strategic planning process and to accomplish this participation in an equitable and consistent manner. External surveys have similar purposes. The advantages and disadvantages of different survey approaches as information-gathering techniques are best left to experts in this subject area (e.g., *Designing and Conducting Survey Research: A Comprehensive Guide* by Louis M. Rea and Richard A. Parker). With the availability and prevalence of electronic communication today and the rise of standard online survey tools, much focused surveying occurs at a relatively low cost.

Focus Groups

The focus group technique is the least frequently used of the three approaches. Focus groups may be convened at any point in the process to gather information on a particular issue, and they may be conducted virtually. Such groups are becoming more widely used in the strategy formulation stage of the planning process and provide excellent forums for multidisciplinary development of strategy on a given issue. The advantages and disadvantages of focus groups versus other research approaches is a larger subject than can be addressed here (e.g., *Focus Groups: A Practical Guide for Applied Research* by Richard A. Krueger and Mary Anne Casey).

Reactor Panels

The reactor panel is a modified version of the focus group. Depending on the substance of the material to which a reaction is being sought, reactor panel members may be key constituents of a particular group (e.g., cardiovascular providers) or more diverse in representation (e.g., the medical executive committee). When conducting a reactor panel during the strategic planning process, the facilitator is usually seeking a found response to a particular recommendation, set of recommendations, or potential alterations under consideration. Reactor panels are appropriate vehicles for these narrowly defined purposes.

KEY STAKEHOLDER INVOLVEMENT

The strategic planning process is more likely to succeed if all key stakeholders understand their roles. The following sections briefly describe each major group's role.

Board Members

The strategic planning committee is usually an ad hoc or standing committee of the board and therefore includes significant representation from the board of directors. Board members are important participants in retreats, and they are involved in internal research. The board should be concerned with the policy implications of strategic planning and is generally and appropriately focused on the organizational direction (i.e., mission, vision, values) portion of the strategic planning output.

Physicians

In hospitals, health systems, and, obviously, medical groups, physicians should be well represented on the strategic planning committee. They are often solicited for input, and typically they provide the most extensive contributions of all internal (and sometimes external) constituencies.

Physicians concern themselves with the clinical implications of strategic planning. In teaching hospitals and academic medical centers, they are also interested in teaching and research interrelationships with clinical services and specific recommendations affecting the academic role of their organizations. Physicians may be most broadly affected by the outputs of the strategic planning process; however, except in some of the second- or later-generation integrated delivery systems, they do not have direct approval authority or clear implementation responsibility.

Few topics are as hotly debated today as how to involve medical staff members in hospital and health system strategic planning. The escalation of competition between independent physicians and hospitals over the provision of outpatient services and, increasingly, entire high-margin clinical service lines, has created enormous complexity and confusion in this area. In addition, some physician groups are bearing risk for the total cost of patient care, sometimes leading them to view the hospital, with its typically higher-cost services, as the enemy. However, with more physicians employed by hospitals and health systems, this dynamic has begun changing in recent years. These alignments and competitive postures yield an ever-evolving mix of tension and cooperation between a hospital and its medical staff that must be considered in its uniqueness in each market.

While no single approach will fit every situation, constructive and careful physician involvement in the planning process is vital to effective planning. Organizations need to make appropriate accommodations for competitive considerations in many instances. Little or no involvement of physicians in strategic planning is not an option. An example approach could include employed physicians on a planning committee or use interviews and reactor panels to engage key independent physician leaders.

Senior Management

Senior management is almost always represented on the strategic planning committee, but these leaders are generally fewer in number and less vocal than board members or physicians. Management, however, plays an important and central role as the coordinator of the strategic planning process—structuring, staffing, keeping it moving along, and overseeing implementation. Senior management's roles and responsibilities in the process generally increase as the planning reaches its later stages.

Other Clinicians

As healthcare organizations seek to retain adequate numbers of high-quality clinical staff, engaging them in strategic planning can be a wise choice to signal their importance. Depending on the nature of the organization, other clinicians (e.g., nurses, physical therapists, psychologists) may play a major or minor role in the strategic planning process. In healthcare organizations not dominated by hospitals or physicians, other clinicians may have significant involvement, including participation on the strategic planning committee of the board. In hospital- or physician-dominated healthcare organizations, other clinicians play a minimal role in the strategic planning process, but they usually get involved when implementation begins or is near.

Other Management

In most cases, other management members only get involved in the strategic planning process prior to implementation if a significant issue or area of concern arises over which they have direct responsibility or expertise.

Although some strategic planning experts advocate a bottom-up strategic planning process that calls for broad-based and extensive participation from all levels of the organization, few healthcare organizations practice such an approach. A summary of the typical involvement of key stakeholder groups in major elements of the planning process appears as exhibit 4.4. While every planning process is carried out somewhat differently, exhibit 4.4 summarizes the

Exhibit 4.4: Typical Stakeholder Participation Grid

Process Elements

Groups/Individuals	Approval	Steering Committee Meetings	Interviews/Surveys	Retreat	Strategy Formulation	Implementation
Entire board	✓	✓	✓	✓	✓	Oversight
Planning Committee of the Board	✓	✓	✓	✓	✓	Oversight
Other Leadership and Management			✓	✓	✓	✓
Physicians		✓	✓	✓	✓	✓
Staff			✓			✓
Community			✓			
Planning staff	← Support entire process →					

information in the previous sections and can be used as an initial framework for structuring involvement at the outset of strategic planning. It may be reconsidered as the process moves along.

EVOLVING AND IMPROVING THE PROCESS

Even today, too many healthcare organizations are wedded to a process that has worked well historically and are reluctant to make significant changes. Some ask, why fix what isn't broken? While there is value and security in the tried and true, regular advances in approaches and methods are occurring in strategic planning in healthcare (and outside of it). Therefore, aspects of a process that is five or ten years old—or even one year—may not be current enough to keep the organization in the forefront. Executives certainly aren't content with yesterday's operations management or financial planning and management approaches, so why shouldn't planning evolve too?

The quality and continuous improvement orientation of an organization's strategic planning process can be evaluated by examining the process at three increasingly challenging levels of inquiry:

1. Is the current process comprehensive, objective, timely, and highly participatory throughout the organization? This question is the most basic.
2. Does the process link effectively to operations and to individual and group performance objectives in the organization?
3. Does the process include continuous learning so that process deficiencies are identified and corrected before the next planning cycle begins?

Organizations with flexible, continuously improving planning processes are able to adapt more readily to the changing environment that is characteristic of healthcare today. These organizations employ planning processes that are far more externally oriented than the typical healthcare organization. They use external factors and forces to create the platform for change that is necessary to keep strategic planning alive and vital.

CONCLUSION

This chapter illustrates that the impact of an effective strategic planning process is at least as important to organizational success as the actual plan itself. When structured and carried out with care, the facilitation, planning retreats, research, and involvement of key stakeholders can lead to a highly successful planning process that maximizes participation and secures a commitment to plan implementation.

REFERENCE

Fogg, C. D. 2010. *Team-Based Strategic Planning: A Complete Guide to Structuring, Facilitating, and Implementing the Process.* Scotts Valley, CA: CreateSpace Independent Publishing Platform.

SUGGESTED READINGS

Krueger, R. A., and M. A. Casey. 2015. *Focus Groups: A Practical Guide for Applied Research*, 5th ed. Thousand Oaks, CA: Sage Publications.

Rea, L. M., and R. A. Parker. 2014. *Designing and Conducting Survey Research: A Comprehensive Guide*, 4th ed. San Francisco: Jossey-Bass.

CHAPTER 5

Encouraging Strategic Thinking

I insist on a lot of time being spent, almost every day,
to just sit and think.

—*Warren Buffett*

Leadership is not just about doing things,
it is also about thinking. Make time for it.

—*Freek Vermeulen*

WHAT IS STRATEGIC THINKING?

This question is puzzling to most, if not all, healthcare executives
and even strategic planning professionals. This question has been
addressed most frequently and successfully outside the context of
healthcare, but the hypotheses and definitions proposed in response
are nonetheless relevant to healthcare executives. This chapter presents a review of writings on the topic, many of them from the late
twentieth century, when the roles of strategic planning and strategic
thinking were being hotly debated. These early insights may be useful
for healthcare leaders seeking to clarify—or refresh—their approach
to the topic. Henry Mintzberg (1994, 107), in his devastating land-
mark critique of strategic planning, says, "Strategic planning isn't
strategic thinking. One is analysis and the other is synthesis . . .
[strategic thinking] involves intuition and creativity. The outcome

of strategic thinking is an integrated perspective of the enterprise, a not-too precisely articulated vision of direction."

Bob Garratt (1995, 8) argues that

> strategic thinking is essentially a process . . . to see, hear and use ingeniously the . . . signals which can give competitive advantage. It requires the ability to create a 'holistic' view of the interconnections between apparently contradictory trends in [the] environment and reframe the current mindsets which you and your competitors hold.

Garratt (1995, 2) further asserts that "'strategic thinking' is the process by which an organization's direction-givers can rise above the daily managerial processes and crises to gain different perspectives of the internal and external dynamics causing change in their environment and thereby give more effective direction to their organization."

Other writers have also contributed to the thinking on the topic. Michael E. Porter (1987, 18) notes that "strategic thinking rarely occurs spontaneously. Without formal planning systems, day-to-day concerns prevail. The future is forgotten. Formal planning provides the discipline to pause occasionally to think about strategic issues." Phil Hanford (1995) adds that "'strategic thinking' in essence amounts to a richer and more creative way of thinking about and managing key issues and opportunities facing your organization. Strategic thinking underscores both the formulation and implementation of your organization's effective strategy."

While executives and board members may have a thorough understanding of and strong skills in operational thinking, Hanford argues that strong strategic thinking skills are essential (see exhibit 5.1), but little has been done to develop these skills. Richard Rumelt (2011, 2) comments that "the core of strategy work is always the same: discovering the critical factors in a situation and designing a way of coordinating and focusing actions to deal with those factors. A leader's most important responsibility is identifying the biggest challenges to forward progress and devising a coherent approach

Exhibit 5.1: Distinguishing Between Strategic and Operational Thinking

Strategic Thinking	Operational Thinking
• Longer term	• Immediate term
• Conceptual	• Concrete
• Reflective or learning	• Action or doing
• Identification of key issues and opportunities	• Resolution of existing performance problems
• Breaking new ground	• Routine and ongoing
• Effectiveness	• Efficiency
• "Hands off" approach	• "Hands on" approach
• "Helicopter" perspective	• "On the ground" perspective

Source: Hanford (1995) in Garratt (1995). Reproduced with permission of The McGraw-Hill Companies.

to overcoming them." Or, as Peter M. Ginter, W. Jack Duncan, and Linda E. Swayne (2018, 17) say it, "Strategic thinkers are always questioning: What are we doing now that we should stop doing? What are we not doing now, but should start doing? And what are we doing now that we should continue to do but perhaps in a fundamentally different way?"

Mintzberg's thoughts have application here as well. He concludes that if strategic planning is to become truly effective and provoke serious organizational change, it needs to move beyond "preservation and rearrangement of established categories . . . and invent new ones. Formal planning has promoted strategies that are extrapolated from the past or copied from others. Strategy making needs to function beyond the boxes, to encourage the informal learning that produces new perspectives and new combinations" (Mintzberg 1994, 109).

How does an organization break out of the box and insert creativity, intuition, a future orientation, new perspectives, and new categories into its process for and results of strategic planning? How can strategic planning rise to Mintzberg's challenge and be a catalyst for critical organizational change?

STRATEGIC THINKING VERSUS STRATEGIC PLANNING

Michel Robert (1998, 30) remarks that "the strategic thinking process can be described as the type of thinking that attempts to determine what an organization should look like in the future." Historically, strategic planning has been primarily concerned with how to get there; operations is all about "how." Robert (1998, 30) comments further: "Strategic thinking identifies the key factors that dictate the direction of an organization, and it is a process that the organization's management uses to set direction and articulate their vision."

Robert identifies four types of companies, as represented by the matrix in exhibit 5.2:

1. Companies in the upper-left quadrant exhibit strong strategic thinking and manage their operations well.
2. Companies in the upper-right quadrant have been successful through good operational management, but they cannot articulate where they are going.
3. Companies in the lower-left quadrant are excellent strategic thinkers, but they cannot implement their vision and generally are weak operationally.
4. Companies in the lower-right quadrant exhibit the worst of both dimensions and usually do not survive very long.

Robert suggests that strategic thinking skills are underdeveloped because most managers and board members have risen to the top ranks based on their skills in operations. In the course of their career development, these individuals did not naturally develop the strategic skills necessary to help lead their companies, and minimal training or support in those areas was provided to them.

Exhibit 5.2: The Strategic Thinking Matrix

STRATEGY (What)

		+	−
OPERATIONS (How)	**+**	EXPLICIT STRATEGIC VISION Operationally Competent	UNCERTAIN STRATEGIC VISION Operationally Competent
	−	EXPLICIT STRATEGIC VISION Operationally Incompetent	UNCERTAIN STRATEGIC VISION Operationally Incompetent

Source: Robert (1998). Reproduced with permission of The McGraw-Hill Companies.

THINKING DIFFERENTLY

Gary Hamel and C. K. Prahalad (1995) state that "to have a share in the future, a company must learn to think differently about three things: 1. the meaning of competitiveness, 2. the measuring of strategy, and 3. the meaning of organization. In many companies, strategic planning is essentially incremental tactical planning punctuated by heroic, and usually ill-conceived, investments. To avoid this situation, we need a concept of strategy that goes beyond form filling and blank check writing."

Hamel and Prahalad argue that strategic planning, as practiced in nearly all organizations, leads to incremental change at best, small gains in market share, and pursuit of modestly profitable niches. Strategic planning is far too focused on *what is*, rather than *what could be.* Deep debates or serious consideration of radical expansion of the boundaries of existing businesses rarely occur, and strategic planning fails to stretch far enough or question fundamental assumptions of the company and its senior staff. Given the rapid rate of change in most industries, strategic planning as described in the previous section is of marginal benefit. Hamel and Prahalad call for a more exploratory and less ritualistic planning process.

In a later publication, Hamel (1998) contends that there are five ways in which more insightful strategy might be brought forth:

1. Involve new voices in the conversation about strategy, including younger employees, new employees, and others outside the inner circle of senior leadership.
2. Create new conversations about strategy, involving diverse perspectives that cut across the usual organizational boundaries.
3. Ignite new passions among individuals involved in the change process that relate to their desires to grow professionally, share in the rewards of success, and play an instrumental role in creating a unique and exciting future.
4. Develop new perspectives about the company, its businesses, its competitors, and its customers that encourage new opportunities to emerge.
5. Encourage new experiments, particularly small-scale forays into new markets and businesses, to gain insights and learning about what strategies might work and which will not.

Above all, Hamel (1998, 8) believes that senior staff must spend less time developing the perfect strategy and more time creating the conditions that could lead to strategy innovation: "In a discontinuous world, strategy innovation is the key to wealth creation. Strategy innovation is the capacity to reconceive the existing industry model in ways that create new value for customers, wrongfoot competitors, and produce new wealth for shareholders." The companies that have grown most successfully in the twenty-first century have either invented new industries (e.g., Google) or dramatically reinvented existing ones (e.g., Amazon). Their strategy is nonlinear.

In an earlier article, Hamel (1996) characterizes linear strategy as ritualistic, reductionist, extrapolative, positioning, elitist, and easy. In exceptional (and unusual) companies, the strategy is inquisitive, expansive, prescient, inventive, inclusive, and demanding. Hamel suggests that strategy making must become subversive and lead to revolution, not evolution, if it is to be an effective mechanism for leading change.

Eric Beinhocker and Sarah Kaplan (2002) make a similar attack on conventional strategic planning and call for new ways to reinvigorate strategic planning through improved strategic thinking processes. In an article whose title, "Tired of Strategic Planning," resonates with many senior executives, they note that "many CEOs complain that their strategic-planning process yields few new ideas and is often fraught with politics" (Beinhocker and Kaplan 2002, 1). They assert that, consistent with Hamel's (1996) observations, a new process to make strategy is required. This process should have two primary goals:

1. *To build prepared minds.* If senior leaders gain a strong understanding of the business, the current and possible future environment, and the rationale for the organizational direction agreed on through the strategic planning process, they are more likely to be able to respond swiftly and effectively to challenges and opportunities that emerge.

2. *To build creative minds.* Beinhocker and Kaplan (2002) agree with Hamel (1996) that strategic experimentation is appropriate and allows for controlled testing of potential future opportunities. They also agree that many of the issues that companies face today are best addressed in multidisciplinary, crosscutting forums that demand new voices, discussions, and perspectives.

Two other articles provide concrete, practical advice on how to insert strategic thinking into the management routines of an organization. Freek Vermeulen (2015) recognizes five big questions that organizational leaders need to ask regularly:

1. *What does not fit?* Are there business units that are peripheral and don't add (or even may detract from) significant value to the organization?
2. *What would an outsider do?* If new external people were in charge, would they jettison legacy products, projects, or beliefs?
3. *Is my organization consistent with my strategy?* Is the company structured to execute the strategy effectively?
4. *Do I understand why we do it this way?* Are practices, habits, operations, processes, and systems appropriate for successful strategy execution?
5. *What might be the long-term consequences?* Have we evaluated the possible substantive effects of this strategy in the long run?

Michael Birshan and Jayanti Kar (2012) suggest a few other basic devices to become more strategic. With the pace of change accelerating in all industries, being on the lookout for potential disrupters must become a regular part of strategic leadership. Technology and new competitors are the most frequent and obvious sources of disruption. Good strategic thinking involves developing an early warning system to identify emerging disruptors. In terms of translating strategic insights into effective action, time spent devising innovative ways to communicate strategy—ways that will break through the postmillennial information glut—is critical.

NEW APPROACHES TO PROMOTING STRATEGIC THINKING

Businesses outside healthcare are years ahead of the healthcare sector in promoting strategic thinking in their organizations. Many companies use the following approaches:

- Contingency planning to address a single uncertainty in a given situation
- Sensitivity analysis to examine the effect of a change in one variable while all other variables remain constant
- Simulation to analyze the effects of simultaneous change in multiple variables

Scenario Planning

Healthcare increasingly employs an even more robust approach: scenario planning. In contrast with contingency planning and sensitivity analysis, scenario planning allows for multiple changes in variables, incorporating both objective analysis (which characterizes simulation) and subjective considerations (which are commonly found in two narrower approaches, contingency planning and sensitivity analysis).

According to Paul J. H. Schoemaker (1995, 27), "Scenario planning attempts to capture the richness and range of possibilities, stimulating decision makers to consider changes they would otherwise ignore. At the same time, it organizes those possibilities into narratives that are easier to grasp and use than great volumes of data." Schoemaker indicates that scenario planning is particularly beneficial for organizations facing the following conditions:

- Uncertainty is high relative to managers' ability to predict or adjust.
- Many costly surprises have occurred in the past.
- The company does not perceive or generate new opportunities.
- The quality of strategic thinking is low (i.e., too routine, too bureaucratic).
- The industry has experienced significant change or is about to.

- The company wants a common language and framework that doesn't stifle diverse thinking.
- There are strong differences of opinion, with multiple opinions having merit.
- The company's competitors are using scenario planning.

Schoemaker observes that because scenarios are designed to construct possible futures, but not specific strategies for dealing with them, some organizations find it beneficial to involve outsiders, such as major customers, key suppliers, regulators, consultants, and academics, in the scenario development process. The objective is "to build a shared framework for strategic thinking that encourages diversity and sharper perceptions about external changes and opportunities" (Schoemaker 1995, 28). Moreover, Schoemaker believes that good scenarios meet four tests: they are relevant, internally consistent, long-term in perspective, and describe clearly different futures.

Decision Analysis and Game Theory

Marion C. Jennings, Scott B. Clay, and Erin P. Carr (2000) advocate decision analysis and game theory as two additional techniques that have been used in business for many years to address future uncertainties creatively. While scenario planning is an excellent approach to addressing a large number of uncertainties, decision analysis works well when a limited number of possible alternatives exist. Game theory allows understanding of interdependencies among affected parties as a result of strategic initiatives, especially the reactions of competitors, strategic alliance partners, customers, and suppliers. These approaches are appropriate in many situations routinely encountered in strategic analysis and should become basic tools in the near future.

Blue Ocean Strategy

W. Chan Kim and Renée Mauborgne's (2005) research led to the coining of the term *blue ocean strategy* to describe the creation of uncontested market space. They argue that most companies pursue incremental improvements by attempting to outcompete their competitors and, in a zero-sum game, increase their share of a crowded market. The more successful approach is to expand the boundaries of their market or invent entirely new market space (the blue ocean). These innovators do not use the competition as a reference point, but instead follow a different strategic logic they term *value innovation*. Value innovation, which defies the conventional competitive paradigm of having to choose between differentiation and cost, combines these two options to find new and uncontested market space (see exhibits 5.3 and 5.4). Value innovation is created in the market space where a company's actions favorably affect both its cost structure and its value proposition to buyers. Cost savings are realized by eliminating

Exhibit 5.3: Value Innovation: The Cornerstone of Blue Ocean Strategy

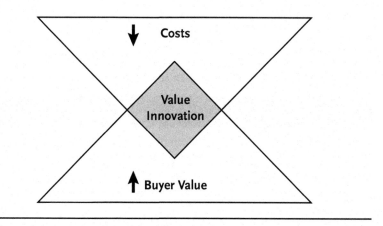

Source: Kim and Mauborgne (2005).

or reducing the factors on which an industry competes. Buyer value is lifted by raising or creating elements that the industry has never offered. Over time, costs are reduced further as scale economies kick in because of the high sales volumes that superior value generates.

This new space creates opportunities for rapid and profitable growth, unlike the *red ocean*, in which nearly all companies operate and compete. Kim and Mauborgne cite many examples of companies applying this kind of strategic thinking to the problem of crowded markets—Uber is one example.

Kim and Mauborgne advise that blue ocean strategy contrasts with traditional strategic planning in the following ways:

- It draws on collective wisdom, unlike top-down or bottom-up planning.
- It focuses on building the big picture more than on number crunching.
- It should be conversational rather than documentation driven.
- It must be creative, rather than largely analytical.
- It should be motivational (resulting in "willing commitment"), instead of bargaining driven (resulting in "negotiated commitment").

Exhibit 5.4: Red Ocean Versus Blue Ocean Strategy

Red Ocean Strategy	Blue Ocean Strategy
Compete in existing market space.	Create uncontested market space.
Beat the competition.	Make the competition irrelevant.
Exploit existing demand.	Create and capture new demand.
Make the value–cost trade-off.	Break the value–cost trade-off.
Align the whole system of a firm's activities with its strategic choice of differentiation or low cost.	Align the whole system of a firm's activities in pursuit of differentiation and low cost.

Source: Kim and Mauborgne (2005).

The Strategic Planning Process

CHAPTER 6

Phase 1: Analyzing the Environment

In God we trust. All others bring data.

—*W. Edwards Deming*

You can never plan the future by the past.

—*Edmund Burke*

LOOKING FORWARD VERSUS LOOKING BACKWARD

Strategic planning typically begins with an analysis of the current situation and recent history of the organization, referred to as the *strategic assessment, situation analysis, or environmental assessment* (see exhibit 6.1).

The strategic assessment should

- identify past successes and failures: what has worked, what has not, and why;
- give trustees and others less knowledgeable about the organization a solid grounding for constructive involvement;
- help determine what factors are subject to the organization's control and influence; and
- identify how external forces might affect the organization in the future.

Exhibit 6.1: Developing the Plan: Strategic Assessment

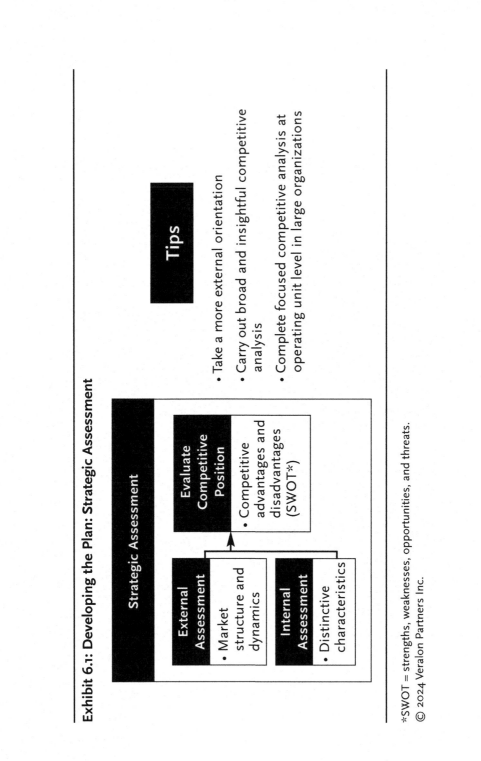

Strategic Assessment

External Assessment
• Market structure and dynamics

Internal Assessment
• Distinctive characteristics

Evaluate Competitive Position
• Competitive advantages and disadvantages (SWOT*)

Tips
• Take a more external orientation
• Carry out broad and insightful competitive analysis
• Complete focused competitive analysis at operating unit level in large organizations

*SWOT = strengths, weaknesses, opportunities, and threats.
© 2024 Veralon Partners Inc.

Although the strategic assessment may be viewed as mere busy-work for the planning staff before the real strategic planning begins, it has valid and important purposes that should be enumerated and highlighted at the start of the assessment. Among them, as the first activity in the planning process, the strategic assessment largely sets the tone for the strategic plan and indicates how the rest of the planning process is likely to unfold by examining the following questions:

- Will the process be comprehensive in scope?
- Which key organizational stakeholders will be involved in a constructive way?
- Will it be highly structured or loosely organized?
- Will it be driven by facts, strive to overcome bias, and focus on critical issues?
- Have the outputs of the strategic planning process been clearly articulated, and will this process drive toward their achievement?
- Is a planning schedule being followed, and will that planning lead to action?

As discussed in chapter 3, many planning efforts get off to a poor start because the planning process and activities lack sufficient advance conceptualization, organization, or explanation to the whole organization. The strategic assessment, if poorly planned and executed, can derail subsequent strategic planning activities. The strategic assessment is characterized by three separate processes: information gathering, distillation of key findings, and translation into conclusions.

Perhaps the most common concern when undertaking an strategic assessment is that the staff may become enmeshed in data gathering and analysis, bogging down the entire planning process early on—a problem known as analysis paralysis. Guidelines and resources for effectively carrying out data gathering—a complicated and controversial task—are provided in exhibits 6.2, 6.3, and 6.4.

Exhibit 6.2: Minimum Data Requirements for the Strategic Assessment

Internal	External
• Characteristics and utilization of major programs and services • Key indicators: facilities, equipment, staff • Clinical and service quality performance • Financial performance and position	• Major demographic and economic indicators • Major technology, reimbursement, and regulatory factors • Competitive position of major programs and services • Profile and analysis of key competitors • Future market size and characteristics

© 2024 Veralon Partners Inc.

While it is important to compile a database that clearly reflects the organization's historical performance and market, strategic planning is not primarily an exercise in plotting historical patterns and then extrapolating. As the Edmund Burke quote at the beginning of this chapter implies, historical performance is not a reliable indicator of the future. Reviewing recent history and analyzing successes and failures is a comforting activity. But organizations gain little from overanalysis of the past, and whatever momentum and excitement it may be able to create at the initiation of strategic planning will likely be lost if historical performance, particularly negative trends or areas of underperformance, becomes the major focus of the strategic planning process. This is particularly true of data for 2020 to 2022, when performance was unusually poor and erratic because of the COVID-19 pandemic, making it difficult to glean meaningful insights from trends during this period. When a "new normal" is established, it will again be possible to gain insights from trend data.

Even then, it will be important not to overanalyze, and to instead maintain a future focus.

Being deliberate and focused in both the type and volume of data that are being sought will not only expedite the strategic assessment but also ensure that excessive time and resources are not spent overanalyzing information simply because it is available. The key takeaways from past results will be reflected in market share and financial position. A few tips for organizing the data collection process follow:

- Create a checklist prior to data collection identifying the specific categories of information that will be most helpful for the organization and situation.
- Limit the historical data to three to five years of trend information.
- Use existing or regularly updated data sets, particularly those that are commonly employed in the organization, as they are more likely to be accurate and are easier to obtain than customized reports.
- Select appropriate benchmarks for comparison.
- Inventory information as it is collected and be sure to clearly label files (e.g., type of information, years included, source) so that information can be easily located and accessed later in the strategic planning process.

While quantitative analytics can tell much about *how* an organization has performed in recent years, data in isolation lack context and perspective on *why* the organization chose a particular path or what environmental factors affected performance. Stakeholder interviews provide valuable insights that will support or supplement data findings. These interviews also shed light on topics that cannot be extracted from analytics, such as culture or an organization's readiness for change (exhibit 6.5). Board members, senior management, and physician leaders are typically the subjects of these interviews.

Exhibit 6.3: Online Healthcare Data Resources

- Agency for Healthcare Research and Quality — www.ahrq.gov
- American Hospital Association — www.aha.org
- American Medical Association — www.ama-assn.org
- Centers for Disease Control and Prevention — www.cdc.gov
- Centers for Medicare & Medicaid Services — www.medicare.gov/hospitalcompare www.medicare.gov/nursinghomecompare
- Dartmouth Atlas of Health Care — www.dartmouthatlas.org
- Health Resources and Services Administration — www.hrsa.gov
- Kaiser Family Foundation — www.kff.org
- National Cancer Institute — www.cancer.gov
- National Center for Health Statistics — www.cdc.gov/nchs
- State-specific hospital discharge databases — (Varies by state)

© 2024 Veralon Partners Inc.

Exhibit 6.4: Creative Data Gathering for the Strategic Assessment: Competitor Intelligence

Hard Data	Soft Data
- State licensure and other state filings - 990 and 10-K reports and other federal filings - Hospital associations - Public vendors - Continuing disclosures for municipal bonds	- Annual reports - Websites - Public relations releases or brochures - Press releases - Presentations by executives - Former employees

© 2024 Veralon Partners Inc.

Interviews should not be limited to internal stakeholders. External constituents, including regional competitors' senior management, major payer representatives, community leaders, and relevant political representatives, can offer perspectives as to how the organization is perceived in the market.

If more extensive feedback is desired or required, online surveys or focus groups can be useful tools to engage a broader group of stakeholders. Although the substantive value of input gathering may diminish significantly as greater amounts of information are collected, the political value of soliciting and carefully listening to organizational leaders' and stakeholders' opinions should not be ignored.

APPROACH TO THE INTERNAL ASSESSMENT

The internal assessment combines data analysis with qualitative information to formulate an accurate profile of the historical performance of the organization. Along with the external assessment, discussed in the next section, it establishes the organization's strengths, weaknesses, opportunities, and threats (SWOT) and identifies competitive

Exhibit 6.5: Internal and External Interview Topics

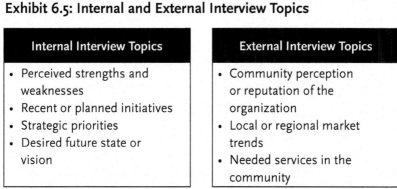

Internal Interview Topics	External Interview Topics
• Perceived strengths and weaknesses • Recent or planned initiatives • Strategic priorities • Desired future state or vision	• Community perception or reputation of the organization • Local or regional market trends • Needed services in the community

advantages and disadvantages that serve as a springboard for subsequent strategic planning activities.

Telling the story of a complex organization is challenging. Information needs to be organized in a way that allows conclusions to be extracted and easily understood by many different constituencies. It is helpful to group the information into summary categories. These categories and the data that are evaluated will be different for every organization. Exhibit 6.6 shows possible categories that can be explored and related key questions that should be answered in the internal assessment.

Larger, more complex organizations may need to evaluate entities or lines of business separately, while smaller organizations may be able to consider the enterprise as a whole. For example, a large health system might profile its acute care business, medical group, post-acute care business, health plan, and so on individually across relevant categories.

Exhibit 6.6: Possible Information Summary Categories

Scale and scope of services	• What is the organization's coverage of the care continuum? • What is the organization's size (revenue and volume) relative to competitors? • What are the breadth and depth of services? • What are the number, nature, and distribution of customer access points? • How is utilization trending by service or entity? • What virtual access points are offered?
Financials	• What is the current financial position? • What has been the recent financial performance and what are the drivers of that performance? • What is the organization's payer mix? • What types of reimbursement contracts are currently in place and what types are being proposed? • Have any major capital needs been identified?

(continued)

(continued from previous page)

Providers	• What is the profile of the medical staff and other providers (e.g., number, age mix, gaps)? • What is the base of employed or tightly aligned providers? • What is the degree of provider engagement?
Value	• How does the organization perform on clinical quality, patient safety, and patient satisfaction measures? • What is the cost of care or service delivery? • Has the organization pursued and succeeded in value-based arrangements with payer? • How are services priced?
Integration	• Do elements of the organization effectively coordinate care or service delivery? • Are organizational goals and incentives aligned across departments or entities? • Is there significant "leakage" or internal referrals to external entities?
Operations	• How efficient is the organization? • Are there any significant facility or staffing needs? • How is the organization positioned in information technology?
Competitive position or market capture	• What is the organization's market share by service and geography? • Who is the market leader by service and geography? • Is there significant outmigration from the service area for any service or consumer group?
Future orientation	• Has the organization prepared for value-based payments? • Can the organization manage change? • What is the organization's structure and does that structure support future growth?

The Internal Assessment's End Product

The product of the internal assessment should be a summary of the results that contains a limited number of charts and tables that are both clear and concise in their key conclusions (see exhibits 6.7 and 6.8 for examples). These conclusions should not simply describe trend information but rather explore implications for the organization's position moving forward. These implications can range from an urgent or immediate need for attention to a source of competitive advantage in any given category. Supporting documentation is required and should be prepared and available as backup. No exact measure for how much supporting documentation is necessary exists, as every internal assessment is unique. A guiding rule is that if a potential table, graph, or analysis does not support or answer a key question identified in the internal assessment, it is likely extraneous.

APPROACH TO THE EXTERNAL ASSESSMENT

The external assessment, like the internal assessment, should be an accurate profile of the organization's historical performance as it relates to the marketplace. The external assessment profiles the historical performance and evolution of the marketplace and begins to look forward by explicitly considering market trends and forecasts. The external assessment has four main components.

Review Population Characteristics
This task identifies the broadest trends and variables that have had and will have an impact on organizational performance. While key community demographic, economic, and health status indicators for the past three to five years should be profiled and forecasts provided for the next five to ten years, if available, it is important to note that minor shifts in these measures are of minimal or no consequence to the strategic planning process. However, some changes have major

Exhibit 6.7: Snapshot of an Integrated System's Health Plan

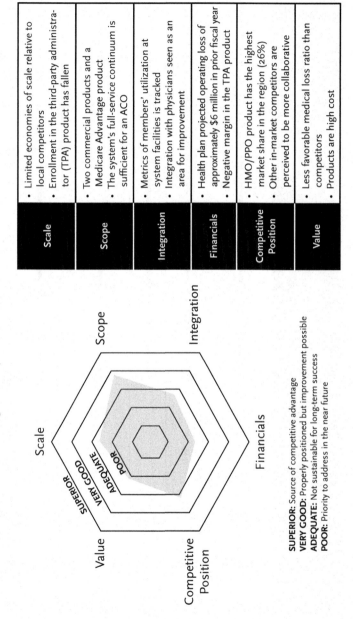

Scale	• Limited economies of scale relative to local competitors • Enrollment in the third-party administrator (TPA) product has fallen
Scope	• Two commercial products and a Medicare Advantage product • The system's full-service continuum is sufficient for an ACO
Integration	• Metrics of members' utilization at system facilities is tracked • Integration with physicians seen as an area for improvement
Financials	• Health plan projected operating loss of approximately $6 million in prior fiscal year • Negative margin in the TPA product
Competitive Position	• HMO/PPO product has the highest market share in the region (26%) • Other in-market competitors are perceived to be more collaborative
Value	• Less favorable medical loss ratio than competitors • Products are high cost

SUPERIOR: Source of competitive advantage
VERY GOOD: Properly positioned but improvement possible
ADEQUATE: Not sustainable for long-term success
POOR: Priority to address in the near future

© 2024 Veralon Partners Inc.

Exhibit 6.8: Community Hospital's Internal Assessment

Categories	Assessment Focus	Urgent Need for Immediate Attention	Major Changes Required for Long-term Sustainability	On the Right Track; Needs Additional Development for Continued Success	Well Positioned for Long-Term Success with Minor Gaps	Well Positioned for Current and Future Competitive Advantage
Scale/scope	– Relative size of operations – Mix and distribution of services and sites – Care continuum coverage				★ →	
Financial position	– Current and historic financial performance, position, and access to capital		★ →			
Market position	– Current and historic market share performance and position			★ →		
Value position	– Quality and service outcomes relative to cost and price – Infrastructure and track record in value-based payer contracts		★ →			
Integration	– Physician alignment – Coordination among services and sites within the system – Care continuum integration	★ →				

© 2024 Veralon Partners Inc.

implications. For example, projected growth of the population aged 65 and older and contraction of the population aged 45 to 64 from 2020 to 2030 is expected to spur a major shift in the payer mix, from better-paying commercial plans to lower-paying Medicare.

Organizations should take care not to overreach and instead should aim to complete a review with a scope that is general and high level rather than detailed. In addition to identifying broad trends, this analysis is occasionally useful in identifying geographical areas or population segments with strong potential for future cultivation.

Review the State of Healthcare Delivery in the Local and Regional Market

This step is perhaps the most important in the external assessment, and it should be afforded requisite attention and resources. The purpose of reviewing applicable healthcare technology, delivery, reimbursement, regulatory, consolidation, teaching, and research trends is to identify any major environmental influences that have affected recent organizational performance and, more important, may affect future performance and strategies. (Examples of such reviews for two areas of the United States are shown in exhibits 6.9 and 6.10.) In addition to identifying an anticipated trend's impact on organizational performance, key statistics or research should be included to support the conclusions.

Analyze Competitors

Analyzing competitors is another critical task—and often the most difficult one. Competitor data in healthcare can be incomplete and out-of-date, although good information can be collected with some hard work and resourcefulness.

Competitors may operate on a variety of levels. Some organizations may compete in most or all service categories, whereas others may do so in one or a few select niches. An increasingly common mistake in competitor assessments, particularly for hospitals and health systems, is an exclusive focus on traditional competitors. In many markets across the United States, new market entrants are

Exhibit 6.9: Select Market Characteristics in the Southeast

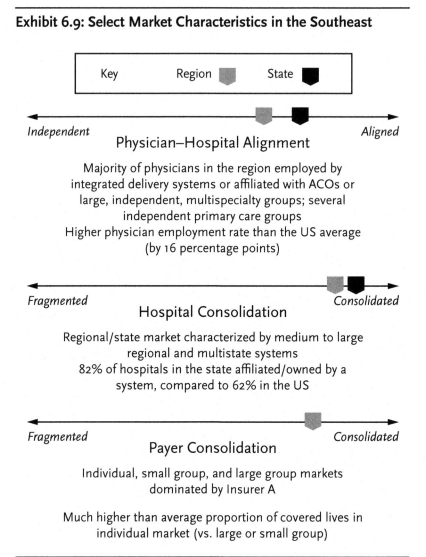

| Key | Region | State |

Physician–Hospital Alignment

Independent — *Aligned*

Majority of physicians in the region employed by integrated delivery systems or affiliated with ACOs or large, independent, multispecialty groups; several independent primary care groups
Higher physician employment rate than the US average (by 16 percentage points)

Hospital Consolidation

Fragmented — *Consolidated*

Regional/state market characterized by medium to large regional and multistate systems
82% of hospitals in the state affiliated/owned by a system, compared to 62% in the US

Payer Consolidation

Fragmented — *Consolidated*

Individual, small group, and large group markets dominated by Insurer A

Much higher than average proportion of covered lives in individual market (vs. large or small group)

competing with acute care providers, particularly in the retail space. Collect competitor data from local, regional, state, and national sources, including those listed in exhibits 6.3 and 6.4. Because of this topic's importance, and because of evidence that many healthcare organizations have historically failed to complete this task adequately,

Exhibit 6.10: Select Market Characteristics in the Midwest

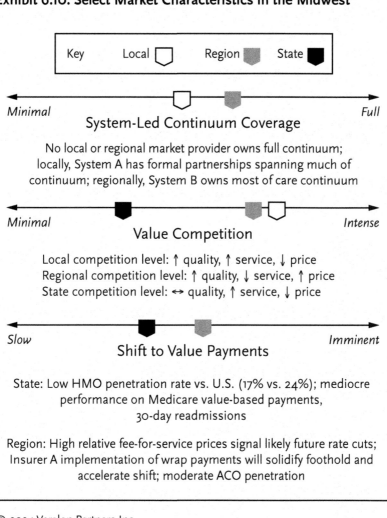

Key   Local ⬠   Region ⬟   State ◆

◀——————————⬠——⬟——————————▶
Minimal   *Full*
System-Led Continuum Coverage

No local or regional market provider owns full continuum;
locally, System A has formal partnerships spanning much of
continuum; regionally, System B owns most of care continuum

◀————————◆—————————⬟⬠——————▶
Minimal   *Intense*
Value Competition

Local competition level: ↑ quality, ↑ service, ↓ price
Regional competition level: ↑ quality, ↓ service, ↑ price
State competition level: ↔ quality, ↑ service, ↓ price

◀—————————◆———⬟————————————▶
Slow   *Imminent*
Shift to Value Payments

State: Low HMO penetration rate vs. U.S. (17% vs. 24%); mediocre
performance on Medicare value-based payments,
30-day readmissions

Region: High relative fee-for-service prices signal likely future rate cuts;
Insurer A implementation of wrap payments will solidify foothold and
accelerate shift; moderate ACO penetration

a three-part example from a strategic plan (exhibits 6.11, 6.12, and
6.13) demonstrates a rigorous analysis for a fictional organization.

Market Forecasts and Implications

In addition to assessing anticipated population, economic, and
health status changes in the market, it may be necessary to forecast

health services utilization. This step is not always required and can constitute overanalysis in some circumstances. Utilization forecasts can be employed if there is a predetermined consensus that the strategic plan will likely focus on a specific segment of services (e.g., outpatient services, cancer services), necessitating more thorough analysis. The forecast will include a baseline level of market utilization for the specific services and projected growth or reduction of those services based on a variety of factors, including population and demographic changes, variations in care delivery (e.g., surgeries shifting to outpatient settings, hospital-at-home models), or the effect of efforts to manage care to reduce avoidable admissions.

The External Assessment's End Product

A summary of the market structure and dynamics should be prepared in parallel with the internal assessment. When possible, comparison to benchmarks can help focus the summary on noteworthy key points. A brief report with several charts and tables accompanied by modest narration or highlighting of key points should suffice. Additional materials may be available for backup support if needed.

TRANSLATION INTO CONCLUSIONS

The internal and external assessments need to produce three main outputs to lay the foundation for subsequent activities: (1) a succinct, pointed, and honest statement of the organization's competitive advantages and disadvantages in the marketplace; (2) assumptions about the future environment; and (3), with the content of the first two outputs in mind, identification of critical planning issues that require resolution in the strategic planning process.

Exhibit 6.11: Analysis of XYZ's Competitors' Strategies

Strategy	System A	System B	AMC A	AMC B	Comm. Hospital	Niche Provider
Value position	●	○	○	○	◐	◐
Market capture	●	◐	◐	●	○	●
Horizontal integration (w/ other health systems)	●	◐	◐	●	◐	○
Vertical integration (w/ payers and physicians)	●	○	○	●	○	○
GME and research	○	○	●	●	○	○
Marketing and consumer preferences	●	○		●	○	◐

Symbol	Description
●	High risk to XYZ
◐	Moderate risk to XYZ
○	Low risk to XYZ

System A and AMC B are XYZ's most significant competitors

Competitive Advantages and Disadvantages

No particular approach or format for determining and displaying competitive advantages and disadvantages is universally accepted. In general, the three most reliable measures of competitive advantage or disadvantage are value position (quality relative to cost), market share, and bond rating. Upward historical trends in these variables usually indicate a strong competitive position. However, trends seen in healthcare organizations are rarely clear-cut. Simply focusing on these indicators, for example, masks major shifts in competitive position because of the lagged effect of capital or human investments. The most commonly used format for displaying competitive advantage and disadvantage is a SWOT analysis. Each category in

Exhibit 6.12: XYZ's Future Competitive Environment and Planning Implications

Strategy	System A	System B	AMC A	AMC B	Comm. Hospital	Niche Provider	Planning Implications for XYZ
Quality or cost differentiation	X				X	X	Enhance value position in core services
Targeted growth in priority geography	X		X	X		X	Strengthen existing referral relationships in priority geography
Network development	X			X			Build and integrate care continuum
Survival mode		X			X		Consider candidates for affiliation or acquisition

XYZ will face difficult competition in its target geography and will need to be active in network development to keep pace with the scale development of its most significant competitors.

© 2024 Veralon Partners Inc.

Exhibit 6.13: Potential Future Competitor Positioning Re: XYZ

Organization	Baseline Forecast	Aggressive Forecast (in addition to baseline)	Declining Forecast
System A	• Continues ambulatory growth • Employs significant number of independent physicians • Adds 1–2 community hospitals to system	• Establishes insurance product • Develops significant base of covered lives; keeps all referrals • National prominence for clinical integration or other innovations	• FTC challenges recent merger • Becomes overextended and pulls back on investments and programs
System B	• Remains strong in their core services • Modest growth attributed to physician practice acquisition	• Out of market parent system infuses major capital resources • Develops integrated service lines	• Financial erosion to a safety-net hospital
Community hospital	• Affiliates with local system • Capital infusion boosts select services	• Affiliates with AMC B to establish strong academic-community network	• Does not draw affiliation interest and reduces scope of services or closes

the analysis has a specific orientation (internal, external) and purpose for examination, as shown in exhibit 6.14. A sample SWOT analysis is provided in exhibit 6.15.

While the team may initially generate a lengthy SWOT analysis, the final list should be refined to a one-page summary. As the exhibits show, items may be drawn from any category of the internal and external assessments, but not every assessment category needs to be represented in the final summary.

The purpose of the SWOT analysis is to provide organizational leadership with a clear assessment of where the organizational stands in its competitive marketplace. Little benefit is derived from applying overly complicated analysis to achieve the results. Leadership must use its skills, experience, and judgment to synthesize all of the external assessment findings and determine the organization's real advantages and disadvantages.

Assumptions About the Future

Up to this point in its process, the strategic assessment has been concerned primarily with the past. The remainder of the assessment and the strategic planning process shifts the focus to the future. The first forward-looking task is to develop a picture of the future environment, at least three to five years hence and perhaps further, in which the organization will operate. This forecast should consider key external factors (some local or regional, others state or national) that may have a significant impact on the organization's future strategies. It should not be strictly numerical (for example, delineating market size and the precise level of reimbursement changes), but rather a qualitative and macrolevel view of significant future and external influences.

The predictions of healthcare futurists and forecasts from publications and associations that track emerging trends can help healthcare organizations formulate their own assumptions (see the suggested readings at the end of this chapter for examples of available resources).

Historically, healthcare organizations and the general business community have predicated much of their planning on one view of the future environment—usually a linear extrapolation from the past—rather than evaluating a wide range of possible futures. Upheavals in healthcare and other fields illustrate how this singular view of the future has led to major errors in organizational strategy and legitimate concern about the wisdom of planning for the future with a narrow view of possible future realities. For

Exhibit 6.14: SWOT Category Orientation

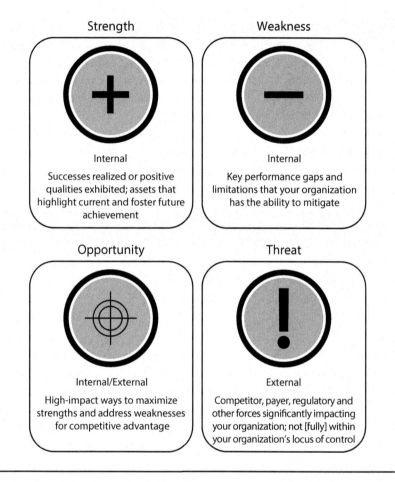

Strength

Internal

Successes realized or positive qualities exhibited; assets that highlight current and foster future achievement

Weakness

Internal

Key performance gaps and limitations that your organization has the ability to mitigate

Opportunity

Internal/External

High-impact ways to maximize strengths and address weaknesses for competitive advantage

Threat

External

Competitor, payer, regulatory and other forces significantly impacting your organization; not [fully] within your organization's locus of control

example, in the 1980s and 1990s, Blockbuster video stores were very successful until the popularity and convenience of Netflix led to its demise.

Even though they wrote during a time of slower-paced change, Hamel and Prahalad (1994, 126) point out that "if senior executives don't have reasonably detailed answers to the 'future' questions,

Exhibit 6.15: An Integrated Health System's Strategic Profile

Strengths	Weaknesses
• Facilities (hospital campuses) • Scope of services • Variety of specialized services • Medical equipment and technology • Owned health plan • Primary care base • Quality outcomes relative to competitors	• Limited debt capacity • Siloed system components • Relationship with medical staff • Condition of post-acute and ambulatory facilities • Leadership in transition • Patient satisfaction
Opportunities	**Threats**
• Rural outreach • System integration • Competitor ownership transition • Shift to customer-focused culture • University affiliation • Insurance product advancement • Affiliations • Transition to value-based environment	• Local/regional economy • Declining or flat reimbursement • Specialist alignment to other systems • Competitor market share gains • Historical perspective of the organization as non-collaborative • Payer mix weakening due to aging population

and if the answers they have are not significantly different from the 'today' answers, there is little chance that their companies will remain market leaders."

Planning for the future in a narrow, limited environmental context may have been acceptable in the more static, highly regulated healthcare environment that prevailed through the early 1990s. However, this approach is no longer feasible, and constitutes one of the main differences between contemporary strategic planning methods and those of even the recent past.

To ensure that a broader perspective is adopted, planning teams should define alternative futures and discuss them fully. Products of the strategic assessment may need to be revised or fine-tuned after completing this task.

Many excellent references offer approaches for developing alternative future scenarios, which can be simplified to the following steps:

- Define the scope of the scenario
- Construct initial scenario options
- Check for consistency, plausibility, and applicability with each critical planning issues
- Develop quantitative models, research or other material for enhanced understanding
- Evolve toward decisions on most likely scenario(s)

This approach enables organizational leadership to consider diverse alternative futures and distill a composite scenario (or scenarios) from this broad view of the future. It is important to consider that while a scenario exercise may have varying degrees of usefulness for management or planning staff, who consider potential futures on a regular basis, it can be a helpful exercise for trustees or physicians, who are not generally focused on specific market or sector trends. Exhibit 6.16 shows a scenario exercise that was used by the Strategic Planning Steering Committee at a hospital in the Southwest.

In contrast, most healthcare organizations typically rely—explicitly or implicitly—on the planning staff to develop a single future environmental scenario by extrapolating current trends and incorporating current hot issues.

Regardless of the approach used, the result should be an explicit set of underlying assumptions about the future, on which the remaining planning analyses and outputs will be based. Exhibit 6.17 presents an example of the results of this process. As the exhibit illustrates, the assumptions should be stated briefly to avoid unnecessarily

Exhibit 6.16: Steering Committee Scenario Exercise: Shift to Value Payments for a Southwestern Hospital

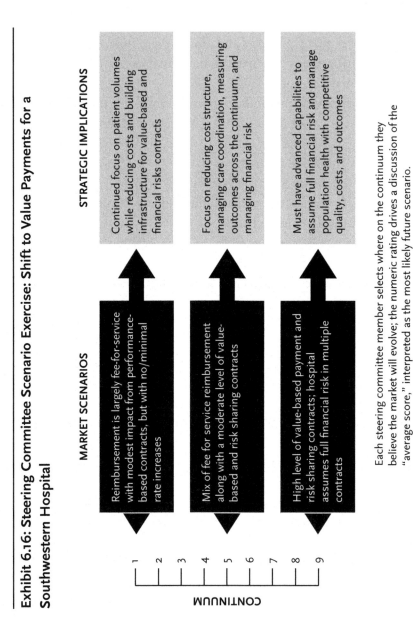

MARKET SCENARIOS

Reimbursement is largely fee-for-service with modest impact from performance-based contracts, but with no/minimal rate increases

Mix of fee for service reimbursement along with a moderate level of value-based and risk sharing contracts

High level of value-based payment and risk sharing contracts; hospital assumes full financial risk in multiple contracts

CONTINUUM

1
2
3
4
5
6
7
8
9

STRATEGIC IMPLICATIONS

Continued focus on patient volumes while reducing costs and building infrastructure for value-based and financial risks contracts

Focus on reducing cost structure, managing care coordination, measuring outcomes across the continuum, and managing financial risk

Must have advanced capabilities to assume full financial risk and manage population health with competitive quality, costs, and outcomes

Each steering committee member selects where on the continuum they believe the market will evolve; the numeric rating drives a discussion of the "average score," interpreted as the most likely future scenario.

complicating the presentation of the future environment in which the organization will operate. This concise, simple summary of a potential future environment is a powerful guide by which to consider, or in many cases reconsider, critical planning issues and, subsequently, organizational mission and vision.

Identification of Critical Planning Issues

The final task in the strategic assessment is to determine what critical planning issues need to be resolved during the strategic planning process. All of the preceding analysis feeds into this final result. The

---

Exhibit 6.17: Future Assumptions Regarding the National and Local Market

- Provider success will be based on delivering value, as defined by high-quality services at a low cost.
- Fee-for-service reimbursement will remain but will account for a lower percentage of most healthcare providers' revenue.
- Regional health systems will become more prevalent, with many markets consisting of only a few large systems.
- Consolidation in the provider and insurance market will give way to a focus on integration of recently partnered organizations.
- Primary care will play an increasingly central role in population health management.
- Nontraditional competitors will more frequently enter the healthcare market, with a focus on differentiating based on technology or customer service.
- Financial pressures will be exacerbated as commercial-payment increases slow to low single-digit levels and states manage budget issues.
- A significant proportion of physicians will be employed by hospitals, systems, or large multispecialty practices.
- Technological advances will continue to shift services to the outpatient setting.

---

determination is subjective and usually evolves through an iterative process of some or all of the steps described in the next paragraph, depending on the size and complexity of the organization, the issues it faces, and the extent to which participative processes are used in strategic planning.

After the planning analyst or planning staff members select an initial list of issues, senior management team members review and revise the list, alone or together. The list may then go to the strategic planning committee members, individually or collectively, who will perform the same review. The issue list may then be accepted as a basis for moving forward or returned to the planning or senior management staff for further work. Exhibit 6.18 shows a worksheet used by a health system in Nevada to facilitate the prioritization of critical planning issues.

Typical critical planning issues that are common to strategic plans today include the following:

- Achieving sufficient scale and scope of services (via organic growth or affiliation)
- Delivering and demonstrating value
- Aligning with physicians
- Constructing an effective and integrated delivery system
- Achieving financial sustainability and/or significant improvement in financial performance
- Managing population health
- Improving health equity
- Preparing for new competitors including investor-backed entities
- Instituting effective information technology, including digital health access and artificial intelligence
- Developing clinical programs
- Improving competitive positioning

A variety of largely operational and quasi-strategic matters frequently emerge as critical issues in the strategic assessment. Leaders

Exhibit 6.18: Critical Planning Issue Prioritization Worksheet

Instructions: Allocate 100 points among the emerging issues to indicate priority (more points = higher priority)

Emerging Issue	Description	Allocated Points
Integration	Seamlessly connect all aspects of the system operationally and electronically, with a focus on shared incentives and accountability	
Financial improvement	Stabilize and improve financial performance and position to ensure the system is able to fund both routine and strategic priorities moving forward	
Organizational design	Redesign the organizational structure, where necessary, to ensure the proper flow of information and decision making	
Culture transformation	Develop a consistent organization-wide culture based on a unique set of values that will make the system attractive to both customers and employees	
Physician alignment	Establish formal relationships with physicians across all specialties that are mutually beneficial and successful	
Service portfolio	Implement the ideal product and market mix to bolster and sustain long-term growth	
Population health management	Set mechanisms and processes to improve the health of a defined population(s) within the service area	
Partnerships	Affiliate with organizations and/or provider groups through a variety of models to extend the system's reach or grow in desired markets and services	
Value	Improve clinical outcomes and customer experience at the lowest possible cost	
	Total Points	100

© 2024 Veralon Partners Inc.

are often tempted to enumerate dozens of "important" issues that need to be resolved to ensure future success. But by doing so, they sacrifice strategic clarity and precision in the name of comprehensiveness and political expediency.

A limited number of issues can and should be dealt with in the strategic planning process if the planning is to lead to a successful outcome. Exhibit 6.19 depicts how one healthcare delivery system subdivided the defined issues into two categories: critical strategic priorities and critical resource priorities. This approach is one reasonable way to handle an otherwise thorny political situation. Few healthcare organizations have so many critical issues that they cannot be condensed into five to seven strategic issue categories. Increasingly, as planning horizons have condensed from five years or more years to three to five years because of increased sector uncertainty, some organizations are limiting their critical planning issues to as few as three key priorities. Failure to limit the number of issues to address in subsequent planning activities almost always dooms the strategic

Exhibit 6.19: One Healthcare System's Critical Issues Categorization

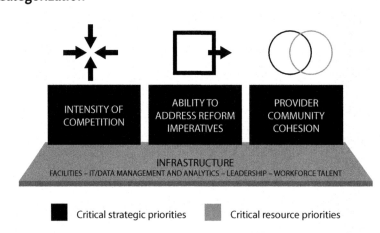

© 2024 Veralon Partners Inc.

planning process. It is impossible to effectively tackle an excessive number of issues concurrently, and doing so may confuse organizational leadership about what issues are truly critical to strategic success.

CONCLUSION

A brief and high-level list of critical planning issues that require resolution is an excellent springboard to the next two planning activities: establishing an overall or corporate direction and formulating core strategies. Such a list reduces voluminous data and other information collected during the strategic assessment to a manageable amount and energizes organizational leadership to move forward on strategic planning with a clear focus on issues of immense importance to the organization.

REFERENCE

Hamel, G., and C. K. Prahalad. 1994. "Competing for the Future." *Harvard Business Review* 72 (4): 122–28.

SUGGESTED READINGS

American Hospital Association. "AHA Environmental Scan." Published annually. www.aha.org/environmentalscan.

Health Affairs. Published monthly. www.healthaffairs.org.

hfm Magazine. Published monthly. www.hfma.org/hfm.

Journal of Healthcare Management. Published every other month. www.ache.org/pubs/journals.

Medicare Payment Advisory Commission. *Report to the Congress: Medicare Payment Policy*. Published annually in March. www.medpac.gov.

MGMA Connection. "The State of Medical Practice." Published annually in the January issue. www.mgma.com/mgma-connection -magazine.

Modern Healthcare. "Healthcare Business and Policy Outlook." Published annually in the first issue of the year. www .modernhealthcare.com.

Society for Health Care Strategy & Market Development and Health Administration Press. *Futurescan: Health Care Trends and Implications.* Published annually. http://shsmd.org/futurescan.

CHAPTER 7

Phase 2: Organizational Direction

If you do not change direction, you may end up where you
are heading.

—*Lao Tzu (attributed)*

When it comes to the future, there are three kinds of people:
those who let it happen, those who make it happen, and
those who wonder what happened.

—*John M. Richardson Jr.*

Good business leaders create a vision, articulate the vision,
passionately own the vision, and relentlessly drive it to
completion.

—*Jack Welch*

The second phase of the strategic planning process, establishing the
organizational direction, initiates in earnest the process of looking forward to chart the organization's future. This activity sets
direction at a high level, encompassing mission, vision, and values.
Subsequent activities address important components of the future
direction and the particular aspects of implementation. Exhibit 7.1
provides a context for the principal outputs of the organizational
direction activity.

Exhibit 7.1: Organizational Direction

Mission	Vision	Values
Reflects an organization's purpose ("why" we exist)	Expresses ideals, standards, and desired future state ("what" the organization wants to be)	Defines the organization's desired culture and behavior

High-level aspirations for the future provide an important context for strategy development.

Organizations that have a clear picture of what they want their organization to look like in five to ten years are better equipped to articulate and implement the more specific components of the strategic plan.

© 2024 Veralon Partners Inc.

REVIEW OF THE LITERATURE

The strategic planning literature highlights the importance of a clear mission and vision to the organization's future success. Peter M. Ginter, W. Jack Duncan, and Linda E. Swayne (2018) note that mission, vision, values, and strategic goals are accurately called directional strategies because they guide strategists in making key organizational decisions. Russ Coile Jr. (1994) describes the interrelationship between vision and strategy as an arrow-to-target process. The shared vision is the target, and strategic planning is the arrow. Timothy R. Clark (2011) writes that organizational vision has three operational functions: a cognitive function to educate, an emotional function to motivate, and an organizational function to coordinate. When all three functions are in place and actively applied, the vision guides the answers to thousands of operational questions and leads to coordinated, effective, and efficient action.

There are, however, caveats to developing mission and vision statements. Christopher K. Bart (2002, 41) writes, "For many senior executives, mission statements don't seem to be worth the paper on which they are written. They don't seem to be of any value." Nonetheless, he goes on to say, "Surprisingly, mission statements (and their accompanying vision and values proclamations) continue to be considered one of the most popular management tools in the world."

As Bart suggests, and as the authors' experiences confirm, the reason for the popularity and prevalence of mission and vision statements is that they make a promise and focus the organization's activities on fulfilling it. Most often, healthcare organizations that clearly express their basic purpose in a mission statement and paint an accurate picture of what they want their organization to look like in five to ten years in a vision statement stand a good chance of articulating and implementing the specific components of the strategic plan, thereby realizing that vision. Failure to specify a mission that is compelling and unique to the healthcare organization, or to define a clear and exciting vision, hinders attempts to resolve strategic issues and to make progress toward a better future.

Robert S. Kaplan, David P. Norton, and Edward A. Barrows Jr. (2008) note that if vision statements are to guide strategy development, they must be inspirational, aspirational, and measurable. To be useful, a statement should also provide a clear focus for the strategy by including a measurable outcome and a distinct target. Kaplan, Norton, and Barrows suggest that a well-crafted vision statement should include three components: a quantified success indicator, a definition of a niche, and a timeline. These three components are evident in an example from Leeds University in the United Kingdom (Kaplan, Norton, and Barrows 2008, 4): "By 2015 (*timeline*), our distinctive ability to integrate world-class research, scholarship, and education (*niche*) will have secured us a place among the top 50 universities in the world (*quantifiable success indicator*)." Leeds did not achieve a top 50 ranking, but that does not mean that its vision statement was "wrong." Vision statements are meant to be aspirational, not easily achieved and a cause for back-patting.

Michael E. Porter (1996, 62) cautions that all too frequently in US industry, "bit by bit, almost imperceptibly, management tools have taken the place of strategy. As managers push to improve on all fronts, they move farther away from viable competitive positions." By failing to focus on what will distinguish their organizations in the future—the essence of effective organizational direction—these companies have difficulty translating gains in operational improvements into sustained profitability.

GUIDELINES FOR DEVELOPING AN EFFECTIVE ORGANIZATIONAL DIRECTION

While specifying direction is necessary and important, developing effective organizational direction statements is a monumental challenge, especially in healthcare organizations. Common problems in direction statements include extreme wordiness; confusion of mission, vision, strategy, and values and a mixture of some in each statement; redundancy among statements; lack of precision; and failure to be farsighted.

Effective statements must be, above all, meaningful, motivational, and memorable. For example, The Joint Commission expects leadership *and* rank-and-file employees in the healthcare organizations it reviews to know their mission statements. But how many mission statements are clear and succinct enough that the organization's employees can readily state them?

Exhibit 7.2 provides a summary of the guidelines for successfully navigating this activity of the strategic planning process. Key points include the following:

- *Sharp, tailored, directional statements are most useful.* These statements should be highly focused and specific to the organization that created them; platitudes and verbosity have no place here.

- *For any complex, multi-entity organization, one vision and one direction are essential.* Successful organizations have a unified direction that is relevant to every entity within them. Establishing an organizational direction at every subsidiary would not only be cumbersome for the strategic planning process, it would also likely lead to inconsistent or conflicting strategies. All subsidiaries must move in the same direction; major, and sometimes minor, differences in vision and direction are divisive and potentially destructive.
- *Organizational direction is the most critical part of the board's and CEO's contribution to strategic planning.* It must emanate from and be fully supported by all elements of corporate or system leadership.

If planning for the future position of the organization starts with poorly conceived, uncertain, or confusing directional statements, the planning process may eventually derail. Getting it back on track will be difficult, if not impossible. Beginning with clear organizational

---

Exhibit 7.2: Developing the Plan: Organizational Direction

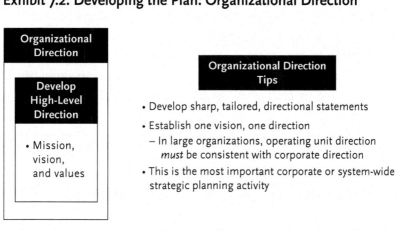

Organizational Direction

Develop High-Level Direction

- Mission, vision, and values

Organizational Direction Tips

- Develop sharp, tailored, directional statements
- Establish one vision, one direction
  - In large organizations, operating unit direction *must* be consistent with corporate direction
- This is the most important corporate or system-wide strategic planning activity

---

direction, on the other hand, helps focus the subsequent detailed strategy-formulation and implementation-planning activities, making it critical to strategic planning success. The organizational direction statements generally fall into two categories: legacy statements (mission and values) and core strategy statements (vision).

Organizations typically have long-standing mission and values statements. A strategic planning process is an opportune time to reflect on these statements and consider whether the mission still represents the reasons the organization exists and whether the values still represent the organization's desired culture and behavior. It is common for these statements to remain wholly unchanged or only slightly modified as a result of this examination. While many of the problems of organizational direction statements referenced earlier may apply to an organization's current mission or values, the two most common reasons for revising these statements are as follows:

- *The mission and values are not concise or clear.* While it is helpful for employees to have knowledge of an organization's future direction via a vision statement, it is essential that all employees know and understand the organization's mission and values, particularly the latter, as these represent how an employee should function on a day-to-day basis. A simple litmus test is to consider whether the mission and values statements can easily be recited by employees at all levels of the organization. If not, then these statements likely need to be reconsidered. This situation does not necessarily indicate the essence of those statements needs to change—simply that the way they are stated can be improved.
- *The mission and values do not reflect significant changes in the organization.* The incremental changes most new business or exits an existing business, the fundamental purpose or culture of the organization may change.

Similarly, if an organization has a major growth spurt (these days, often the result of inorganic growth) or merges with another organization, these legacy statements may not be applicable.

The following sections outline some things to consider in the event that the mission or values statements require reexamination.

DEVELOPMENT OF THE MISSION STATEMENT

Mission statements should be relatively timeless in the absence of significant organizational change. Some organizations' current statements will not require alterations as part of the strategic planning process. However, if reexamination and retooling of the mission statement are called for, the starting point should be the current statement.

Mission Statement Characteristics

Effective mission statements are brief and fundamental statements of organizational purpose. A mission statement should clearly communicate to the board, employees, and other internal and external constituencies why the organization exists and what important purpose it intends to achieve. Influential management consultant, writer, and professor Peter Drucker is reputed to have said that the content of a mission statement should be small enough to fit on a T-shirt. Also, mission statements commonly stray into strategy, which should be avoided. If a mission statement addresses "how" an organization will proceed or act, it should be reconsidered.

Exhibit 7.3 presents several examples of mission statements for healthcare organizations, as well as examples from major companies outside the healthcare field. Note the precision, clarity, and brevity of the nonhealthcare mission statements compared with even these exceptional examples of healthcare mission statements. Interesting, too, is how Tesla, Nike, and Google capture the essence of their purpose without resorting to descriptions of the business, products, or markets. These statements should inspire healthcare leaders to think carefully and creatively about the true purpose of their organizations.

Mission Statement Development Process

The mission statement development process varies by organization, but in any organization, significant input is the board's most fundamental contribution to organization policy and strategic direction. Development begins with the strategic planning committee, which may hold two to three sessions at least partly devoted to a discussion of mission. These sessions typically encompass

Exhibit 7.3: Mission Statement Examples

Nonhealthcare
Google: To organize the world's information and make it universally accessible and useful.
Nike: To bring inspiration and innovation to every athlete* in the world.   *If you have a body, you are an athlete.
Tesla: To accelerate the world's transition to sustainable energy.
Healthcare
Banner Health: Making health care easier, so life can be better.
Cleveland Clinic: Caring for life, researching for health, educating those who serve.
CVS Health: Bringing our heart to every moment of your health.

- scenario development and generation of a composite future scenario (as discussed in chapter 6),
- review of the definition of a mission statement and examination of the current statement,
- review of other healthcare organizations' mission statements (and possibly some nonhealthcare mission statements), and
- review and modification of a new draft mission statement.

Strategic planning committee or board members should not be wordsmiths for the proposed mission statement. They should instead concentrate on what the mission statement is trying to convey, focusing on substantive changes in content. A group discussion is not the place to rewrite, in whole or in part, the mission statement, as it is a cumbersome, tedious, and ultimately unproductive approach. Drafting or redrafting the document should be left to an individual or a small group once the discussion sessions have yielded the statement's focus.

DEVELOPMENT OF THE VALUES STATEMENT

Like the mission statement, the values statement is widely disseminated to internal and external constituencies. In the absence of significant organizational or environmental changes, this statement is relatively timeless and may not require major modification.

With the proliferation of mergers and other forms of affiliation; the growth of integrated delivery systems; and, for some, disaffiliation and disintegration, few healthcare organizations have been untouched by the waves of change sweeping the field. In these new, larger organizations, diverse cultures are brought together, and existing values are blended with, or in some cases imposed on, the new entity. The core of the values statement is a representation of the desired character of the new organizational culture and sets forth the manner in which that character is conveyed to employees and other stakeholders. As some organizations downsize, restructure, and divest themselves of component parts, the values of the surviving entities often must be reexamined.

In stable, successful healthcare organizations, a values statement can be gleaned from organizational behavior. Observation of the day-to-day practices of the employees and of board policy and performance will lead to a fairly clear picture of the organization's values. In this type of strong-valued organization, the development of a values statement can be driven through a bottom-up approach, led by staff and overseen by leadership. Allowing staff ownership of this type of process (where appropriate) can be beneficial and further contribute to a strong culture with buy-in from the front line. Then the board can make final decisions about the values statement.

For other healthcare organizations (e.g., brand-new organizations, those with high organic growth, those in rapid organic decline), a values statement should be developed through a top-down process similar to that recommended for the mission statement. Where current organizational values are determined to be inadequate or not conducive to providing high-quality healthcare and new or significantly different organizational values must be instituted, leadership must discover how the existing values came into being. Then the organization must conduct a self-examination to create a new values statement for the future.

Examples of values statements from two health systems, typical of what many healthcare organizations aspire to, are illustrated in exhibit 7.4. Note, as well, the Amazon and Mercedes-Benz USA values statements, and given the general public knowledge of these organizations, how tailored and descriptive a values statement can be.

The vision statement represents core strategy elements and, unlike the mission and values, should be developed anew in virtually every strategic planning process. These statements progress beyond why the organization exists and describe what the organization wants to be or to achieve at the end of the planning cycle.

Exhibit 7.4: Values Statement Examples

Nonhealthcare
Amazon
• Customer obsession rather than competitor focus
• Passion for invention
• Commitment to operational excellence
• Long-term thinking
Mercedes-Benz USA
• Integrity, openness, and respect
• Inspired, empowered, and diverse people
• Financial and social responsibility
• Customer focus
• Commitment to excellence
• Sustainability

Healthcare
Beth Israel Lahey Health
• Well-being
• Empathy
• Collaboration
• Accountability
• Respect
• Equity
Mayo Clinic
• Primary value: The needs of the patient come first.
• Other values: Respect, Integrity, Compassion, Healing, Teamwork, Innovation, Excellence, and Stewardship

DEVELOPMENT OF THE VISION STATEMENT

Planning teams should consider vision statements and mission statements simultaneously, and the development of the two should follow the same process and general principles. The main distinction between mission statements and vision statements is that mission is about purpose (Why does the organization exist?) and vision is about the future (What does the organization want to be or achieve?). In addition, mission statements are not time limited, whereas vision statements refer to a particular future point or period and generally must be updated and revised with each complete strategic planning process.

Vision Statement Characteristics

Unlike the mission statement, the current vision statement likely requires substantial change if it is to be an effective guide for the organization's future direction. But many vision statements share two main problems with mission statements—cumbersome length and inappropriate inclusion of strategy.

Effective vision statements conform to the guidelines listed in exhibit 7.1. The vision statement should be a vehicle by which to communicate a preferred future state of the organization to internal constituencies. Historically, organizations have considered vision statements ten years or more into the future. However, given the rapid change in the healthcare field—recently and possibly for the foreseeable future—many healthcare organizations are limiting their vision statements to five to ten years. The statement should be aspirational given current circumstances and conditions, and it should represent such an exciting and desirable state of being that it motivates and energizes all elements of the organization through the ground-level strategies and actions that support it. Exhibit 7.5 shows concepts that frequently appear in vision statements of various types of healthcare organizations.

The vision statement should project far enough into the future that the point of unpredictability is reached. This extended time frame should encourage organizational leaders to be imaginative in their views of the future characteristics of the organization while avoiding the urge to analyze their way into the future.

Exhibit 7.5: Vision Statement Concepts

Organization Type	Common Vision Concepts
Community hospital	• Improve patient/customer experience • Provide best value in healthcare services • Become a preferred physician partner
Academic medical center	• Innovate • Become a research or education leader • Provide world-class care
Integrated health system	• Transform healthcare delivery • Improve population health • Be a leading community partner
Post-acute provider	• Shift the care setting to home • Improve quality of life
Insurer	• Reduce healthcare costs • Improve the total healthcare experience • Provide access to care for broad populations

© 2024 Veralon Partners Inc.

Several examples of healthcare organization vision statements that conform to this description are presented in exhibit 7.6, along with a few classic and contemporary examples from major corporations outside the healthcare field.

Here, as with the mission statement examples, the precision, clarity, and brevity of the nonhealthcare examples are striking. Those examples also illustrate the recommended vision principles—stretching, motivating, and inspiring the organizations to achieve what nearly all experts would have deemed improbable, if not impossible, at the time they were developed. Healthcare organizations are making progress in vision development, and the examples in exhibit 7.6 illustrate this effort.

Exhibit 7.6: Vision Statement Examples

Nonhealthcare (Historical)
Honda (1970s): We will destroy Yamaha.
Ford (early 1900s): Democratize the automobile.
Sony (early 1950s): Become the company most known for changing the worldwide poor-quality image of Japanese products.
Stanford University (1940s): Become the Harvard of the west.

Nonhealthcare (Contemporary)
American Express: Provide the world's best customer experience every day.
Ikea: To offer a wide range of well-designed, functional home furnishing products at prices so low that as many people as possible will be able to afford them.
LinkedIn: To create economic opportunity for every member of the global workforce.

Healthcare (Contemporary)
Corewell Health: A future where health is simple, affordable, equitable and exceptional.
Jefferson Health: Reimagining health, education and discovery to create unparalleled value.
University Hospital (New Jersey): Partnering with our communities, University Hospital improves health for generations to come.

The 20-year strategic plan of Banner Health provides an example of the power of a bold organizational vision. In 2000, Banner was struggling financially and organizationally after the merger of two disparate health systems. Banner Health aspired to be in the top tier of medical centers nationally, but it recognized that given its current

Exhibit 7.7: Banner Health's 20-Year Vision

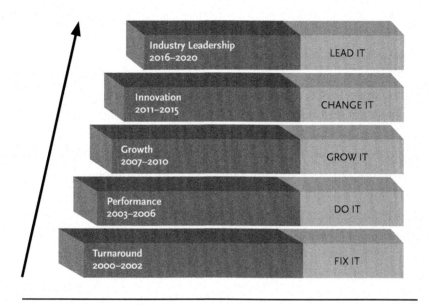

Industry Leadership 2016–2020	LEAD IT
Innovation 2011–2015	CHANGE IT
Growth 2007–2010	GROW IT
Performance 2003–2006	DO IT
Turnaround 2000–2002	FIX IT

© 2024 Veralon Partners Inc.

situation, this vision could be a journey of 20 years or longer (see exhibit 7.7). Banner set its long-range vision and also established interim targets (Compass Clinical Consulting 2011). The organization is largely living up to the vision it set in 2000—an impressive feat that it now must work to sustain.

Vision Statement Development Process

The suggestions discussed earlier related to the mission statement apply to the development of a vision statement, too. Interactions among the board, strategic planning committee, and other key leaders should produce an effective vision statement without excessive attention to wordsmithery.

CONCLUSION

Organizational direction produces three critical outputs—mission, vision, and values statements—that are developed during phase 2 of the strategic planning process. With direction identified, productive movement into the next level of detail in strategic planning—strategy formulation (made up of major initiatives, goals, and objectives) to address the important issues outlined in phase 1—may begin.

As the organization moves further into the how of strategic planning, the roles and responsibilities of management expand. The board, both directly and through its strategic planning committee, may have had significant input into the organizational direction because it represents the major policy elements of the strategic plan; with the completion of the organizational direction activities, the transition from board-driven strategic planning to staff-driven strategic planning begins.

REFERENCES

Bart, C. K. 2002. "Creating Effective Mission Statements: Recapturing the Power and Glory of Mission Is Possible with Careful Planning and Implementation." *Health Progress* 83 (5): 41–55.

Clark, T. R. 2011. "The Power of Vision Provides Organizations with Direction, Inspiration." *Deseret News*. Published February 14. www.deseretnews.com/article/705366518/The-power-of-vision -provides-organizations-with-direction-inspiration.html.

Coile, R. C., Jr. 1994. "Making Strategic Planning a Vision-Driven Process." *Hospital Strategy Report* 6 (10): 8.8.

Compass Clinical Consulting. 2011. "A Fine Choice." Published March 11. www.compass-clinical.com/wp-content/uploads/2013 /10/fine-monograph3.pdf. [The graphic presented in exhibit 7.7 can now be found on page 5 of Banner University Medicine's

"Care Management Overview" at https://medicine.arizona.edu
/sites/default/files/5-theodorou_new_faculty_10_15.pdf.]

Ginter, P. M., W. J. Duncan, and L. E. Swayne. 2018. *Strategic
Management of Health Care Organizations*, 8th ed. Hoboken,
NJ: John Wiley & Sons.

Kaplan, R. S., D. P. Norton, and E. A. Barrows Jr. 2008. *Developing
the Strategy: Vision, Value Gaps, and Analysis.* Boston: Harvard
Business School Publishing.

Porter, M. E. 1996. "What Is Strategy?" *Harvard Business Review*,
November–December, 61–78.

CHAPTER 8

Phase 3: Strategy Formulation

"We always overestimate the change that will occur in the
next two years and underestimate the change that will occur
in the next ten. Don't let yourself be lulled into inaction."

—*Bill Gates*

Sound strategy starts with having the right goal.

—*Michael Porter*

FROM VISION TO GOALS

Once leaders have defined the overall direction of their organization,
they can begin determining its goals, objectives, and future strategic
development. As emphasized in chapter 7, significant progress must
be made in a number of key areas to achieve the vision of the next five
to ten years. Exhibit 8.1 illustrates the critical relationship between
organizational direction and strategy formulation and defines the
outputs of each strategic planning activity.

Exhibit 8.2 highlights a few important points about the strategy
formulation phase of strategic planning. Broadening the number
and types of internal participants involved in plan development
and bringing diverse perspectives to bear on strategy formulation
will increase the probability of success. In large, multi-entity organizations, the strategy formulation framework usually begins at the

system or corporate level and cascades down to the operating units for their respective strategy formulations.

For many organizations, the most difficult part of strategic planning is moving from the vision to the next level of detail: the goals. Identifying hundreds of goals that support the vision is tempting but should be avoided, as doing so creates an unwieldy plan that is impossible to implement. Healthcare organizations also struggle with setting measurable, clear goals, instead tending to specify a series of activities or processes or a vague directional intent (e.g., "improve quality"). This chapter addresses these problems directly.

Strategic planning is, in essence, the process of making difficult choices among competing priorities and focusing the organization's limited resources on the areas that will yield the greatest payoff. For strategic planning to be effective, that focus must be maintained

---

Exhibit 8.1: From Organizational Direction to Strategy Formulation

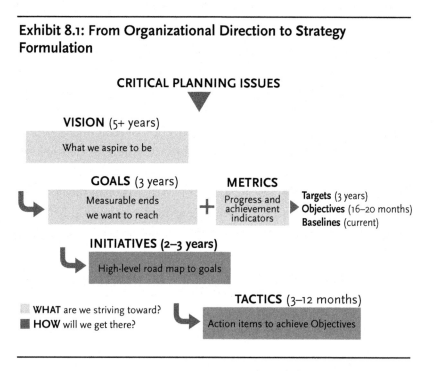

CRITICAL PLANNING ISSUES

VISION (5+ years)

What we aspire to be

GOALS (3 years)

Measurable ends we want to reach

METRICS

Progress and achievement indicators

Targets (3 years)
Objectives (16–20 months)
Baselines (current)

INITIATIVES (2–3 years)

High-level road map to goals

WHAT are we striving toward?
HOW will we get there?

TACTICS (3–12 months)

Action items to achieve Objectives

Exhibit 8.2: Developing the Plan: Strategy Formulation

Strategy Formulation

Establish Goals and Objectives

- For critical areas identified in preceding activities

Strategy Formulation Tips

- This is an excellent time/phase to get broad involvement of internal constituents
- Overall corporate or system goals direct operating unit goals and objectives
- To be effective, strategy needs to address a limited number (no more than ten and desirably as few as three to five) of the most critical issues

© 2024 Veralon Partners Inc.

throughout the process—and especially in the transition from vision to goals. Successful organizations identify only a small set of goals that are imperatives for realizing the vision—preferably no more than five, and certainly no more than ten.

Moving from vision to goals is most readily accomplished through a three-phase process:

1. Determine or affirm critical issues
2. Formulate strategic options and recommendations
3. Identify goals

Revisit Critical Planning Issues

Critical planning issues are determined by examining the organization's mission and vision in light of the initial critical planning issues defined in the strategic assessment (see exhibit 8.3). Often, the critical planning issues that the organization defined in phase

Exhibit 8.3: Strategy Formulation Process

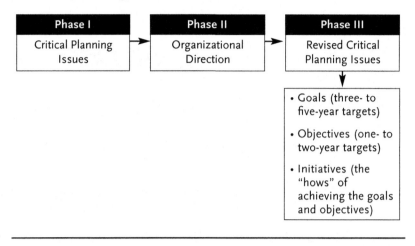

I survive largely intact as the final set of revised critical planning issues. Sometimes the issues may need to be reshaped because of conclusions reached in the organizational direction phase.

Determining what constitutes a critical issue is clearly subjective, and healthcare executives are commonly confused by this step. Typically, critical issues stand out as central to achieving the vision, have a deep potential impact on the organization, and cannot be addressed easily or resolved in the short term. Another common distinction is that these issues deal primarily with concerns outside the realm of day-to-day operations.

One of two approaches is typically used to determine the final list of critical issues. The more process-intensive approach, used most often when the initial list of issues is large or controversial, consists of three steps. First, each member of the strategic planning committee identifies the top three or so issues, and they compile a master list. Assuming the priorities are not obvious from this first step, a second step is to have some discussion of what each issue is and why it is important. Some issues may fall off the list or be consolidated as a result. Third, the committee members are asked to vote for the top three issues; the most frequently named three to five issues make the final list.

The second approach is for planning staff or a small group of members of senior management to narrow the number of issues down to five or fewer and present the findings of their analyses to the strategic planning committee for review and modification. It is important to specify why the selected areas are strategically significant and why other areas are not.

Two representative lists of critical issues that resulted from these processes are shown in exhibit 8.4.

Preparing Strategic Options and Recommendations

Once critical issues are identified, the focus moves from issues to goals. A process-intensive approach is most likely to identify the best goals, objectives, initiatives, and actions and to build support for plan implementation and action. The more process-intensive the approach, the more time required to complete it. A highly intensive approach can take as long as two or three months, while the least intensive approach can be completed in as few as three or four weeks.

Exhibit 8.4: Critical Planning Issues

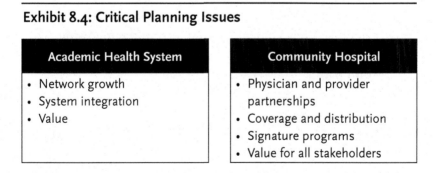

Academic Health System	Community Hospital
• Network growth • System integration • Value	• Physician and provider partnerships • Coverage and distribution • Signature programs • Value for all stakeholders

If the time frame for planning is a concern, the planning team should carefully consider the approach selected for this activity.

Leaders can choose from three basic paths to transition to goal setting:

1. *Move directly from critical issues to goals.* Planning staff, senior management, or the strategic planning committee (with assistance from the previous two constituencies) develop the goals without further analysis or process.

2. *Prepare strategic options and recommendations.* Preparing in-depth reports that consider strategic options can help to distinguish and prioritize alternatives. Planning staff prepare supporting documentation on each issue and recommend goals for review and modification by senior management and the strategic planning committee.

3. *Convene task forces to prepare strategic options and recommendations.* This option is similar to option 2, except that a multidisciplinary group of organizational representatives convenes for a limited period to assist in preparing the supporting documentation.

   The task force alternative has an additional benefit: It exposes important organizational stakeholders to the outline of the emerging strategic plan and constructively engages them in further definition of organizational strategy in areas that are personally significant and relevant. A few guidelines, presented in the following paragraphs, can help organizations to manage this third path.

Assemble the Task Force with Care

No foolproof formula exists for assembling task forces, but recognizing all the ends that the organization is trying to accomplish and the potential incompatibility of those ends is a good starting point. A typical set of principles for task force composition includes the following:

- Gain broad representation from potentially affected constituencies
- Include enough diversity so that the task force is not biased toward any single perspective
- Achieve relatively good chemistry among the members
- Keep the group small enough that it is not unwieldy
- Select members who are interested enough to participate actively
- Choose a leader who will lead but not dominate

The task forces typically will meet three to four times over a period ranging from six to eight weeks (or longer). The members should understand and appreciate that their task is time limited and that they are not making decisions, only presenting alternatives and making recommendations to the strategic planning committee.

Give Task Force Guidelines and Support

Although active participation and free-flowing discussion are to be encouraged, some structure and staff support are necessary to achieve sound output and leave the participants feeling that they were constructively involved in the process. Expectations of the task forces need to be defined clearly at the outset, including the time frame for deliberation, questions to answer or issues to address, and the likely structure of the output needed. In particular, task force members need to hear why the strategic planning committee identified a critical issue that the task force is addressing.

Exhibits 8.5 and 8.6 give samples of guidance that might be provided to task forces. Appendix 8.1 presents an example of a full set of strategic options and recommendations developed using this outline. The planning team should assemble data and other relevant information collected in earlier planning activities and provide them to task force members before their first meeting. The planning staff should be introduced as staff support to the task forces and play a major role in logistical support, data support, and production of the strategic options and recommendations.

Exhibit 8.5: Task Force Overview: ABC Health System

Strategic Issue	Issues to Be Explored	Proposed Leadership and Membership Profile

1. Primary care network	• Size and distribution of the network
	• Operational and financial expectations
	• Care delivery models
	• Value-based care strategy
		• Leader: Primary care physician
		• Members:
		  – Managed care
		  – Marketing
		  – Senior management
		  – Nurse practitioners
		  – Practice managers

2. Cost position	• Cost target required to compete successfully
	• Schedule to attain targeted costs
	• Approaches to cost management and reduction
		• Leader: Chief financial officer
		• Members:
		  – Department chairs
		  – Senior management

3. Medical education	• Role of medical education within system
	• Expectations of medical education and criteria for evaluating residencies
	• Need for an academic affiliation
		• Leader: Teaching physician
		• Members:
		  – Physicians trained at system programs
		  – Other physicians
		  – Senior management

© 2024 Veralon Partners Inc.

Exhibit 8.6: Outline: Critical Issue Strategic Options and Recommendations

- Issue definition
- Background (including importance of resolving the issue)
- Strategies being employed by others faced with similar situations
- Options available, pros and cons, evaluation of options
- Recommended option(s) to pursue
- Major goals for a three- to five-year planning horizon; objectives for next year (or two); major initiatives (categories of activities) to achieve goals and objectives
- Barriers and constraints to achieving goals and objectives

© 2024 Veralon Partners Inc.

Identifying Goals

Ideally, the strategic options and recommendations will thoroughly review all aspects of the critical issue they address and present recommendations that allow a goal—or, occasionally, multiple goals—to be readily identified. It is the strategic planning committee's job to select a goal that will constructively and creatively deal with the critical issue and contribute to achieving part of the vision.

Typically, each task force leader presents the team's report to the strategic planning committee for review, modification, and, ultimately, acceptance. A goal is then identified, discussed, and modified before strategic planning committee approval. Exhibits 8.7 and 8.8 show the relationship between critical issues and goals. Goals should be stated in measurable forms, whenever possible, and as targets for the future. However, this approach is not always practical or possible. The Regional Health System example shows goals that are described as qualitative future positions rather than quantitative endpoints. In such cases, it is important to define metrics related to the goals that can be monitored as a measurement of progress. Exhibit 8.9

Exhibit 8.7: Current and Desired Future State: Regional Health System

Critical Issue: Coordinate care to deliver value	
Current State	**Desired Future State**
Care across the health system is siloed or fragmented	Care is coordinated across the health system
Physicians not aligned on value-based care	Employed and independent physicians aligned with health systems on value
Operates in a volume-driven fee for service environment	Focus on value-based care
Ability to take risk is limited	Able to take on risk for the entire population; impact on overall population health is significant
Critical Issue: Expand partnerships	
Current State	**Desired Future State**
There are few alignment options to promote partnerships with physicians and other providers	Various strategies to align/ partner with physicians and other providers are defined and implemented
Historical tendency to be an insular organization	Develop and strengthen partnerships to improve the health of the community
Seek to maximize hospital outpatient volume despite lower cost alternatives	Partner with physicians/others for freestanding ambulatory services that support value-based care
Critical Issue: Grow across the full continuum of care	
Current State	**Desired Future State**
Focus on traditional acute care services and programs	Service portfolio appropriately meets the needs of the community through internal services or partnerships

(continued)

(continued from previous page)

Geographic reach extends beyond the primary service area, but focus tends to be local	Geographic focus extends beyond the primary service area to include a variety of populations throughout the region
Ad hoc approach to innovation	Innovative solutions are encouraged and routinely executed and embraced throughout the health system

Exhibit 8.8: Critical Issues and Goals: Regional Health System

Critical Issues	Goals
Coordinate care to deliver value	Deliver high-value, coordinated services across the health care network to effectively manage the health of our community
Expand partnerships	Strengthen relationships with key internal (employees, medical staff members) and external stakeholders (customers, community groups, government organizations, and businesses)
Grow across the full continuum of care	Build a critical mass of services across the full continuum of care provided by the health system

provides an example of such metrics. Goals and objectives should be framed as ends to be achieved on the way to the vision, leaving how to achieve them to be determined by the initiatives and the tactical details in the action plan. An example of the relationship among the three major outputs of strategy formulation—goals,

Exhibit 8.9: Critical Issues and Key Metrics for Goals: Regional Health System

Critical Issues	Key Metrics for Goals
Coordinate care to deliver value	• Top decile nationally in clinical quality • Top decile nationally in service excellence • Top decile in the state in value-based care contract results • Service area counties perform in the 90th percentile nationally for the majority of health-related indicators
Expand partnerships	• 80% of affiliated providers (physicians, care extenders, etc.) are accountable for performance measures • 25% more incremental providers and staff • 50% increase in annual philanthropic contributions
Grow across the full continuum of care	• Grow net revenue by 25%+ to ensure the appropriate scale to execute strategic initiatives • Increase market share by 5% (on average) across all services • Increase total covered lives by 30%

objectives, and initiatives—from a medical center strategic plan is shown in exhibit 8.10.

Typically, the task force's strategy formulation process identifies 10 to 20 initiatives for the organization to pursue over the next three to five years in implementing its strategic plan. Because organizations rarely have the resources to pursue so many initiatives vigorously and equally, the strategic planning committee may need to prioritize the initiatives. An example of prioritization during a regional referral center's creation of a strategic plan is

Exhibit 8.10: Strategy Recommendations: Our Health System

Goal	Initiatives
The preferred partner—employee, affiliate, or ally—in the delivery of superior quality and experience for a competitive price	• Transform care and delivery management models (with care partners)
	• Price competitively
Objectives	• Capture first dollar healthcare spending
	• Create an accountable care culture—reward value perfor-mance
• Annual associate retention rate improves from 85% to 88%	• Integrate functions and key leadership
• Covered lives in a risk or value-based contract increase by 10%	• Manage waste to maximize price leverage
• Cost per equivalent discharge is <100% of Medicare	

shown in exhibit 8.11. Such a prioritization process will help set the stage for a realistic and achievable implementation plan. The completion of goals and the selection of initiatives are significant steps; they put in place the final piece of the strategic plan with which the board should be principally concerned. Collectively, the mission, vision, strategy, values, goals, and initiatives constitute the strategic portion of the plan, whereas the remaining components—objectives and actions—are more tactical and operational. It may be helpful to think about the strategic plan as composed of two parts: strategy, which has been the subject of chapters 7 and 8 up to this point, and the management action plan, which remains to be completed.

Few not-for-profit boards understand or appreciate the distinction between the strategic and tactical parts of the process. Although the work of the strategic planning committee as a whole should be

Exhibit 8.11: Example Prioritization of Five-Year Initiatives

Imperative	• Expand primary care network • Continue performance excellence journey • Execute long-range facility plan • Expand workforce development
Critical	• Strengthen clinic relationships • Grow university relationships • Develop centers of excellence • Build ambulatory care clinics • Consider modifying scope of services • Enhance appeal to physicians
Important	• Collaborate with hospital-based physicians • Establish stronger presence in county • Expedite transfers and referrals

Note: Imperative initiatives receive 75% of resources in implementation; critical initiatives receive 20% of resources in implementation (some may need to be deferred); important initiatives receive 5% of resources in implementation (very modest effort or deferral required).

wrapped up at this point and management should take responsibility for completing the remaining plan tasks and components, some strategic planning committees continue to function in an increasingly dysfunctional way until the plan is complete.

In this situation, a compromise may be in order. Rather than finish the committee's work at this point or allow the committee to continue to provide similar oversight as in prior tasks, the senior management team should thank the committee for completing the overwhelming majority of its important work and offer to reconvene it when the objectives and actions are drafted. Management can then present its draft management action plan and an executive summary of the plan to the committee. Following the committee's review, the action plan and executive summary are submitted to the full board for approval and adoption.

ESTABLISHING OBJECTIVES

If the suggested approach is followed, the remaining planning tasks are carried out under the direction of senior management. These tasks typically involve broader representation of management team members than has been the case up to this point.

Essentially, each goal needs to be dissected into smaller, more manageable components:

- Objectives: short-term targets in each goal area
- Actions: the principal tactics that need to be accomplished to achieve the objectives (and relate to parts of the initiatives)

The objectives and actions (the latter are discussed in chapter 9) collectively compose the near-term game plan to move the organization's strategic plan forward.

Sometimes the objectives are well developed in the critical issues, strategic options, recommendations, and task force discussions. In other cases, senior management staff need to determine the objectives, individually or collectively. In either event, the objectives need to provide intermediate, preferably measurable targets on the path to achieving the goals. Review the example of goals and related objectives of one organization shown earlier in exhibit 8.10.

CONTINGENCY PLANNING

Stepping back once or twice during the strategic planning process to consider how the expected direction and strategy will hold up under the likely alternative future conditions identified at the end of the strategic assessment is helpful (see chapter 6). Some events may be incorporated explicitly into the strategy formulation process for specific goals and objectives resulting from the barriers and constraints analysis mentioned in exhibit 8.6. Other changes could affect a broad range of strategy formulation outcomes.

Typical contingencies to consider today include the following:

- Shifting national and state policy priorities
- Expedited transition from fee-for-service to value- or risk-based reimbursement, or a reversal of that trend
- Market consolidation, including hospitals, health systems, insurance companies, and physician groups
- Entrance of new competitors, including retailers and private equity–backed providers

These situations should be fully considered during planning to ensure that future strategies will still apply in the event of a market or other strategic shift. If some scenarios would require significant adjustments to strategy, the board and executive leadership will be better prepared to pivot to a new strategy. This way, plan implementation can move forward expeditiously and with greater ability to adapt should conditions change during implementation.

Furthermore, contingency planning is built into the planning process as a component of the annual update process, in which the organization regularly reviews the market and internal environment. These steps will help ensure the plan remains a living document that is fully relevant to the organization, even in changing times.

FINANCIAL ANALYSIS

One final topic in strategy formulation deserves discussion. A long-standing controversy exists among strategic planners and other healthcare executives about the appropriate depth and breadth of financial analysis in the strategic planning process. This book describes a moderate approach; however, other texts recommend that something close to a financial feasibility forecast or integrated strategic financial plan is necessary. Appendix 8.2 offers an example of the level of financial analysis required in a typical strategic planning process.

The strategic plan should have a high-level strategy focus; any substantial financial analysis should occur in at the implementation stage or later. However, one note of caution is important: The approach recommended in this book is one that is continually vigilant in recognizing resource limitations, making choices, and focusing effort. This approach can be accomplished by following a process that has financial awareness and concerns as parts of its infrastructure so that financial implications are implicitly part of each step. If such high awareness and astuteness is not routinely part of the organization's work, some substantive financial tasks may need to be included in the strategic planning process. (For further discussion of this topic, see chapter 13.)

CONCLUSION

When phase 3 is complete, the organization will have a sound framework, through its goals, initiatives, and objectives, for the work that lies ahead in implementing the plan. But, even more important, if the planning process has been successfully carried out, one of its by-products will be shared learning among organizational leaders about how to address each critical issue. Consensus or near consensus on managing these issues will facilitate problem-free approval of the strategic plan and a rapid transition from planning to implementation.

Example: Issue Documentation

Grove Medical Center (GMC), a midsize community hospital located in the Midwest, identified "physician alignment" as a critical planning issue. A task force charged with developing strategic options and recommendations produced this report for the planning committee.

ISSUE DEFINITION AND SITUATION DESCRIPTION

GMC's medical staff has grown in recent years and now includes a variety of specialties and primary care. While some medical staff members are employed by GMC through Grove Physician Group (GPG), the majority of medical staff members are independent (i.e., in private practice). As the financial environment becomes increasingly challenging, many physicians in GMC's market are seeking closer alignment with hospitals or health systems. The following list includes the factors influencing the market:

- GPG is growing, but there is a need to improve cohesiveness and standardize both clinical and operational processes.
- GMC often has limited options for alignment with independent physicians.
- A shortage of primary care physicians in the market exists, and GMC has gaps in several specialty physician services.

- There are some independent physicians in the market who are seeking to align with a health system in some form but also maintain their private practice.
- Mountainview Health System (MHS), GMC's competition, has been aggressive in acquiring physician practices and is offering participation in its clinically integrated network. Nontraditional investor-backed competitors are turning away from GMC alignment.

STRATEGIES EMPLOYED BY OTHERS

Many hospitals across the country are challenged by medical staff alignment issues, including a lack of critical mass in certain specialties, clinical quality or customer service inconsistencies, insufficient care coordination, and frustration in independent practices. These issues commonly linger in an organization because the solutions are perceived to be cost prohibitive. Successful hospitals and health systems use multiple strategies to address alignment concerns, including the following:

- Offer a variety of alignment options, ranging from tighter alignment (e.g., employment, practice leases) to looser alignment (clinically integrated network membership, provision of electronic health records)
- Provide leadership and professional development opportunities for medical staff members
- Pursue clinical integration to align independent and employed practices to achieve high-value care
- Offer incentive-based compensation structures for employed physicians
- Standardize clinical practice procedures and processes and hold medical staff members accountable for quality and patient satisfaction performance

OPTIONS AVAILABLE TO GROVE MEDICAL CENTER

The planning committee considered the options available to GMC. Based on the rapidly evolving market dynamics and the need to respond to physicians' preferences, the members decided that a purposeful and aggressive physician alignment strategy is required for not only continued success, but for ongoing sustainability.

Options	Pros	Cons
1. Pursue an aggressive employment strategy to expand GPG	Tightest form of alignment; counteracts MHS strategy	High cost; significant infrastructure requirements
2. Create a "menu" of alignment options	Appeals to nearly all physicians in the market	Many menu options fall short of meaningful alignment
3. Form a clinically integrated network	Provides financial incentive for alignment without employment hurdles	Time and resource intensive; requires expertise to implement

GMC'S PROPOSED STRATEGY

The proposed strategy calls for GMC to use aspects of options 1 and 2 for a focused employment strategy for specialties that are a high priority for the organization and to offer alternative alignment models targeted to primary care practices. As GMC's number of aligned medical staff members increases, the quality of services provided needs to be standardized while the organization prepares to engage in value-based contract arrangements. The task force developed and presented to the planning committee the following recommendations, goals, objectives, measurement criteria, and barriers.

Recommendation

- Target high-priority specialties for employment in GPG
- Develop several (two or three) alignment alternatives focused on attracting primary care physicians
- Increase physician outreach activity
- Establish clinical and service quality standards, and link physician compensation to performance in these areas

Goals

- Increase the number of medical staff members in formal economic or clinical alignment relationships by 75 percent
- Coordinate high-quality services across all specialties

Objectives

- Expand GPG's infrastructure to accommodate planned future growth
- Establish clinical quality and service standards through a collaborative process between administrative and medical staff leaders
- Determine and implement alternative alignment models
- Identify target physician practices for alignment via strategic and financial criteria; align high-priority practices or engage them in discussions with GMC

Measurement Criteria

- Number of physicians in formal alignment arrangements
- GPG revenue

- Clinical quality and service indicators
- Physician engagement survey scores

GMC's Barriers and Constraints

- Resource requirements to acquire high-priority practices
- MHS's aggressive physician employment strategy
- Ability to execute new and unfamiliar alignment models

Example: Strategic Plan Financial Analysis

At the outset of its strategic planning process, GMC recognized that its baseline operating income estimates (exhibit A.1) would not allow it to achieve its vision. After identifying initiatives in phase 3 of its strategic planning process, GMC estimated the financial impact of each (exhibit A.2) and determined that the initiatives were not expected to generate the required financial improvement. Several initiatives were then reconsidered and refined to achieve the desired financial result.

Exhibit A.1: Strategic Financial Analysis Projected Baseline Income Statement

	Budgeted Fiscal Year (2024)	Projected Fiscal Year (2025)
Revenue	$492,230	$599,460
Expenses	$495,840	$601,260
Operating income	($3,610)	($1,800)
Operating margin	(0.73%)	(0.30%)
Non–operating gains	$4,930	$5,410
Net income	$1,320	$3,610
Net margin	0.27%	0.60%

Note: Dollars in thousands.

Exhibit A.2: Net Financial Impact from Initiatives

	Fiscal Year 2024	Fiscal Year 2025	Fiscal Year 2026	Fiscal Year 2027	Fiscal Year 2028	Net Impact from Initiatives
Baseline net income	$1.3	$1.5	$2.1	$2.8	$3.6	
Estimated impact from initiatives						
Inpatient volume growth	$0.1	$0.3	$0.6	$1.0	$1.5	$3.5
Ambulatory surgery volume growth	$0.2	$0.3	$0.5	$0.7	$1.0	$2.7
Downstream ancillary volume growth	$0.5	$0.9	$1.4	$1.8	$2.0	$6.0
Technology investments	($0.5)	($0.5)	($0.5)	($0.5)	($0.5)	($2.5)
Other infrastructure investment	($0.8)	($0.8)	($0.8)	($0.8)	($0.8)	($4.0)
Revised net income	$0.8	$1.7	$3.3	$5.0	$6.8	$5.7

Note: Dollars in millions.

© 2024 Veralon Partners Inc.

CHAPTER 9

Phase 4: Transition to Implementation

> When it comes to getting things done, we need fewer
> architects and more bricklayers.
>
> —*Colleen C. Barrett (attributed)*

> Never confuse movement with action.
>
> —*Ernest Hemingway*

No strategic planning topic today is more controversial than how
to successfully manage the transition from planning to implementation. While developing a good strategic plan is difficult, many
feel that implementation is far more challenging. The transition
from strategic planning to implementation is a point where plans
frequently stray off course.

Most experts concur with Peter M. Ginter, W. Jack Duncan, and
Linda E. Swayne (2018, 421), who postulate that "effective strategy
implementation requires the same determination and effort that is
devoted to situational analysis and strategy formulation."

More specifically, Martin Corboy and Diarmaid O. Corrbui
(1999, 29–30) identify the following "seven deadly sins . . . that
doom effective strategy implementation":

1. *The strategy is lacking in terms of rigor, insight, vision,
    ambition, or practicality.* If the strategy is simply more of

the same, comfortable, and incremental, it will not create the excitement needed for successful implementation.

2. *People are not sure how the strategy is to be implemented.* Leaders are too impatient to make the strategy happen, so they don't communicate details about how implementation is to proceed. They sometimes consider communication to be time-consuming indecisiveness.

3. *The strategy is communicated on a need-to-know basis.* It is not disseminated freely throughout the organization.

4. *Some or all aspects of strategy implementation lack a specific person in charge.* Failure to carefully manage all aspects of implementation results in oversights and confusion.

5. *Strategic leaders send mixed signals by dropping out of sight when implementation begins.* The absence of strategic leadership implies that implementation is not worthy of leaders' attention and, therefore, unimportant.

6. *Unforeseen obstacles to implementation occur.* When they do, responsible people are not prepared to overcome them in creative and innovative ways.

7. *Strategy becomes all-consuming*, and details of day-to-day operations are lost or neglected. Strategy is important, but so are operations.

This chapter provides guidance on transitioning effectively from planning to implementation. Exhibit 9.1 highlights several key elements of this final activity of the strategic planning process: the necessity of increased involvement of those who will be important participants in implementation of the plan, the need to specify and adhere to an ongoing tracking system for plan implementation, and the critical role in larger healthcare systems of the corporate organization in defining and mediating demands for resources required to carry out implementation.

The five major activities involved in a successful transition from planning to implementation are briefly described in the next section,

Exhibit 9.1: Developing the Plan: Action Planning

Implementation Planning	Strategic Planning Tips

Identify Actions Required
 	
• Implementation plan
  – Schedule
  – Priorities
  – Resources
  – Responsibilities
	• Increased involvement of clinicians and managers in this activity to build support for implementation
	• Before completion of the plan, an ongoing progress-tracking system should be defined and agreed on by leadership
	• Corporate sets priorities, especially among competing resource needs of operating units

© 2024 Veralon Partners

followed by a more detailed discussion of each in subsequent sections of this chapter.

DEVELOP A DETAILED YEAR 1 IMPLEMENTATION PLAN FOR THE NEW STRATEGIC PLAN

Many people mistakenly believe that implementation should address all three to five years of the strategic plan. That is neither practical nor effective. Too much will change during implementation, so detailed steps identified now would not be effective in two or three years. Rather, the implementation steps should cover 12 to 18 months and should be developed for each year of the plan. The annual update is described in chapter 10.

Strategic goals, objectives, and initiatives developed during strategy formulation must be operationalized through a set of tactics with associated time frames and standards of accountability that serve as the implementation road map and link with budget development activities for year 1.

- *Prepare and submit the proposed strategic plan to the board of directors for review and approval.* Depending on the full board's level of participation in the strategic plan development process, one to three working sessions to present key findings, discuss future market assumptions, and review proposed strategic priorities might be required prior to board adoption.
- *Roll out the new strategic plan to internal and external audiences.* Organizational leaders should prepare a comprehensive communication plan that is ready to go once board approval has been obtained, including the identification of target audiences, key messages, and presentation materials.
- *Establish systems for monitoring and reporting progress.* Tracking changes in key metrics via a formal reporting system and timetable helps to maintain the focus on strategic priorities, instill accountability for results, and prompt midcourse corrections to get back on track as conditions warrant.
- *Update the strategic plan on a regular basis, no less than annually.* In today's dynamic world of healthcare, organizational strategy must be flexible enough to accommodate unanticipated changes in the environment—unforeseen challenges as well as opportunities. Strategic priorities should be revisited at least annually, so that important adjustments can be made when necessary.

The development of a detailed first-year implementation plan is a critical component of transitioning successfully from planning to action. This task involves translating the strategic goals, objectives, and initiatives developed during strategy formulation (see chapter 8) into a set of thoughtful activities that will lead to progress toward a set of desired outcomes. Exhibit 9.2 illustrates the cascading

Exhibit 9.2: Relationship Between Strategy and Implementation

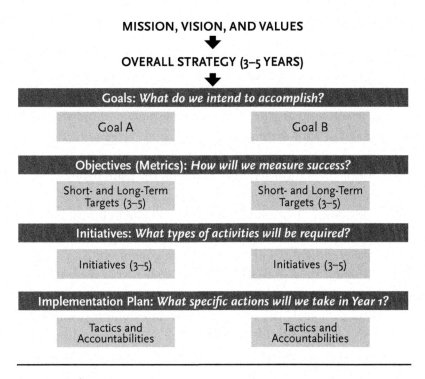

MISSION, VISION, AND VALUES
⬇
OVERALL STRATEGY (3–5 YEARS)
⬇

Goals: *What do we intend to accomplish?*
Goal A	Goal B

Objectives (Metrics): *How will we measure success?*
Short- and Long-Term Targets (3–5)	Short- and Long-Term Targets (3–5)

Initiatives: *What types of activities will be required?*
Initiatives (3–5)	Initiatives (3–5)

Implementation Plan: *What specific actions will we take in Year 1?*
Tactics and Accountabilities	Tactics and Accountabilities

relationship between the strategy formulation outputs and the year 1 implementation plan.

During the course of the strategic plan development process, primary responsibility shifts from the board, whose focus is overall strategic direction (Where do we need to go?), to the senior management team, whose responsibility is to make that direction happen (How will we get there?). Development of the initial-year and subsequent-year implementation plans, therefore, rests with the senior management team.

Exhibit 9.3 provides an example of content for a specific strategic goal, including short- and long-term objectives, initiatives, and year

1 implementation activities and accountabilities. In this section, we suggest that senior management use a four-step process to create a compelling and effective implementation plan.

- Step 1: For each strategic goal, appoint one or more executive champions from the senior management team to draft the year 1 implementation plan. The executive champions then assemble a team of individuals to assist with the process for each goal. Depending on the complexity of the assigned area and scope of implementation activities required, the team may consist of just two or three people or as many as 20. At this point, it is appropriate and advisable to broaden team membership to include middle managers and other individuals likely to be heavily involved in implementation. Each team will meet two or three times to flesh out the initial implementation details for its assigned goal. The example shown in exhibit 9.3 contains minimal details, which will be fine for many organizations, but others may prefer to break down tactics into smaller steps and time frames.
- Step 2: Each team reviews its respective draft goal statement, objectives, and initiatives for clarity, alignment, and completeness. As shown in exhibit 9.3, each team should begin by carefully reviewing, and refining as necessary, the proposed framework to make sure it is clear and compelling. Does the goal statement clearly explain what the organization wants to achieve? Have short-term and long-term objectives been identified, and are they quantifiable? Do the initiatives lend themselves to specific activities that will move the needle on achieving the proposed goal and objectives? Note that the component most often needing additional work by the team is defining and quantifying the objectives. What exactly will you measure, and what data source will you use? Do you

have baseline data to know where you are starting? What should the future targets be and why? It is important that the teams complete step 2 before jumping to step 3.

- Step 3: Each team identifies a set of proposed projects and tactics to be undertaken during year 1 of implementation. The group needs to delineate specific tactics the organization will engage in during the year, as well as the expected time frame for each tactic (e.g., six months, one year), the individual who will take lead responsibility, and a high-level estimate of resource requirements and expected impact. It is better (and usually more challenging) to identify a limited number of tactics that collectively will result in significant impact, rather than a long list of projects that provide limited return on investment.

- Step 4: Senior management reviews all draft implementation plans to ensure internal alignment with appropriate prioritization and allocation of resources. After all teams have completed their proposed year 1 implementation plans, senior management is responsible for evaluating the plan in its entirety. Are any of the proposed tactics in conflict with other tactics? Are there areas of overlapping tactics that need to be clarified? Does the organization have the resources to take on all suggested tactics in year 1, or should some be deferred for a later time? Most important, if all items identified in the implementation plan are accomplished, does it significantly advance the organization toward its strategic goals and objectives?

A couple of additional thoughts about the importance of creating buy-in for implementation are in order at this point. The initial framework of the strategic plan (goals, objectives, initiatives) is developed largely by the board and senior management, but one key to successful implementation is commitment at the operations

Exhibit 9.3: Strategic Goal with Detailed Objectives and Year 1 Implementation Plan

Strategic Goal #1

Our health system successfully participates in alternative reimbursement models that emphasize coordinated and longitudinal care for patients

Objectives for Strategic Goal #1

	1-Year Target	5-Year Target
Reduction in inpatient stays for ambulatory sensitive conditions	–10%	–30%
Reduction in readmission rates	–10%	–40%
Reduction in per member cost of care for ACO attributed lives	–5%	–15%
Positive overall operating margin from risk-based reimbursement contracts	2%	5%
Growth in total net revenue attributed to risk-based reimbursement models	+10%	+60%

Major Initiatives for Strategic Goal #1

- Refine care models to focus on providing "Right care, Right time, Right place"
- Improve coordination and efficacy across care locations, within our system and with external partners
- Enhance operational capabilities to assume financial risk under alternative reimbursement models
- Seek out new and expanded opportunities to participate in alternative reimbursement models

(continued)

(continued from previous page)

Implementation Plan for Year 1

Projects and Tactics for Year 1	Time Frame	Lead	Resource Requirements[1]	Estimated Impact[2]
Implement three new care coordinator positions for primary care offices	Q1	JS	Medium	High
Implement nurse hotline service for ACO members	Q2	JS	Low	Medium
Utilize ACO data to identify opportunities to improve care delivery	Q1–Q4	GJ	Low	Medium
Institute Lean as a means for streamlining and improving care processes	Q1–Q4	SD	Medium	Medium
Improve continuity of patient care by providing community partners with an appropriate level of access to patient information	Q3	GJ	Low	Medium
Develop cost accounting system for alternative payment models	Q3–Q4	BL	High	Medium
Explore opportunities for alternative reimbursement contracts with commercial payers	Q3–Q4	DD	Low	Low

[1]Time and/or financial resources: Low < 0.20 FTE and/or <$250K and/or <$250K during the year; Medium=0.2 –1.0 FTE and/or $250K–$500K; High > 1 FTE and/or >$500K

[2]Net impact from incremental revenue and/or decreased costs: Low=<$100K during the year; Medium=$100K–$500K, High=>$500K

© 2024 Veralon Partners Inc.

level, primarily with middle management. To facilitate buy-in and make sure implementation expectations are realistic, those managers need to actively participate in shaping the parts of the plan for which they will be principally responsible (i.e., actions, schedule). Another important recommendation is to proceed with implementation as quickly as possible to avoid losing momentum. Multiple tactics and projects can typically be initiated even before the strategic plan is formally adopted by the board, with adjustments made down the road, as necessary, to maintain consistency with the final version of the plan.

BOARD REVIEW AND APPROVAL OF THE STRATEGIC PLAN

Following completion of the year 1 implementation plan, submit the new strategic plan to the board of directors for review, discussion, and consideration for approval. If planning activities have proceeded smoothly up to this point, adoption of the strategic plan is fairly straightforward. In this section, we discuss five recommended steps in the board review and approval process.

Step 1: Prepare the Draft Strategic Plan Document and Presentation Materials

Preparing two versions of the strategic plan is helpful—a three- to five-page executive summary that can be used as a stand-alone document, as well as a longer, more comprehensive version that contains more extensive documentation.

In the rush to move from planning to implementation, organizations sometimes overlook the need for an executive summary. However, this document is often the only strategic plan output read by board members and other important stakeholders. When new board members and senior executives join the organization, the executive summary of the strategic plan provides an insightful snapshot of current challenges and strategic priorities. The executive summary should include the rationale for preparation of the strategic plan, an overview of the planning process, key findings, critical issues addressed, and a summary of proposed strategic goals, objectives, and initiatives. Exhibits 9.4 and 9.5 present examples of summary strategic plan documents. Some organizations issue the executive summary as a discrete document, while others place it as the first section in the complete strategic plan report. Appendix 9.1 represents an example of a more comprehensive strategic plan document.

In addition to the executive summary, organizational leaders should prepare a full strategic plan report at the conclusion of the planning process. This document should include the output of all planning activities and a description of important process steps (e.g., interviews, retreats). This document serves as the record for all that occurred during the planning process and as a reference source for analyses and supporting information that may be germane to implementation and to the next full strategic planning process.

Step 2: Obtain a Resolution by the Strategic Planning Committee Recommending Board Approval of the Plan

Although it may only be a formality if the strategic planning process has proceeded smoothly, nearly all healthcare organizations convene the strategic planning committee for a final meeting to review the draft plan and recommend adoption to the board. After making any additional refinements in wording or format, the committee passes a resolution to forward the draft strategic plan to the board for review and consideration for approval. The final meeting can also be used to discuss next steps and implementation and to outline how the committee will be involved in subsequent strategic plan updates or implementation monitoring.

Exhibit 9.4: Sample Summary of Overall Strategic Direction for District Hospital (DH)

Organizational Direction

DESIRED FUTURE STATE

— Key stakeholders (board members, physicians, employees) aligned and committed to a *shared vision*

— *Strong primary care base* aligned with DH and integrated in the community

— *Specialty physician services* that provide value and are *sustainable*

— *Inpatient volume and market share* stabilized and *trending upward*

— *Operating independently* with a *strong financial position*

— *Multiple partnerships/collaborations* to ensure that community needs are met and DH is viewed as a strong community partner

VISION STATEMENT

To be your First Choice for First Class Health Services.

MISSION STATEMENT

The mission of District Hospital, in partnership with its Medical Staff, is to provide health services with a personal approach to care that enhances the quality of life.

VALUES

HONESTY AND INTEGRITY – RESPECT – EXCEPTIONAL SERVICE – COMMITMENT TO EXCELLENCE AND TEAMWORK

(continued)

(continued from previous page)

Three-Year Strategic Goals and Major Initiatives

	GOALS	INITIATIVES
1	**FOUNDATIONAL STRATEGIES** Maintain excellence in hospital operations, infrastructure, and financial performance as foundational strategies for future growth and development	• Ensure the availability of a high-quality workforce and medical staff • Achieve ongoing improvements in quality, patient safety, and patient satisfaction • Maintain a strong financial position • Provide up-to-date facilities and technology • Forge strong connections with the communities we serve
2	**SCALE AND SCOPE** Achieve thoughtful and sustainable growth in scale and scope of services	• Increase the availability of both primary care and physician specialty services based on community need and operational viability • Expand outpatient services when appropriate and feasible—new and wider distribution of services • Reduce patient outmigration for inpatient care that we can provide locally • Work with partners to address gaps in non–acute care services; prevention/wellness through post-acute care
3	**PATIENT AND CONSUMER FOCUS** Redesign care delivery models to meet the changing expectations of our patients and communities	• Improve access to timely and convenient care • Increase transparency in pricing, quality, and patient safety • Facilitate multiple ways for patients to provide input about their satisfaction with and expectations for care delivery • Engage patients and families as partners in their healthcare
4	**SHARED VISION AND TEAMWORK** Create a shared vision for DH that resonates throughout the organization, inspires teamwork, and promotes professional camaraderie	• Generate support for a unified vision that positions DH for continued long-term success • Invest in leadership development for management and medical staff • Strengthen employee and physician engagement with DH • Align internal policies and processes to support organizational values and priorities
5	**POPULATION HEALTH** Position DH to be successful in the transition to alternative payment models based on coordinated and longitudinal care	• Refine care models to focus on providing "Right care, Right time, Right place" • Improve coordination and efficiency across care locations—with DH and with external partners • Pursue opportunities to participate in alternative payment models as appropriate

© 2024 Veralon Partners, Inc.

Step 3: Provide an Opportunity for Medical Staff Review and Input (for Hospitals and Health Systems)

Prior to final approval, most hospital and health system boards want to see some level of medical staff review and feedback on the draft strategic plan as a part of the process, although there is substantial variation in how organizations approach that task.

Medical staff participation in this stage may range from a few individual or small-group meetings with physician leaders (especially in highly competitive environments) to meetings with the medical executive committee or other medical leadership groups to broad-based input with widespread participation. The purpose of the dialogue with the medical staff is to obtain high-level feedback as opposed to a more detailed or parochial discussion, although some of that will likely occur anyway. Finally, unless the board directs otherwise, it is important to communicate that the requested role of the medical staff is to offer perspectives on the draft strategic plan, rather than approval.

Step 4: Hold Formal and Informal Work Sessions with the Board to Review and Discuss the Proposed Strategic Plan

In most healthcare organizations, at least one presentation of the complete draft strategic plan to the board is scheduled prior to formal review and consideration for approval. This educational session, which is frequently conducted in a retreat setting, provides an opportunity for the full board to review and question the plan's analyses, findings, and recommendations. The purpose is to increase the board's understanding of the plan and its implications for the organization, and to allow any important issues about the development process and subsequent implementation to surface and be resolved.

For most organizations, this one educational session is the only major activity required before the board feels prepared to formally consider the proposed plan for approval. At times, however, the board may require additional time and discussion to become comfortable with the plan before taking formal action. In that case, it is usually productive to schedule another educational session, small group discussions, or one-on-one meetings between board members and the CEO before proceeding further. Senior management and leaders of the strategic planning committee need to do whatever is necessary to ensure that board members understand and support the strategic plan. They should be especially sensitive to board members' concerns, confusion, or discomfort and attempt to address each board member's needs, so that the full board is genuinely enthusiastic about strategic plan adoption and implementation.

Step 5: Board Votes to Adopt the Strategic Plan

The board's review and approval of the strategic plan may encompass a limited number of steps carried out over a few weeks, or a significant number of steps over a few months. This variation is largely a function of the complexity of the plan, its recommendations, and organizational style, such as the degree of deliberateness in the review and approval process.

Rarely are strategic plans not approved, although there are instances in which the plan is rejected by the board because of a change in the strategic environment or returned to the planning staff or committee for reworking. When the staff, senior management, and strategic planning committee have done their jobs well, including gathering extensive input and communicating effectively throughout the plan development process, board approval should proceed without any serious roadblocks. In most cases, approval is

Exhibit 9.5: Strategic Plan Summary

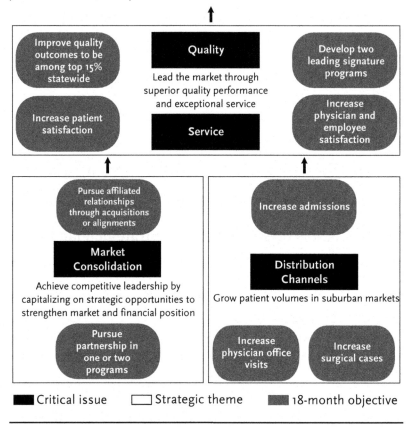

OHS Organizational Direction

Our Health System will be the healthcare leader in the region, providing exceptional medical care and service for every patient, every day, in a patient-centered, family-focused environment.

Quality

Lead the market through superior quality performance and exceptional service

Service

Improve quality outcomes to be among top 15% statewide

Increase patient satisfaction

Develop two leading signature programs

Increase physician and employee satisfaction

Market Consolidation

Achieve competitive leadership by capitalizing on strategic opportunities to strengthen market and financial position

Pursue affiliated relationships through acquisitions or alignments

Pursue partnership in one or two programs

Distribution Channels

Grow patient volumes in suburban markets

Increase admissions

Increase physician office visits

Increase surgical cases

■ Critical issue ☐ Strategic theme ▨ 18-month objective

© 2024 Veralon Partners

unanimous. If the strategic plan is not adopted when it is brought forward for formal consideration or if it is adopted with significant opposition, it is likely that either appropriate preparation did not occur or sensitivity to board concerns was lacking.

STRATEGIC PLAN ROLLOUT AND COMMUNICATION

The next key element of a successful transition from strategic planning to implementation is a strong communications process. Some organizations do an exceptionally good job of communicating the results of strategic planning and moving into the implementation phase, while others do not.

Few would argue against the importance of communicating the results of strategic planning as a critical component of the transition from planning to implementation—so why is there such wide variation in attention to this task? What appears to be at issue is the degree of formality and the extent of the communications process, as well as the rigor and need for structure in transitioning to implementation.

Organizations that move smoothly and effectively from planning to implementation communicate broadly and use completion of the strategic plan to signal to key stakeholders that a new era is beginning. The use of celebration as a communications element garners attention and interest, raising expectations and energy in support of implementation.

The communication process should inform and involve constituents. By sharing strategic plan findings, recommendations, implementation priorities, and sequencing of initiatives with key individuals and groups, the prospects for plan acceptance and implementation support are enhanced.

C. Davis Fogg (2010) outlines some of the most important considerations in designing and effectively carrying out a strategic plan communications process. The following section discusses three central aspects of the communications plan.

1. Audiences that need to be addressed
   – Senior management and boards
   – Their subordinates

- Other employees (in most healthcare organizations, this includes medical staff members and key external constituencies)
2. How to frame the message for each audience
   - Tailor information to their jobs and positions.
   - Take into account the information that they need to carry out their part in the plan.
   - Be sensitive to their need to know proprietary information or planned strategies.

   As a general rule, the more people know about the vision and strategic plan, their role in it, and its effect on their job, the better. This knowledge helps direct spontaneous action, plans, and programs at lower levels in the organization. It also reduces working at cross-purposes and misunderstandings about what is strategically important (e.g., quality versus cost reductions).
3. The best method of communicating the plan
   - Develop scripts and visual aids for each major target audience so that a uniform message is conveyed.
   - Have a senior manager, preferably a member of the planning team, present the plan to each target group.
   - Leave time for employees (and others) to ask questions and get answers, preferably in small groups facilitated by managers who are also recording issues.

Refer to the ideas listed in exhibit 9.6 as potential strategies and materials to incorporate into a comprehensive communications plan. Appendix 9.1 provides an example of a strategic plan summary document that was developed by an organization as a communications tool to share with key constituencies. When developing written materials about an organization's strategic priorities and plans, senior leaders must balance the desire and need to share enough information to create buy-in and enthusiasm with the risk of compromising competitive advantage by prematurely divulging too much information.

Exhibit 9.6: Potential Ideas to Incorporate into Communications Plan

Internal Communications	External Communications
• Communicate directly with frontline employees as often as possible to ensure system-wide buy-in of strategic initiatives • Train executives and managers to convey strategic initiatives and core values in a consistent manner • Articulate accountability so that staff members have a clear understanding of responsibilities • Reinforce strategic initiatives through symbolic representation, such as posters or signs • Use multiple networks: town hall meetings, employee newsletters, intranet postings, webcasts/podcasts	• Create summary document for marketing materials and media distribution • Post succinct and clear outline of strategic plan on website • Create presentation with a review of strategic plan for CEO to give to community groups • Schedule appearances before various community constituencies (e.g., church groups, chamber of commerce) • Consider producing a video with staff at all levels explaining the plan

A well-organized communications plan will be an essential part of the strategic plan rollout.

Fogg (2010) also suggests that strategic plan communication is not a one-time event and that consistent effort and attention of the CEO and senior management are necessary to carrying out this task successfully. While the planning process may be technically complete when the board approves the strategic plan, all the hard and creative work may be for naught if these efforts are not complemented by a solid communications plan.

SYSTEMS FOR MONITORING AND REPORTING PROGRESS

Every organization should develop a formal system for monitoring and reporting progress even before the strategic plan is approved. In the first year of implementation, many organizations monitor progress on a monthly or every-other-month basis. Assuming that good progress is being made and significant external or internal changes are not occurring, formal progress tracking and monitoring may be conducted with decreasing frequency, but it probably needs to occur at least quarterly to remain effective. Chapter 10 includes a detailed discussion and specific format suggestions regarding progress reports. Tracking and reporting progress are related to reviewing and updating the plan, both of which are discussed in the next chapter.

CONCLUSION

This chapter addresses a successful transition from planning to implementation and completion of the strategic plan. A thorough, structured approach to this transition is recommended in five key steps:

1. Develop a detailed year 1 implementation plan for the new strategic plan.
2. Prepare and submit the proposed strategic plan to the board of directors for review and approval.
3. Roll out the new strategic plan to internal and external audiences.
4. Establish systems for monitoring and reporting progress.
5. Update the strategic plan on a regular basis, no less than annually.

Because the transition from planning to implementation is especially difficult for many healthcare organizations, a leadership-driven, carefully managed, and clearly articulated approach to this phase is required. As a result, the transition should be smoother, and it should position the organization for a higher degree of implementation success.

REFERENCES

Corboy, M., and D. O Corrbui. 1999. "The Seven Deadly Sins of Strategy." *Management Accounting* 77 (10): 29–33.

Fogg, C. D. 2010. *Team-Based Strategic Planning: A Complete Guide to Structuring, Facilitating, and Implementing the Process.* Scotts Valley, CA: CreateSpace Independent Publishing Platform.

Ginter, P. M., W. J. Duncan, and L. E. Swayne. 2018. *Strategic Management of Health Care Organizations*, 8th ed. Hoboken, NJ: Wiley.

Regional Health System: Strategic Plan

INTRODUCTION

Regional Health is a first-generation integrated delivery system. It has annual revenues of about $1.6 billion and consists of five hospitals, including a tertiary medical center, an employed medical group with about 300 providers, and an insurance company with 150,000 members.

Regional Health is based in a small city but serves a large rural area of about 1 million residents. It competes with a not-for-profit community hospital, two smaller for-profit hospitals that are part of national chains, a statewide Blue Cross plan, other national insurance companies, and a variety of niche players. Regional Health's recent expansion initiatives have strained its relations with smaller providers and communities in the region.

With the arrival of a new CEO, Regional Health began a comprehensive strategic planning effort.

Major activities in the strategic planning process included the following:

- Conducting 125 stakeholder interviews
- Evaluating 600 survey responses from three stakeholder groups (management, board, physicians)
- Assessing each business entity within the Regional Health structure

- Facilitating input sessions with medical staff leaders and subsidiary boards
- Holding monthly working sessions with the strategic planning committee

FACTORS DRIVING THE NEED FOR CHANGE

A number of external environmental factors helped drive the identification of the areas of focus that Regional Health must address:

- Consumerism: Publicly available information will increasingly influence consumer choice; quality, service, and cost will become more significant considerations for patients when selecting providers.
- Delivering value: Reimbursement methodologies will be more significantly tied to outcomes; greater integration of system components will be necessary to provide care efficiently.
- Reimbursement: At best, modest increases can be expected; cost shifting to commercial plans to subsidize low payments from other payers will diminish; there will be continuing pressure to reduce costs.
- Scale and scope: Regional Health needs to scale up and develop differentiated centers of excellence to successfully compete with national organizations and niche players.

ORGANIZATIONAL DIRECTION

The strategic plan determined that Regional Health will position itself as a market innovator and differentiate itself from others based on value. The plan outlined Regional Health's mission, vision, and values as follows:

Mission

Regional Health improves the health and well-being of the people and communities we serve

Vision

In partnership with others, Regional Health will lead the way to better health

Values

Caring—We are compassionate and caring
Integrity—We treat others with integrity and respect
Collaboration—We collaborate with our customers, peers, partners and communities
Excellence—We strive for excellence in all we do

GOALS

Regional Health identified three broad goals for the five-year planning horizon:

Coordinate care to deliver value	Deliver high-value, coordinated services across the healthcare network to effectively manage the health of our community
Expand partnerships	Strengthen relationships with key internal (employees, medical staff members) and external stakeholders (customers, community groups, government organizations, businesses)
Grow across the full continuum of care	Build a critical mass of services across the full continuum of care

SUMMARY OF INITIATIVES

Regional Health then developed initiatives to achieve the goals.

Coordinate care to deliver value	Develop a system-wide framework for managing populations and coordinating care, with a focus on improving operational efficiency, reducing unnecessary care, and using evidence-based protocols
	Strengthen electronic medical records and analytical capabilities to improve care management and outcomes
	Engage medical staff in creating systems of shared accountability for performance indicators: clinical, patient experience, and financial
	Provide education for patients and families to take charge of their personal health
	Continue to develop population health capabilities, including arrangements that involve shared financial risk
Expand partnerships	Develop an array of options for physician alignment
	Leverage relationship with academic partner to expand scope of services
	Formalize educational training programs for nursing and allied health personnel
	Update approaches to employee recruitment and retention to better attract top talent
	Implement systematic and proven approaches to philanthropy for increased donations
Grow across the full continuum of care	Expand continuum of care services to better meet community needs
	Strengthen regional referrals for tertiary services
	Increase number of insured lives with targeted geographic and product development strategies
	Enhance geographic distribution of ambulatory services
	Create innovations lab for testing new approaches to care delivery

METRICS FOR MEASURING PROGRESS

Metrics were developed to track progress on goal achievement over time.

Coordinate care to deliver value	Top decile nationally in clinical quality
	Top decile nationally in service excellence
	Top decile in the state in lowest cost of care
	Service area counties perform in the 90th percentile nationally for the majority of health-related indicators
Expand partnerships	80% of affiliated providers (physicians, care extenders, etc.) are accountable for performance measures
	25% more incremental providers and staff
	"Employer of choice" in the market
	50% increase in annual philanthropic contributions
Grow across the full continuum of care	Grow net revenue by 25%+ to ensure the appropriate scale for executing strategic initiatives
	Increase market share by 5% (on average) across all services
	Increase total covered lives by 30%

CHAPTER 10

Annual Review and Update

Even if you're on the right track,
you'll get run over if you just sit there.

—*Will Rogers (attributed)*

In today's healthcare delivery environment, a meaningful strategic planning process should result in a plan that has a useful life of at least three years. This timeline appears to parallel the broader business world, wherein it is typical that a comprehensive plan update or overhaul is required about every four to five years (Fogg 2010). Regardless of the specific planning horizon, the plan should be reviewed at least annually, to determine whether the intended results are being achieved and to update the annual tactics. This step is important—not only to keep abreast of progress and manage performance but also to stay attuned to the environment and to maintain momentum for execution. In addition, doing so will be viewed positively by potential partners, bond rating agencies, regulatory bodies, and other external stakeholders. A well-executed annual update helps ensure that a strategic plan does not just sit on the shelf.

The annual review entails a high-level evaluation of progress toward the vision and goal achievement. The annual update makes appropriate adjustments to ensure the relevance of goals based on the pace and amount of progress made and in light of significant changes in the market, regulations, and the industry, as well as any major internal changes. The outcome of the annual review may be a substantial update to the plan, however. Typically, for at least one and often for two years after a comprehensive strategic planning process has been completed, a far less extensive update is called for. If it is unlikely that a robust update of the plan will be warranted, the refresh is done only to facilitate a productive review process and to inform next year's action plan. This action plan, like the one developed after full plan completion and described in chapter 9, should identify appropriate projects and tactics for the coming year, project leads, anticipated time frames, required resources, and expected impact.

Organizations should be clear on how much and what type of process is called for, and they should be thorough but judicious in determining the degree of update warranted for each of the four main phases of the plan. The following sections provide guidance on making these decisions.

REVIEW AND UPDATE APPROACH

Preliminary Assessment

To conduct a focused review and update, it is helpful to set the stage by gauging progress to date, degree of change since plan completion, and continued relevance of key plan elements. The following set of questions (and answers) is very useful to preliminarily identify how much of an update is called for and what kind of preparation and process may be most applicable:

- Have we made sufficient progress toward each of our strategic goals in the past year as measured by our performance on year 1 objectives?
- Are there recent or pending developments (internally or externally) that have or will have a *major* impact on organizational direction and priorities?

- Do current goals and metrics still reflect our most important strategic aims?
- Do initiatives still represent the key ways we will pursue our goals?

Exhibit 10.1 shows several possible scenarios for answering the four questions and provides insight into how answers translate into the degree and type of update required. While not an exhaustive set of scenarios by any means, it is helpful to see that patterns of answers emerge from asking these questions. For example, if insignificant internal and external change has occurred since the development of the last full plan, and even if progress to date on the plan has not been exceptional, an extensive update is unlikely to be required. On the other hand, even if progress on the existing plan has been adequate, a high degree of change may meaningfully reduce the relevance of goals and initiatives and thus create the need to update more extensively.

Using the questions and your answers in conjunction with the framework should give you a baseline sense of how much updating will be required, which in turn will inform how much preparation and process is needed.

Organizing and Setting Expectations

No matter how much updating is required, the process and outcomes of both the review and update should be recorded and maintained. Documentation is critical if a substantive update is in order, as formal board input on and approval of modifications will likely be needed.

As with the comprehensive planning process, the review and update processes are most efficient and productive when preparation is done in advance. Of the four key categories of preparation outlined in chapter 3—communication and expectations, management and leadership, context, and mindset—the first three, and only specific steps in each, are most relevant to the review and update processes.

1. *Communication and expectations.* The most important step in this category for the review and update is defining desired outcomes. In cases in which minimal updating is anticipated, the annual update should yield changes sufficient to justify continuing per the original plan. Typical desired outcomes in these circumstances include a thorough understanding of progress to date and successful execution of fairly minor course corrections. When significant change has occurred, plan implementation never started in earnest or has stalled, or the organization is in crisis, the annual update must be designed to yield more effective outcomes that restore plan relevance, reset priorities, and incite more or different action.

2. *Management and leadership.* The key to this category is defining roles and responsibilities of the leadership and management team. The extent to which executive leadership and the board are actively involved should correlate to the degree of update deemed necessary. If the desired outcome is a routine review and update, roles and responsibilities of the C-suite and board will be both time and scope limited and focused on ensuring appropriate progress and approval of next year's action plan developed by the management team.

3. *Context.* Appropriate context for the review and update must be established by some indication that the process is kicking off. Generally, if only minimal updating is in order, the update can begin with an informal meeting paired with written or electronic communication in which the desired outcomes and roles are explained. An extensive update, however, calls for a more formal kickoff with a broader audience and a more structured update process, timeline, and roles. Ensuring sufficient context also entails any preparatory activities related to gathering the performance data required to conduct the review and identifying any additional data needed to support strategic assessment updates.

	Potential Answer Scenarios			
	Scenario 1	Scenario 2	Scenario 3	Scenario 4
1. Good progress?	Y	N	N	Y or N
2. Lots of change?	N	N	Y	Y
3. Goals still relevant?	Y	Y	Y (Mostly)	N
4. Initiatives still appropriate?	Y	Y	N	N
Updating Required	Minimal	Minimal	Moderate	Significant
Approach	• Least process • Primarily affirm outputs, minimally update as necessary • Develop new action plan; make sure next year's objectives are appropriately aggressive based on progress to date	• Least process • Primarily affirm outputs, minimally update as necessary • Develop new action plan that is more structured, with clearer accountability and more consistent progress checks	• Moderate process • Update strategic assessment outputs • Tweak goals and metrics; revise initiatives • Develop new action plan with clear accountabilities and progress checks	• Most process • Update outputs of strategic assessment and strategy formulation, including drafting new initiatives • Review organizational direction (primarily to affirm but modify as necessary) • Develop new action plan

Process Options

In nearly all cases, the process used in the annual update will be far less extensive than that employed in the initial development of the strategic plan. However, it is hard to accurately assess the minimum amount of work required to adequately update plans, and there are no hard-and-fast rules for this determination. Clearly, if a more robust update is called for, a more substantive process will be required. But even knowing this, what a "more substantive process" entails is subjective and depends on organizational dynamics and leadership preferences, among other factors. Thus, there are almost unlimited options for what and whom to include in the process and how to approach and carry out the update. To avoid getting overwhelmed by all of the process options available, the authors of this chapter have categorized process intensity into three points on a process-intensity continuum.

1. *Informal and very abbreviated process.* Even when a limited update is warranted, some attention should be paid to the outputs of each of the four strategic planning stages. Though this attention may be cursory in nature, affirming the continued relevancy of all key plan outputs is important; it is also vital to document doing so. If staying at the minimalist end of the process-intensity continuum makes sense, the work can typically be done by planning staff with oversight from a few senior leadership champions. These individuals assume responsibility for carrying out the review and update activities, with modest input or participation from others. Select input may be sought to validate the externally oriented portion of the strategic assessment, specifically future environmental assumptions, and to identify any finetuning of initiatives underway to address the critical planning issues. A summary of the review process and proposed modifications may be prepared and provided to additional

members of the senior team or the planning committee for endorsement before commencing action planning for the following year.

2. *Formal but somewhat abbreviated process.* This option is likely best suited to situations such as scenario 3 in exhibit 10.1, in which change has occurred or new environmental threats are looming, but the overall direction, goals, and initiatives are still largely relevant. Completion of the update requires more senior management and staff effort and more input and participation are needed. This process includes a more thorough update of the strategic assessment outputs to confirm that critical planning issues still reflect priorities. Adjustments to strategy formulation outputs—goals, metrics, initiatives—are appropriate. To carry out these activities, a few structured review-and-update sessions should be held to get input and participation from a range of key internal stakeholders. Critical issue champions should spearhead these efforts, and the strategic planning committee should be engaged to review and affirm the changes proposed before passing along for C-suite or board approvals.

3. *Formal and lengthy update process.* Here, as in scenario 4 of exhibit 10.1, significant internal or external change has occurred, and more is likely to come. In these situations, the update process will involve a fairly hard look at the environment and assumptions about the future and may call for redefining the critical planning issues. As such, the products of strategy formulation—goals with metrics and initiatives—will need thorough review and likely substantive modification. A review of organizational direction—vision and overall strategy—should be undertaken and possibly tweaked. In proportion to the amount of update contemplated, input and participation from senior executives is needed, as is fairly extensive involvement of the strategic planning committee. It may

be most effective to create task forces, overseen by key members of the strategic planning committee, charged with proposing changes to the results of the strategic assessment, strategy formulation, and organizational direction. Recommendations from the task forces should be formally presented to the entire planning committee, including C-suite leaders, for their feedback and decision-making. The transition to developing action plans for the next year should also involve more extensive participation than typically necessary.

Many organizations have found that retreats (see chapter 4) are an excellent vehicle for accomplishing a significant portion of the input and participation called for in the annual strategic plan update. Obviously, the need for and desirability of retreats will vary somewhat depending on the scope and extent of the update required. Nonetheless, a growing number of healthcare organizations have at least one annual strategic planning retreat as an important element of the annual update process.

Tips for Review and Update by Planning Stage

Strategic Assessment

Given that the inputs to this planning stage are indicative of the current state and emerging trends, the strategic assessment is likely to appear (and be) out of date most quickly. However, what matters most to the rest of the plan are the three main outputs of this stage: competitive advantages and disadvantages, future environmental assumptions, and critical planning issues. Therefore, while it is advisable to review and update the organizational performance and position information that drives these work products, doing so should be a focused activity. More specifically, the time and energy expended should be proportionate to the degree to which these input updates are likely to significantly affect the three main outputs. C. Davis Fogg (2010) suggests that, assuming the internal and external environment has not radically changed since plan completion, the strategic assessment should be "surgically updated." That is, the review and update should focus on the specific elements that have been affected by change and that are likely to affect the primary outputs.

Many provider organizations use national trend reports, such as *Futurescan: Health Care Trends and Implications* (published annually by the Society for Health Care Strategy & Market Development of the American Hospital Association and the American College of Healthcare Executives), to identify key shifts in the field and to determine the degree to which these shifts are relevant and visible in their market and to their organization. Summaries of these types of materials also lend themselves well to kicking off the review and update process, as they can generate productive, high-level dialogue on trends with potentially critical strategic implications. Brief reviews of key local, regional, state, and national developments over the past year may also be helpful for staff to prepare, as may be a list of major organizational accomplishments. A structured discussion of these developments and of organizational accomplishments is recommended with the senior management team.

In circumstances of low to moderate change (scenarios 1 and 2), it is likely sufficient to review and tweak parts of the strength, weakness, opportunity, and threat (SWOT) analysis as appropriate, modify the list of future environmental assumptions as necessary, and affirm the critical planning issues. In circumstances of moderate to high change (scenarios 3 and 4), it is appropriate to revise the SWOT more fully, create a new list of future environmental assumptions, and revise existing critical issues to be more relevant, or to develop a revised list of critical planning issues. Whether the changes are minor or significant, reviewing them in a format that shows what has changed and what remains unchanged can help quickly clarify how the changes to the strategic assessment may point to necessary updates to goals, metrics, and initiatives.

Organizational Direction

Ordinarily, this component of the strategic plan requires the least attention in the annual update; organizational direction outputs should remain largely intact from update to update. The mission and values statements are the most timeless and least likely to require modification. Even in today's tumultuous environment, the vision and overall strategy should last at least five years for the majority of healthcare provider organizations.

Strategy Formulation

If the preliminary assessment responses align with scenarios 1 or 2 (see exhibit 10.1), the focus of reviewing and updating the strategy formulation is exclusively on examining progress related to the plan's goals and objectives. Revisions may be warranted because of actual implementation success or failure, including pace of progress, roadblocks encountered, and the like.

If the preliminary assessment responses align with scenarios 3 or 4, the review and updating of strategy formulation may be conducted in a manner similar to that followed in the complete planning process or, depending on current circumstances, in a less or more process-intensive fashion. Assuming new critical issues were identified in the update of the strategic assessment stage, new goals, metrics, and initiatives will need to be developed for these new critical issues. Even if critical issues remain largely the same, some updating of goals, metrics, and initiatives should be carried out to account for the significant change since completion of the last plan. Similar to the strategic assessment, senior management, at minimum, discusses and reviews strategy. Typically, and if using a more process-intensive approach, the strategic planning committee is briefed and reviews the strategy formulation outcomes.

Implementation Planning

Regardless of how much updating has been done to the products of the other planning stages, this stage should entail development of a new action plan for the next year. Even if there are only minimal updates in the strategy formulation phase (scenarios 1 or 2), it is always necessary to update action plans to account for progress made and challenges encountered in the previous year. See "Approach" for scenarios 1 and 2 in exhibit 10.1 for detail on the types of updates to the implementation plan that are most applicable.

In the case of scenario 2, in which progress has been inadequate, this time is advantageous for making sure that accountability is focused on individuals as opposed to groups and that the right individuals are chosen. When individuals realize that their implementation performance will be reviewed, the culture of an organization can shift toward accomplishment of each step toward strategic goals and the organizational vision.

Significant strategy formulation output updates (scenarios 3 or 4) require developing a brand new action plan to identify new objectives for each goal and metric and to establish new tactics.

At the conclusion of the annual update, board approval of the new strategic plan may be required. The scope and extent of the changes to the plan ordinarily will dictate how involved the approval process needs to be. Even if the board does not need to approve the changes, organizations can increase board commitment to the planning process and organizational strategy by apprising the board of progress on the plan, and informing them when the plan has been actively and thoughtfully revised.

A Few Examples

Academic Health

Academic Health is located in a major East Coast city and serves as the clinical delivery system for a major university. It comprises multiple health systems, the result of a series of mergers. Academic Health updates its three-year rolling strategic plan annually. The strategic planning calendar is integrated with the organization's key operational and fiscal routines and staged over the course of the fiscal year, which begins in June.

The annual strategic plan update begins in the summer, when management reviews the organization's progress against its plan for the previous year. At this time, it also assesses environmental changes and develops new or modified assumptions for the future. High-level system goals are also reviewed and revised as appropriate. With these system parameters set, planning at the business-unit and critical-issue levels takes place over the next few months. Typically, teams for key service lines and organization-wide initiatives, such as service excellence and quality or safety improvement, develop detailed plans in each area. All this effort rolls up to create the next version of the organization's strategic plan in December.

Following this phase, the plan presents issues to be considered during the budget development process and the annual operating plan in the second half of the fiscal year. The results provide the balanced scorecard for use during the next fiscal year. Research and information gathering, including surveys and data collection, are also carried out during the second half of the fiscal year to inform the plan update in the following fiscal year.

Catholic Health System

Catholic Health, a large Catholic healthcare system, has an annual process called the Integrated Strategic, Operational, and Financial Plan (ISOFP) for the system and its members. In the past, the process resulted in a five-year plan, but recently, given the dynamic nature of healthcare and rapid changes in the environment, the system converted to a three-year plan. However, it noted that the strategic horizon for the ISOFP should still be five years, with a focus on strategies that affect each fiscal year's operational and financial plans.

Strategic planning begins by reconsidering overall system direction, including Catholic Health's strategies, guiding principles, and key assumptions. Then, detailed planning occurs in the defined regions that the system serves. Catholic Health provides strategic plan content and process guidance via a content guide that contains templates, process steps, and a schedule. The process at the regional level kicks off in December, about midway through the fiscal year.

Market leaders are provided with a content guide that

- promotes rigor, accountability, and consistency across each market ISOFP;
- guides each market on the strategic, operational, and financial content that should be in the ISOFP;
- helps market leaders conduct meetings with system leaders to review their annual ISOFP;
- provides a template for the ISOFP; and
- includes other resources to simplify the process.

As the parts of the ISOFP are drafted, a fairly intensive process of region-specific strategic and financial planning and regular interactions with system strategy and finance staff ensues over the next few months.

Each Market ISOFP addresses strategy, capital requirements, operational plans, and financial plans and budgets. Therefore, in each Market, the ISOFP process involves clinical, finance, operational, strategy, and business development leadership. The system then develops a full draft of each region's ISOFP by late March, and after reviews by system leadership, the regional plans are finalized by mid-April. Over the next two months, the plans are consolidated into a system-wide plan and reviewed and approved by the office of the president, board committees, and board of directors.

Final Thoughts on the Review and Update Processes

An Art, Not a Science
Unfortunately, how frequently a comprehensive strategic plan should be completed, compared with less intensive annual updates, depends on the organization and its environment, particular circumstances, leadership style, cultural norms, and an array of other factors. In

addition, as described earlier, even once it is determined that the update route is preferable, there is no one-size-fits-all approach that can be prescribed.

The need for an annual update is usually evident because the organization or its environment has changed markedly, the update process has started to become stale, the organization has largely accomplished (or has made substantial progress toward) its key goals, or some combination of all three.

Integration Improves Effectiveness

The annual strategic plan update should be integrated with financial and operational planning to the extent possible. For most healthcare organizations, the annual update occurs during the first half of the fiscal year. When beginning an annual update process, many healthcare organizations erroneously delay the start (and completion) of the update process until later in the year and find that the information needed for the budgeting process is not available in a timely manner. Experience indicates that an early start in the fiscal year provides for smoother integration with financial planning. As a practical matter, the workflow needs to be staged and sequenced throughout the year, so that all elements of the management plans receive appropriate and thorough attention. Typically, the bulk of the work on the strategic plan update should be completed before financial and operating planning begins. However, some flexibility must be built into the process so that revisions of all plans can be made as necessary before finalization, depending on the results of each element of this process. The third and (principally) fourth quarters can be used for iterative revisions to the strategic, financial, and operating plans.

Getting Perspective on the Role of the Update

The annual update helps ensure that a strategic plan doesn't just sit on the shelf. The annual update should be treated as a mechanism and forum for formalizing appropriate adaptation, and it should be viewed as the component of broader strategic plan implementation that reconciles change over time. Inevitably, as implementation occurs, variation from what was envisioned will be called for and put into practice. Some of these ideas and opportunities may be so compelling or emergent that they are acted on before the next plan update occurs. Others may be held for consideration at the time of the update, though this delay is certainly not necessary. In either case, the annual update is the time and place to document these events and to test for their consistency with and relevance to the strategic plan. Some innovations to the review process that may provide a stronger foundation for sustainable execution are described in detail in chapter 11.

REFERENCE

Fogg, C. D. 2010. *Team-Based Strategic Planning: A Complete Guide to Structuring, Facilitating, and Implementing the Process*. Scotts Valley, CA: CreateSpace Independent Publishing Platform.

SUGGESTED READING

Society for Health Care Strategy & Market Development and American College of Healthcare Executives. 2021. *Futurescan 2022–2027: Health Care Trends and Implications*. Chicago: Health Administration Press.

Optimizing Strategic Planning

CHAPTER 11

Enabling More Effective Execution

Things don't just happen, they are made to happen.

—*John F. Kennedy*

To-morrow let us do or die.

—*Thomas Campbell*

THE CHALLENGES OF IMPLEMENTATION

Strategic planning has been criticized for its detachment from day-to-day operations and its inability to effect significant change in an organization. While comprehensive, well-designed plans may be prepared with exceptionally strong supporting documentation and the use of thorough, inclusive consensus development processes, implementation seems to be elusive and ultimately out of reach for many organizations.

Implementation difficulties are not unique to healthcare organizations. Studies suggest that 60 to 90 percent of strategic plans fail to launch (Olsen 2022). Why is there such a high failure rate in the transition from planning to implementation? It appears to be a function of four main factors:

1. *Loss of energy and focus.* In many organizations, strategic planning engages a broad spectrum of leadership.

It is a high-level, high-visibility process that garners considerable attention and effort. Once the strategic plan has been completed and approved, the show is over, and implementation occurs out of the spotlight. This loss of energy and focus may cause implementation to be inconsistent and to dissipate over time.

2. *Lack of management.* As described later in this chapter, implementation needs to be actively managed. It does not just happen, but rather requires a significant amount of hard work, direction, and oversight. Yet, in the aftermath of many strategic planning efforts, implementation is assumed rather than actively managed; in these cases, the implementation failure rate is high.

3. *Disconnect from operations.* Strategic planning is often viewed as an add-on to day-to-day operations; if done periodically, rather than continually, the fragmentation is aggravated. In these situations, the implementation plan does not belong to anyone, and it is not a part of the organization's routine operations. This disconnect makes it difficult to maintain a focus on implementation and regularly and consistently make progress.

4. *Lack of resources.* Many strategic plans are overly ambitious and unrealistic. They call for too many activities and actions to be implemented concurrently and propose strategies that exceed the organization's resources. Frustration emerges as it becomes clear that implementation is in jeopardy.

This chapter describes methods and processes to achieve a higher rate of implementation success; integrate strategic planning into regular, ongoing organizational management; and ultimately evolve from the periodic strategic planning processes of the last several decades to more effective and contemporary strategic management processes.

FOSTERING IMPLEMENTATION SUCCESS

Making a smooth, effective, and successful transition from planning to implementation starts with a sound, well-understood implementation plan. Many organizations tend to rush into implementation at the conclusion of the strategic planning process and fail to prepare thorough, thoughtful implementation plans. In such plans, the roles and responsibilities of staff must be understood and accepted, as well as the time frame and interrelationships of implementation activities. Finally, and possibly foremost, a management structure and approach to implementation needs to be in place. This structure and approach must include, at minimum, a designated overall implementation leader and regular progress reviews. These reviews could involve senior management, corporate staff (in a system), or the strategic planning committee of the board. Effective implementation is an iterative process, so that review often leads to revision followed by subsequent implementation, further review, more revision, and so on, in a continuous cycle.

Successful plan implementation comprises ten steps:

1. *Understand that plan execution starts during the preplanning stage.* The tone, content, and approach of an organization's strategic planning process all influence the likelihood of its success. Involve key stakeholders—board members, board planning committee members, physicians, other clinicians, senior leadership, middle management, and planning staff. Communicate the importance of the strategic planning process and make sure everyone understands the benefits (community, financial, product or market, operational) of a well-executed plan. If you sought consulting assistance for development of the strategic plan, consider retaining that assistance to monitor implementation.

2. *Consider execution while formulating strategy.* Execution is not something to worry about later; it must be an

underlying theme during strategy formulation. However, execution worries should not dampen the creative spirit of strategy formulation. Instead, execution must be one of the many considerations of planning and doing that occur later in strategic planning. Think about whether high-level strategies can be subdivided and executed at the operational level. Individual actions should be aligned with organizational strategies.

3. *Choose execution leaders wisely.* Having the right leaders with the right skills in place during plan execution can be the difference between success and failure. When you are selecting execution leaders, carefully consider skill level, ability to engender a sense of strategy ownership, and capacity for communicating. Ensure that leaders have the tools, resources, and training they need. More important, give them the time to finish the job—a chief complaint among execution leaders is a shortage of time. Finally, make sure that leaders can resist the urge to meddle. When execution committees are managing implementation well, leaders need to know when to get out of the way.

4. *Mobilize the team and communicate.* Clarify the roles and responsibilities of those involved in plan execution. In many organizations, there will be an oversight group of senior executives, leaders of individual initiatives and tasks, and supporting staff and groups. Make sure the implementation team is in place and clearly charged with carrying out its responsibilities as this phase begins.

5. *Mark the implementation phase in a formal, celebratory way.* As planning concludes and execution begins, organizations should select a formal approach for communicating to their staff that implementation is beginning. Most important, plan an inclusive rollout event to show that the planning is complete and a new era is beginning. A celebratory occasion can help draw attention, raise

expectations, and build enthusiasm that will be needed during implementation.

6. *Drive the plan down into the organization.* Strategy execution is most successful when it is seen as an organization-wide effort rather than an executive office exercise. Individuals throughout the organization must be given clear directions about what they are expected to achieve. Build implementation tasks into performance objectives and give rewards when they are completed. Using implementation subcommittees—with no more than 12 members—may help. Consider having these subcommittees in place during the strategic planning process, then transitioning them to a new role in the implementation phase. Organizations may also need to provide training to individuals responsible for implementation.

7. *Watch out for the warning signs of execution failure.* Some common red flags that implementation is not progressing as it should include persistent political infighting, a loss of focus, a sense of inertia, pervasive resistance to change, and a disconnect between planning objectives and operational realities. If any of these issues crop up, quickly defuse the situation and work aggressively to get implementation back on track.

8. *Communicate, communicate, communicate.* Strategy execution involves even more people than strategy formulation, making communication crucial. Establish a common message about the strategic plan, make the plan summary widely available, and provide updates and internal communications online or by e-mail. The CEO and other senior managers should meet with key stakeholders directly to provide feedback and respond to concerns.

9. *Have a monitoring system in place.* To track the implementation schedule, budget, and progress, use a monitoring system that is relevant, accurate, and useful for

organization. Consider using a system that also measures the intangibles, such as management effectiveness, innovation, and potential for further progress. A good monitoring system will help you review the progress of the plan's implementation. The review should help the organization ensure that progress is being made, priorities stay on track, obstacles to progress are resolved, and resources are reallocated if necessary.

10. *Consider moving from strategic planning to strategic management.* Strategic planning has been criticized for its detachment from day-to-day operations and its inability to produce real, sustainable change in organizations. Many organizations use strategic *management* approaches to integrate core management processes. Strategic management, discussed further later in this chapter, has clear benefits, such as integration (rather than coordination) with finance and operations and the fact that day-to-day management occurs in a strategic framework rather than in separate management processes. Organizations that use strategic management often find that their organizational culture starts adapting to change more easily.

ONGOING REVIEW OF PROGRESS

C. Davis Fogg (2010, 215) suggests that ongoing review of progress "helps you keep the plan on track once implementation is under way, reallocate resources as you accomplish goals or your strategic situation changes, embed accountability for program accomplishment with every implementer, and reward results to ensure commitment and continued top level performance." He believes that the key to success is

- "review, review, review;
- revise, revise, revise; and
- reward, reward, reward."

There are five main reasons for conducting regular progress reviews:

1. To shine the spotlight on the ongoing importance of implementation to the organization's success
2. To encourage and motivate individuals and teams involved in implementing action plans through visibility, recognition, and praise
3. To make sure that appropriate progress is being made and priorities stay on track
4. To discuss and resolve problems and internal obstacles to progress, particularly those that require interdisciplinary intervention
5. To allow reallocation of valuable resources to the areas that most need them

Both formal and informal mechanisms can be used to effectively review ongoing progress. Regular meetings of senior management or the strategic planning committee of the board are one common approach to this task. For many organizations, monthly progress review meetings for the first year or two after completion of a major strategic planning effort help ensure progress and accountability. Frequent progress review meetings are the best way to ensure that implementation occurs and that timely adjustments are made to individual action plans.

Once the organization has accepted a disciplined approach to implementation, meeting frequency may be reduced. Mature strategic planning organizations find that quarterly, or in some instances semiannual, progress review meetings are sufficient to keep implementation on track.

A structured approach to implementation progress reviews often yields the best results. Such structure involves taking action plan formats, such as those provided in chapter 9, and marking them up in advance of each meeting, charting expectations versus actual results, schedules, resource consumption, and so on (see exhibit 11.1).

Many organizations use a red, yellow, and green light schema to facilitate review of progress relative to the plan at a glance. Explanations of variances from expectations should be provided. New issues or concerns, or those that transcend individual action plans, can be noted in a comments section. Recommendations for changes to the implementation plan should also be noted. These progress reports should be circulated to all progress meeting attendees in advance. Key to making these meetings more effective is a structured approach to meeting conduct. An important consideration is allowing enough dialogue to occur about action plans and issues that require group attention while minimizing discussion about things that do not require group discussion. In the absence of such focus, progress review meetings tend to be overly long and have diminished effectiveness as a result. In other cases, the meetings are too short and perfunctory.

The meeting leader needs to carefully craft the agenda to balance competing concerns and needs, all in a time frame that is appropriate to the importance of the topics being discussed. Advance preparation and awareness of pitfalls in this process help ensure that the progress review meetings achieve the intended outcomes and are a highly effective mechanism for ongoing plan implementation support.

Individual performance reviews also can enhance the effectiveness of plan implementation. If the action plan objectives are built into individual performance objectives, these annual or semiannual reviews provide an opportunity to review progress and make adjustments with individuals responsible for implementation.

Informal progress reviews can and should occur on an ongoing basis. Contact among senior leadership, some of whom may have direct implementation responsibilities, and between senior leadership and other staff with implementation responsibilities, should be frequent in most organizations. Such regular contact provides yet another opportunity for periodic but less formal review of progress against plan.

Even with the active monitoring process outlined in the earlier section, senior management may need to intervene directly in

Exhibit 11.1: Action Plan Progress Review Example: Service Excellence Action Plan

Objective	Leader	Threshold	Target	Superior	Status Update
			Performance Level		
1. Improve the level of patient/customer satisfaction with Community Health (a partner)	AB	Have a combined patient/client satisfaction score average of 94	Have a combined patient/client satisfaction score average of 95	Have a combined patient/client satisfaction score average of 96	Patient satisfaction score is 95%
2. Achieve high level of patient satisfaction with medical center services as measured by inpatients, outpatients, emergency department, and physician practices	CD	Demonstrate improvement in the average scores of two of the satisfaction surveys	Demonstrate improvement in the average scores of three of the satisfaction surveys	Demonstrate improvement in the average scores of four of the satisfaction surveys	Third quarter patient satisfaction improved in all four areas: • Inpatients YTD: 87.7 (vs. 2012 score of 86.7) • Outpatients YTD: 93.4 (vs. 2012 score of 93.1) • Medical practices: 92.1 (vs. 2012 score of 91.9) • Emergency department: 89.1 (vs. 2012 score of 87.9)
3. Increase average patient satisfaction with services at Imaging Associates and Center for Surgery	NH	Increase average Press Ganey scores by 0.5	Increase average Press Ganey scores by 1	Increase average Press Ganey scores by 1.5	Third quarter combined average was 93 vs. 2012 average of 93.6
4. Achieve high level of employee engagement	KM	Achieve 50th percentile "Engaged" ranking	Achieve 65th percentile "Engaged" ranking	Achieve 75th percentile "Engaged" ranking	Employee Engagement Survey has been finalized; achieved 58th percentile for employee engagement
5. Achieve high level of physician engagement	VK	Survey employed and independent physicians using engagement tool	Using results of survey, develop a plan to improve physician engagement	Implement at least one strategy to improve engagement	Physician Engagement Survey closed with a 44% participation rate; a plan to improve physician engagement is being developed

Key: ■ On target   ▨ In process   ▨ Behind target/needs attention

© 2024 Veralon Partners Inc.

implementation to keep initiatives on track. Fogg (2010) notes four types of interventions that may be required:

1. Counseling an individual or team, providing advice for dealing with problems or problematic team members
2. Exerting influence to remove obstacles or obtain the resources needed to move forward
3. Improving skills, such as through training or by enhancing functional expertise
4. Providing direction, especially to get an individual or group back on track

Rewards also play an important role in facilitating achievement of implementation tasks. Individual and group performance may both be rewarded, and rewards can be both financial and nonfinancial in nature. Psychological rewards, including publicity for achievements or effort and recognition for winning organizational contests, can play a key role in motivating individuals and teams to make good progress in implementation.

THE BALANCED SCORECARD

The balanced scorecard is a tool to assist with ongoing progress monitoring and implementation. It is estimated that more than 50 percent of large US companies use a balanced scorecard (Balanced Scorecard Institute 2023). Developed in industry in the early 1990s by Robert S. Kaplan and David Norton (1996a, 75), it is intended to supplement traditional performance measurement systems by tracking "financial results while simultaneously monitoring progress in building the capabilities and acquiring the intangible assets [organizations] would need for future growth." John R. Griffith and Jeffrey A. Alexander (2002) describe the balanced scorecard as an integrated set of measures, driven by the organization's vision and strategy, typically covering the following dimensions in healthcare organizations:

- *Financial.* Financial performance and management of resources (including intangible resources such as workforce capability and supplier relations)
- *Internal business processes.* Cost, quality, efficiency, and other characteristics of goods and services
- *Customer.* Measures of satisfaction, market share, and competitive position
- *Learning and growth.* Measures of the ability to respond to changes in technology, customer attitudes, and economic environment

The balanced scorecard complements financial measurements with measurements of progress in three key areas: customer satisfaction, internal business processes, and learning and growth. Improvements in the balanced scorecard approach have rendered it a valuable tool for some companies that have used it as a key part of a strategic management system (see next section). Kaplan and Norton (1996a, 75) suggest that "used this way, the scorecard addresses a serious deficiency in traditional management systems: their inability to link a company's long-term strategy with its short-term actions."

A number of healthcare organizations have adopted the balanced scorecard to aid in strategy implementation. Noorein Inamdar and Robert S. Kaplan (2002) cite five potential benefits of this approach for healthcare organizations:

1. It aligns the organization around a more market-oriented, customer-focused strategy.
2. It facilitates, monitors, and assesses the implementation of the strategy.
3. It provides a communication and collaboration mechanism.
4. It assigns accountability for performance at all levels of the organization.
5. It provides continual feedback on the strategy and promotes adjustments in response to marketplace and regulatory changes.

In a review of the literature on the use of the balanced scorecard in healthcare, Bob McDonald (2012) cites a few additional benefits of the balanced scorecard for healthcare organizations, including avoiding overemphasis on financial measures, enhancing focus on customer service, and improving outcomes.

In a review of the application of the balanced scorecard approach to healthcare organizations, Inamdar and Kaplan (2002) chart the steps involved in developing and implementing the balanced score-card (see exhibit 11.2). Kaplan and Norton (1996a) suggest that the process of managing performance via the balanced scorecard consists of four sequential steps (see also exhibit 11.3):

1. *Translating the vision.* The mission and vision are often too abstract to be useful to employees as effective guides to day-to-day operations. Identifying concrete measures related to the mission and vision translates these lofty statements into a more effective form.

2. *Communicating and linking.* Involving employees from all levels of the organization in developing the scorecard initiates the process of integrating it into the organization. Ultimately, linking the scorecard measures to subgroup and individual performance measurements is the most effective approach.

3. *Business planning.* In this step, the overall strategy is translated into the objectives, measures, targets, and initiatives that link the strategy with operations and implementation. Similarly, integration of strategic and budgeting or financial planning is inherent in the creation of the scorecard.

4. *Feedback and learning.* A balanced scorecard incorporates a process for review and evaluation of progress and modification of plans as necessary.

Exhibit 11.2: The Balanced Scorecard Development and Implementation Process

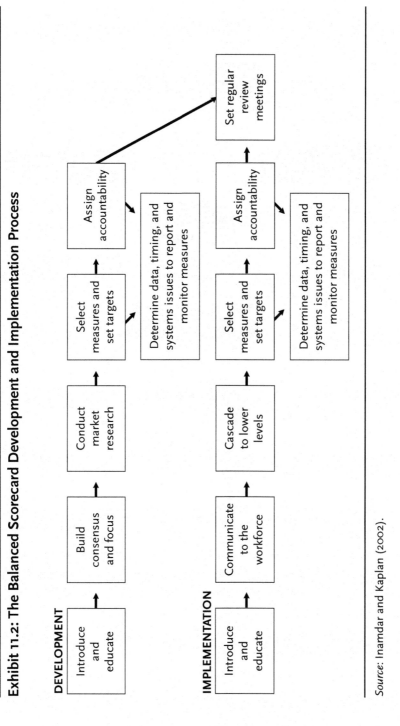

Source: Inamdar and Kaplan (2002).

Exhibit 11.3: Effectively Using the Balanced Scorecard to Manage Performance

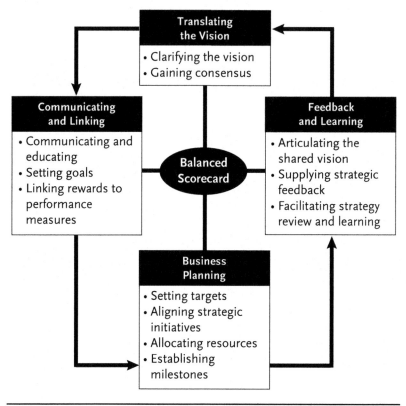

Source: Kaplan and Norton (1996b).

While using the balanced scorecard approach improves on previous performance measurement approaches, Kaplan and Norton (1996a, 85) argue that it is even more valuable "as the foundation of an integrated and iterative strategic management system." In these situations, companies are using the scorecard to

- clarify and update strategy,
- communicate strategy throughout the company,

- align unit and individual goals with the strategy,
- link strategic objectives to long-term targets and annual budgets,
- identify and align strategic initiatives, and
- conduct periodic performance reviews to learn about and improve strategy.

FROM STRATEGIC PLANNING TO STRATEGIC MANAGEMENT

Increasingly, healthcare organizations are moving beyond periodic strategic planning and adopting more systematic approaches carried out regularly and integrated with other core management processes (see exhibit 11.4). Clear benefits may be derived in implementation rigor and implementation success. Also, the quality of strategic planning and implementation is improved as a result of better coordination with finance and operations in ongoing strategic planning processes. Additional benefits are obtained by those organizations that evolve to strategic management and integrate (rather than

Exhibit 11.4: Transitioning the Strategic Planning Process to Strategic Management

Periodic Strategic Planning	Ongoing Strategic Planning	Strategic Management
• Plans prepared every three to five years; no annual updates	• Full plans every three to five years; updates annually	• Continuous, evolving plans; refined annually
• Implementation is unsystematic	• Implementation is managed	• Continuous, managed implementation
• Operations divorced from planning	• Finance/operations interfaced with planning	• Finance/operations integrated with planning
• Finance at odds with planning	• Management unsystematically strategic	• Management mostly strategic

© 2024 Veralon Partners Inc.

coordinate) finance and operations with strategic planning as part of their regular management routines. Further, in strategic management, day-to-day management is carried out in a largely strategic framework, rather than the traditional separate management processes for operations, finance, and planning.

The balanced scorecard is one proven approach to strategic management. Exhibit 11.5 presents another approach used by healthcare organizations. This approach is a logical extension of a strong strategic planning process transitioning into strategic management. Annually, three concurrent activities take place:

1. The strategic plan is developed or, following a comprehensive strategic planning process, updated in subsequent years. The plan update typically occurs in the first half of the fiscal year. In the second half of the year, planning initiatives provide inputs to capital and operating budgets and plans, and an iterative process leads to the finalization of all budgets and plans.

2. Throughout the year, implementation of the previously developed strategic plan occurs. This process is managed, with ongoing support and oversight of implementation— including formal review of progress and adjustment of implementation. Contingency plans for certain initiatives may be required.

3. Operations proceed routinely throughout the year. The implementation is managed within regular management structures and processes, and new strategic opportunities are reviewed and tested (with great frequency in some organizations) against the strategic plan. Such reviews may dictate adjustment of the plan's strategies and actions to accommodate new, emerging initiatives.

Whatever process organizations employ, strategic management represents a powerful tool with substantial benefits for both a stronger

Exhibit 11.5: Annual Strategic Management Process Components

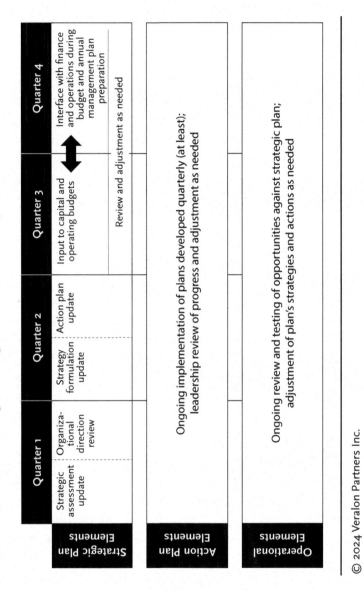

	Quarter 1	Quarter 2	Quarter 3	Quarter 4
Strategic Plan Elements	Strategic assessment update / Organizational direction review	Strategy formulation update / Action plan update	Input to capital and operating budgets	Interface with finance and operations during budget and annual management plan preparation
			Review and adjustment as needed	
Action Plan Elements	Ongoing implementation of plans developed quarterly (at least); leadership review of progress and adjustment as needed			
Operational Elements	Ongoing review and testing of opportunities against strategic plan; adjustment of plan's strategies and actions as needed			

© 2024 Veralon Partners Inc.

strategic planning function and a more successful implementation and integrated operations management function.

CONCLUSION

Effective implementation has proven to be difficult for most organizations. A common misperception is that implementation just happens, when in fact it must be carefully managed if the organization is going to meet its goals and objectives. Ongoing review of progress and new approaches, such as the balanced scorecard, should help keep implementation on track. Strategic Management offers greater integration of strategic planning, finance and operations.

REFERENCES

Balanced Scorecard Institute. 2023. "Balanced Scorecard Basics." Accessed October 6. https://balancedscorecard.org/bsc-basics/.

Fogg, C. D. 2010. *Team-Based Strategic Planning: A Complete Guide to Structuring, Facilitating, and Implementing the Process.* Scotts Valley, CA: CreateSpace Independent Publishing Platform.

Griffith, J. R., and J. A. Alexander. 2002. "Measuring Comparative Hospital Performance." *Journal of Healthcare Management* 47 (1): 42–43.

Inamdar, N., and R. S. Kaplan. 2002. "Applying the Balanced Scorecard in Healthcare Provider Organizations." *Journal of Healthcare Management* 47 (3): 179–95.

Kaplan, R. S., and D. P. Norton. 1996a. *The Balanced Scorecard: Translating Strategy into Action.* Boston: Harvard Business Review Press.

———. 1996b. "Using the Balanced Scorecard as a Strategic Management System." *Harvard Business Review*, January–February, 75–85.

Olsen, Andrea Beck. 2022. "4 Common Reasons Strategies Fail." *Harvard Business Review*. Published June 24. https://hbr.org/2022/06/4-common-reasons-strategies-fail.

Wells, D. L. 1996. *Strategic Management for Senior Leaders: A Handbook for Implementation*. Total Quality Leadership Office, US Department of the Navy. Accessed January 11, 2017. http://gov-info.library.unt.edu/npr/initiati/mfr/managebk.pdf.

CHAPTER 12

Future Challenges for Strategic Planners

The best way to predict the future is to invent it.

—Alan Kay

The future will soon be a thing of the past.

—George Carlin

THE STATE OF THE ART IN HEALTHCARE STRATEGY AND STRATEGIC PLANNING

In a highly provocative article, Michael E. Porter, one of the leading authorities on strategy, and his coauthor Thomas H. Lee (2015, 1681), state, "Until recently, most health care organizations could get by without a real strategy, as most businesses understand that term. They didn't need to worry about how to be different or make painful decisions about what not to do. As long as patients came in the door, they did fine, since fee-for-service contracts covered their costs and a little more."

Success came from operational effectiveness: working hard, embracing best practices, and burnishing the organization's reputation to attracted both patients and talent. Typically, "strategy," by default, meant having the scale and market presence to secure good rates and participate in networks.

But if that era is ending, the time has come for healthcare organizations to rethink the meaning of strategy. Strategy is about making the choices necessary to distinguish an organization in the competition to meet customers' needs.

When compared to strategic planning practices outside of the healthcare field, it is clear that healthcare strategic planning has not advanced to sophisticated levels and is far behind what are considered state-of-the-art practices. In fact, the areas in which healthcare organizations seem to do best—development of mission statements and goals and participation of senior management in the planning process—are rudimentary in strategic planning outside the healthcare field. Organizations exhibiting more advanced strategic planning would merely think of these areas as the basics, not best practices or even strengths.

Companies that demonstrate pathbreaking strategic planning practices outside of healthcare already embody what are considered bleeding-edge strategic planning approaches among healthcare organizations today, such as attacking critical issues, developing clear strategies, achieving real benefits, and managing implementation.

More important, outside of healthcare, pathbreaking planning practices are characterized by five qualities:

1. *Systematic, ongoing internal and external data gathering leads to the use of knowledge management practices.* Rather than the ad hoc data assembly and analysis frequently observed in healthcare organizations, pathbreaking companies outside of healthcare have highly structured systems for continuously gathering information that drives strategic planning. Data gathered have a breadth and depth rarely seen among healthcare organizations. Once data are gathered, nonlinear analysis is conducted using sophisticated modeling, artificial intelligence, game theory, and other advanced approaches that far exceed the linear techniques and correlations used in healthcare organizations. Data collection and analysis focus on the

market and external factors and forces, so that decision-making is largely driven from the outside, as opposed to the inward-looking approach more common in healthcare organizations.

2. *Innovation and creativity are prized.* Pathbreaking companies demonstrate the high value they place on innovation and creativity by building a work environment that is receptive to new ideas and looks at alternatives, especially when they create new products and market space. Risk-averse healthcare organizations understand the concepts of innovation and creativity, but putting them into action is another matter. The key issue here is less what to do but rather how to do it. Demonstrating leadership instead of followership and becoming risk tolerant are important first steps for healthcare organizations. Developing a culture that supports—or better yet, encourages—risk-taking is a prerequisite for progress. (The challenge of encouraging risk-taking in a culture focused on avoiding errors is addressed in chapter 14.)

3. *Strategic planning is more bottom-up than top-down.* Leading firms outside of healthcare use a planning process that is increasingly focused in the business units or subsidiaries, with corporate leadership providing high-level direction. This approach allows strategic planning to be more broadly based, meaningful, and substantial, with the real action of planning taking place closer to the customer. Organizational support for initiatives is nurtured when planning has a bottom-up orientation, and implementation may be more successful when planning has been vigorous at lower levels of the organization. Healthcare strategic planning is still too often a top-down process that engenders insufficient participation, awareness, or support from the majority of employees. As health systems consolidate into ever larger entities, there is a risk of even greater top-down planning.

4. *Evolving, flexible, and continuously improving strategic planning processes help organizations adapt more readily.* Pathbreaking companies embrace the inevitability of change and use planning processes with an external orientation. They use external forces and factors to create a platform for change that keeps planning responsive and vital. They regularly revise and upgrade their planning processes and techniques based on their own experiences, observations of other leading companies, and academic research. Many healthcare organizations are content to use tried-and-true strategic planning processes that have worked well historically. Most healthcare professionals are not content with yesterday's operations management and financial planning approaches, so why shouldn't they support similar levels of change in their strategic planning processes?

5. *Dynamic strategic planning has replaced static planning.* Many companies in rapidly changing industries recognize that strategic planning must be dynamic—vision statements must inspire and stretch the organization, goals may need to be revolutionary, strategic thinking is encouraged, decision-making is driven down to all levels, and strategic planning is embedded throughout the culture. Strategic planning becomes everyone's job, every day, not just an annual or periodic exercise by executive leaders.

Healthcare leaders must look beyond their own backyards to learn how other highly competitive sectors are spurring organizations to greater levels of growth and success with more rigorous and sophisticated planning. The five qualities discussed here, even when executed at rather basic levels, will go a long way toward helping healthcare organizations experience the benefits that pathbreaking companies realize from their planning processes.

THE NEW STRATEGIC PLANNER

These new perspectives on healthcare strategic planning argue for careful reconsideration of this role in guiding and shaping the strategic planning process. As we consider where the healthcare field is in terms of strategy development and strategic planning, and where it needs to go, the results of a survey about strategy practices outside of healthcare may be enlightening. Authors Chris Bradley, Martin Hirt, and Sven Smit (2011) believe that good strategy has ten fundamental qualities:

1. Will your strategy beat the market?
2. Does your strategy tap into a true source of advantage?
3. Is your strategy granular about where to compete?
4. Does your strategy put you ahead of trends?
5. Does your strategy rest on privileged insights?
6. Does your strategy embrace uncertainty?
7. Does your strategy balance commitment and flexibility?
8. Is your strategy contaminated by bias?
9. Is there conviction to act on your strategy?
10. Have you translated your strategy into an action plan?

In an international survey of more than 2,000 executives, these scholars found that nearly two-thirds believed that their company's strategy passed three or fewer of these tests, with only about 10 percent saying that they passed seven to ten. Given healthcare organizations' relative lack of sophistication in strategic planning, it is likely that they perform even worse. In work focused specifically on healthcare, the Society for Health Care Strategy and Market Development (SHSMD 2016) completed a major examination of the future role of the healthcare strategic planner. The study sought to answer the question, "Given the evolving changes in the healthcare environment and our desire to enhance the value we bring to the enterprise, how might we, as strategy professionals, reimagine our work?" In summary, SHSMD recommended five areas of future emphasis for healthcare strategic planners:

1. *Be nimble to exceed the rate of change.* Evolve as quickly as the external environment does. Frame problems, ask provocative questions, and move the organization to action.
2. *Create consumer experiences. Tell powerful stories.* Understand needs and motivations in order to compel storytelling. Intentionally design experiences to influence consumer behavior.
3. *Integrate and co-create.* Facilitate conversations in multilayered and complex organizations, create coalitions, and seek out a diversity of perspectives.
4. *Erase the boundaries of business.* Help develop accessible, integrated systems of care assembled through creative means, such as partnerships and technology.
5. *Generate data-driven insight.* Identify the best tools for collecting, interpreting, and communicating information to deliver insights and better decisions with data.

Looking further ahead and drawing on the more advanced state of strategy development and strategic planning outside of healthcare, Martin Reeves, Knut Haanaes, and Janmejaya Sinha (2015) call for leaders to resist the natural tendency of organizations to hold fast to familiar or historically successful strategies. Instead, readers should encourage a focus on an external perspective, challenging internal biases. Further, with the multiple complex environments of today's markets, leaders need to be the animators of a dynamic combination of multiple approaches to strategy. To carry this out effectively, leaders need to wear eight different hats.

1. *Diagnostician.* Continuously take an external perspective to diagnose the degree of predictability, malleability, and harshness of each business environment and match

this with the required strategic approach for each part of the firm.

2. *Segmenter.* Structure the firm to match the strategic approach to the environment at the right level of granularity, balancing the trade-off between precision and complexity.

3. *Disrupter.* Review the diagnosis and segmentation on an ongoing basis, in line with shifts in the environment, to protect the organization from becoming rigid and to modulate or change approaches when necessary.

4. *Team coach.* Select the right people for the job of managing each element in the collage according to their capabilities and help develop their understanding of the strategy palette, both intellectually and experientially.

5. *Salesperson.* Advocate and communicate the strategic choices as a whole in a clear and coherent narrative to investors and employees.

6. *Inquisitor.* Set and retune the correct context for each particular strategic approach by asking probing questions—not dictating answers—to help stimulate the critical thinking flow that is appropriate to and characteristic of each approach.

7. *Antenna.* Look outward continuously and selectively amplify important signals to ensure that each unit stays in tune with the changing external environment.

8. *Accelerator.* Put weight behind select critical initiatives to speed up or bolster their implementation, especially when the required approach has changed, is unfamiliar, or is likely to be resisted.

Reeves, Haanaes, and Sinha also suggest some tips and traps (see exhibit 12.1) for carrying out the new strategic roles.

Healthcare leaders can find inspiration in the more sophisticated strategic planning approaches of more competitive, market-driven fields. The qualities discussed earlier, even when executed at rather

Exhibit 12.1: Tips and Traps: Key Contributors to Success and Failure for Leaders in Navigating Diverse and Changing Strategic Environments

Tips	Traps
• *Embrace contradictions.* The demands of the many approaches you lead may be diametrically opposed, and that's okay—but tailoring your messages to each environment is critical.	• *Single-color palette.* Any large organization is probably too complex for a single, unchallenged, and unchanging view of strategy. Avoid oversimplification and uniformity.
• *Embrace complexity.* Introduce complexity in your organization where this will improve the match between environment and strategy without incurring excessive coordination costs.	• *Managing instead of leading.* Getting too deeply involved in managing each approach can prevent you from shaping the strategy collage at a higher level, as encapsulated in the eight roles of leaders.
• *Explain simply.* The resulting strategic collage may be confusing to workers and investors; find the common thread to communicate a clear story.	• *Planning the unplannable.* In a world that changes quickly and unpredictably, overinvesting in precise predictions and plans can backfire. An effective leader recognizes that sometimes plans are not the sign of good leadership.
• *Look outward.* Use your unique position to counteract the self-reinforcing tendencies of your organization to perpetuate dominant beliefs by keeping the organization externally focused and fluid.	• *Rigidity.* Some leaders select an approach but are unwilling to change as new information arises, even though the original course will likely not survive the tides of change.
• *When in doubt, disrupt.* Organizations naturally become entrenched in their established ways of doing things. In a dynamic world, an overemphasis on continuity is a larger danger than unnecessary disruption.	

Source: Reprinted from Reeves, Haanaes, and Sinha (2015).

basic levels, will go a long way toward helping healthcare organizations experience the benefits that pathbreaking companies realize from their planning processes.

CONCLUSION

The good old days of a relatively calm and stable healthcare environment are long gone. A highly competitive and dynamic healthcare ecosystem demands robust strategic planning to ensure organizational success. Intuition and educated guesses are no longer viable substitutes for sound planning methods. Change is occurring so rapidly that it is impossible to fully understand its scope and impact. With organizations no longer able to rely on the accuracy of long-range forecasts, they must improve their ability to respond to unanticipated changes in the market.

To quote George Bernard Shaw, "To be in hell is to drift, to be in heaven is to steer." Strategic planning is the vehicle that enables healthcare organizations to steer and have control over their futures. Yet strategic planning is a journey without a specific destination. It will take soul-searching, courage, and commitment to face a future full of uncertainty and potential threats. Strategic planning can also inspire, helping organizations create a road map to guide them through the unknown, balancing the need for articulated and compelling vision and direction with the flexibility to adapt and respond as healthcare is transformed in the coming years.

Effective strategic planners of the future are more than information gatherers or guardians of the planning process. They are leaders in management and organizational transformation; catalysts of organizational change; and strategy finders, enablers, and leaders. This transformational agenda is ambitious for many healthcare strategic planners, but it carries huge potential for personal and professional growth and success.

REFERENCES

Bradley, C., M. Hirt, and S. Smit. 2011. "Have You Tested Your Strategy Lately?" *McKinsey Quarterly*, January, 40–53.

Porter, M. E., and T. H. Lee. 2015. "Why Strategy Matters Now." *New England Journal of Medicine* 372 (18): 1681–84.

Reeves, M., K. Haanaes, and J. Sinha. 2015. *Your Strategy Needs a Strategy: How to Choose and Execute the Right Approach.* Boston: Harvard Business Review Press.

Society for Health Care Strategy & Market Development of the American Hospital Association (SHSMD). 2016. *Bridging Worlds: The Future Role of the Health Care Strategist,* 2nd ed. Accessed October 9, 2023. www.aha.org/sites/default/files/shsmd/bridging -worlds-second-edition.pdf.

Key Issues for Healthcare Organizations

CHAPTER 13

Strategic Financial Planning

Hope is not a financial plan.

—*Ric Edelman*

The strategic plan focuses the organization's attention and determines how its limited resources, including financial resources, will be allocated. The strategic plan serves both to advance the organization's mission and to ensure its long-term health and viability.

Integrating financial planning into the strategic planning process is an effective way to ensure that the organization uses resources wisely and increases the likelihood that the organization will accomplish its goals. For those embarking on a strategic planning process that includes financial planning, it may be helpful to understand financial planning in a little more depth, as presented in this chapter.

Heading into the process, it is important to assess the finance department's capability to carry out the necessary financial planning. Some finance departments excel at financial operations (revenue cycle, accounts payable, producing financial reports) but are not as good at financial modeling or business planning. In other circumstances, the finance department may have the knowledge and skill to do the financial modeling required for financial planning but not the time or staff to focus on it. In this case, it may be helpful to obtain outside support for the financial modeling aspects of strategic planning. In some instances, a strategic planning consultant can provide financial planning support as well. It is best to determine the finance department's capability early in the strategic planning process so that the organization can obtain outside support if needed.

KEY ELEMENTS OF FINANCIAL PLANNING

The financial planning process, independent of strategic planning, can take many forms, but it should comprise at least three key steps: developing a baseline scenario, quantifying the impact of the planned strategies, and completing scenario and sensitivity analyses. These steps are described in exhibit 13.1. Exhibit 13.2 illustrates how these steps fit into the strategic planning process.

Healthcare organizations should consider financial planning as part of the strategic planning process for a number of reasons. First, an integrated financial plan better informs strategic decision-making and prioritization of strategies. Now more than ever, boards want to know: If we pursue these strategies, how will that affect our financial position? Integrating financial planning into the strategic planning process is the only way to answer this question.

Second, a financial plan helps the organization assess each opportunity using a consistent methodology—for example, measuring the incremental financial impact of an opportunity and the time needed to realize that impact. This analysis, when considered as part of the opportunity's contribution to the organization's mission, can aid in setting priorities.

Third, financial planning informs long-term capital allocation decisions, which should be guided by a strategic plan. Some strategies will not require significant up-front or ongoing capital, while others will require more substantial investments. A financial analysis that highlights capital expenditures (both routine and strategic), cash flows, and the resulting cash position across several planning scenarios will guide decision-making.

Fourth, a financial plan allows the organization to assess and prepare for continually evolving financial challenges that have an

Exhibit 13.1: Sample Financial Planning Work Steps

Develop a Baseline Scenario	Quantify the Impact of Planned Strategies	Complete Scenario and Sensitivity Analyses
• Outline current-state operational and financial performance trended forward • Consider the impact of known or expected market changes (e.g., opening of a new competitor facility)	• Quantify the incremental financial impact of new strategies to be pursued (e.g., service line growth plan, market share capture, physician recruitment, operational efficiencies)	• Develop a small number of planning scenarios based on the variables with the greatest financial impact (e.g., successful vs. unsuccessful implementation of a key initiative) • Perform sensitivity analyses for each scenario to show the range of outcomes based on changes in other key variables • Depict the results as prospective financial estimates and key metrics (e.g., days cash on hand, debt to capitalization, operating margin, etc.)

Exhibit 13.2: How Financial Planning Fits into the Strategic Planning Process

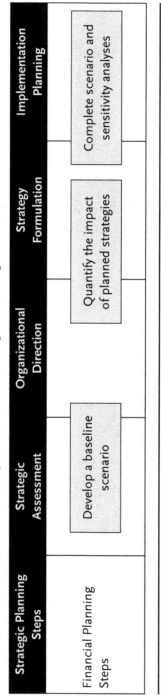

Strategic Planning Steps	Strategic Assessment	Organizational Direction	Strategy Formulation	Implementation Planning
Financial Planning Steps	Develop a baseline scenario		Quantify the impact of planned strategies	Complete scenario and sensitivity analyses

© 2024 Veralon Partners Inc.

impact on overall operations and strategy. These challenges might include inflation, labor market trends, reimbursement rate pressures, economic and financial market fluctuations, public health crises, and shifts in the payer mix (e.g., from commercial to Medicare as a result of population aging). As the organization determines how aggressively or cautiously to pursue new initiatives or conserve resources, a multiyear financial plan is a critical tool for considering risks and setting strategy.

THE FINANCIAL-PLANNING PROCESS

Developing a Baseline Scenario

In the first step of the financial planning process, the finance team develops a financial model for a baseline planning scenario. This scenario shows how the organization is expected to perform financially in the next three to five years assuming that there are no significant changes to its current operations, except for any initiatives that are already underway. For example, if the organization will be onboarding a group of new orthopedists in the coming months, that incremental volume should be counted in the baseline scenario, as the impact of the initiative is imminent and highly likely. Other than planned initiatives that are highly likely to occur in the near term, no significant changes in volume, reimbursement, or expense structure should be considered in the baseline scenario. The finance team generally leads the development of the financial model and the baseline scenario with input from other operational, clinical, and planning team stakeholders. The following are key components of the baseline scenario:

- *Prospective estimates of patient volume.* These are estimates of patient volume by service line and/or by major patient service category (e.g., inpatient, emergency room, same-day surgery). These estimates are based on factors such as population growth and demographics, trends in healthcare utilization, and competition. Volume estimates should include strategic initiatives that are already underway.

- *Prospective estimates of revenue.* These are estimates of all the expected revenue streams for the healthcare organization. Revenue is typically estimated for each defined patient service category and based on historical reimbursement trends, adjusted to reflect anticipated changes in the payer mix, patient acuity, and other factors. Other non–patient service sources of revenue (e.g., value-based payments and other quality programs) are estimated based on historical trends and anticipated future experience. Although many healthcare organizations have shifted their focus to value-based payments and population health, only the most advanced health systems in these areas actually budget revenue based on population payments; others simply estimate add-on payments.

- *Prospective estimates of operating expenses.* These are estimates of the direct and indirect expenses (e.g., labor, supplies, equipment, professional services) associated with providing healthcare services. These estimates take into consideration historical trends, projected inflation, and the variable and fixed components of each expense category.

- *Prospective estimates of capital expenditures.* These estimates include expected routine capital expenditures (e.g., ongoing investments in equipment) as well as investments in strategic initiatives, such as new buildings and technology required to support the organization's strategic objectives.

- *Regulatory considerations.* Hospitals and health systems are subject to a complex regulatory environment; therefore, the baseline scenario should take into account the impact of known and ongoing regulatory changes on the hospital's operations and finances.

- *Prospective financial estimates.* Using the foregoing components and assumptions, prospective estimates of income, financial position, and cash flow, in addition to key financial ratios, should be developed for the baseline scenario.

The development of the baseline scenario is a critical component of the strategic assessment phase of strategic planning (see chapter 6). The baseline scenario provides a starting point for the strategic assessment by identifying the key assumptions and trends that will drive the organization's financial performance and position. The baseline scenario sets the stage for an assessment of the organization's prospective financial performance and position through the development of income statements (performance) and balance sheets (position), as well as financial ratios calculated from these financial statements (e.g., days cash on hand, debt to capitalization). As exhibit 13.2 illustrates, it is best to develop the baseline scenario during the strategic assessment phase of the strategic planning process because it can inform the internal assessment and make it easier to evaluate strategies later.

Quantifying Goals and Initiatives

As the strategic planning process evolves, the desired future state of the organization (i.e., the organizational direction) is clarified, and goals and initiatives are developed (i.e., the strategy formulation) to address the critical planning issues identified in the strategic assessment. The financial impact of each goal or initiative is then quantified to further inform strategy formulation and implementation planning, including the prioritization and timing of initiatives. In addition to the organization's own initiatives, it may be important at this stage to quantify the impact of other significant market factors, such as changes in the strategies of payers or competitors.

The planning team takes the lead in the development of strategies and then works closely with the finance team to describe the nature of the initiatives (e.g., timing, investment, volume). This process allows the finance team to integrate these strategic assumptions into the financial model and to quantify the financial impact of each initiative. This is different from the first step, developing the baseline scenario, where the finance team takes the lead. In this step, the financial impact is quantified in terms of the expected increase or decrease in volume, revenue, expense, and profitability. For each initiative or market factor, the following questions must be considered:

- Impact on volume
  - *How will the new initiative or market factor directly impact patient volumes?* Consideration should be given to the organization's current and planned capabilities, market demand for services, and services offered by competitors.
  - *How will the new initiative or market factor indirectly impact patient volumes?* For example, will there be a downstream increase or decrease in the volume of other services? Will the new service at one location cannibalize volume from another facility?
  - *Over what time horizon will the impact on patient volumes be realized?* For example, if the organization is adding a new service, how will the new volume ramp up over time? The impact of a new initiative may take time to materialize; therefore, it is important to incorporate the anticipated time horizon into the volume estimates for the new initiative.
- Impact on revenue
  - *How will reimbursement change as a result of the new initiative or market factor?*

- *What impact, if any, will the new initiative or market factor have on value-based care initiatives and/or performance?*
- *What impact will the new initiative or market factor have on the organization's future payer mix?*
- Impact on expenses
  - *How will the underlying cost structure of the organization change, if at all?*
  - *How will the organization's variable costs change?*
  - *What new fixed costs, if any, will be incurred?*
  - *What cost efficiencies, if any, might be gained?*
- Impact of capital investments
  - *What capital investments will be required to implement the strategic initiative?* This may include investing in new equipment, expansion of facilities, or technology upgrades.
  - *What is the anticipated timing of any needed capital investments?*

Once the incremental financial impact has been quantified for each new initiative, the initiatives can be added to the baseline model. Financial modeling software tools can help the finance team quantify the impact of the new initiatives rather than doing this work in spreadsheets. Even if financial modeling software is used, what comes out is only as good as what goes in—key assumptions about the initiatives still need to be nailed down before beginning the analysis.

The financial model should now show the incremental impact of each new initiative as well as the impact on the baseline scenario. At this stage, the analysis should examine each initiative's overall impact on the estimated financial performance and financial position of the organization. This includes reviewing key financial ratios, such as operating margins, days cash on hand, debt to capitalization, and other measures.

Completing Scenario and Sensitivity Analyses

After modeling the baseline scenario and quantifying the impact of strategic initiatives, a small number of planning scenarios (two or three) are developed to test the impact of different future events or conditions, particularly those that have significant financial implications. These planning scenarios are usually identified in the strategic assessment. For example, one planning scenario could assume that an organization experiences lower than expected demand for services because another organization opens a competing facility.

In addition to scenario analysis, financial planners also perform sensitivity analysis. This approach involves changing one or more of the input variables in a financial model to see how sensitive the output is to those changes. A sensitivity analysis is typically applied to each planning scenario. For example, a sensitivity analysis might assess the financial impact of a greater than expected shift in the payer mix from commercial insurance to Medicare.

The impacts of scenario and sensitivity analyses are measured using the prospective financial estimates and associated financial ratios. These analyses are often developed concurrently with the strategy formulation and/or implementation phases of the strategic planning process, as the outcomes of these exercises can help planners identify potential risks and opportunities and adjust accordingly.

CONCLUSION

A financial plan completed as part of the strategic planning process can inform the organization's decision-making about resource allocation and the timing and magnitude of its strategic investments. While the strategic plan outlines the organization's overall direction and goals, the financial plan provides the necessary financial strategies and resources to achieve those goals. Together, the strategic and financial plans can be used to develop prospective financial estimates that forecast the organization's future financial performance

Exhibit 13.3: Sample Financial Ratio Analysis

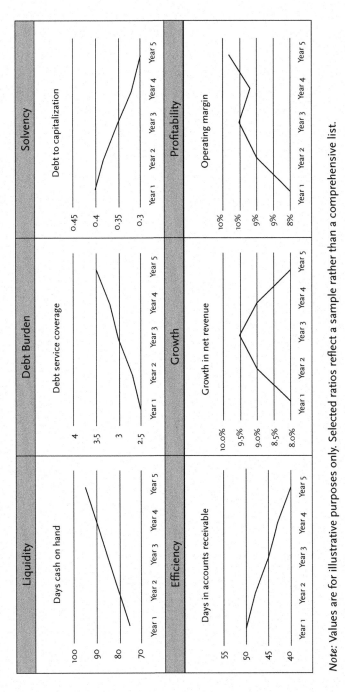

Note: Values are for illustrative purposes only. Selected ratios reflect a sample rather than a comprehensive list.

across the planning horizon. Using these estimates, the organization can anticipate its future financial position, assess its ability to meet financial obligations, and evaluate key financial ratios, as illustrated in exhibit 13.3.

With these tools in hand, the organization can make better strategic decisions, management can demonstrate and explain financial performance in the context of agreed-upon expectations, and the board can monitor improvements in financial results and financial position achieved through the strategic plan.

CHAPTER 14

Innovation

The arrogance of success is to think that what you did yesterday will be sufficient for tomorrow.

—*William Pollard*

Hospitals and health systems have historically focused on stability, consistency, quality, and reliability. Innovators, however, typically focus on disruption, flexibility, and creativity. As more innovators penetrate the healthcare field, traditional providers must decide whether to innovate and how to do so in ways that do not undermine their core promise of quality and reliability. To navigate the culture clash between reliability and innovation, it is helpful to consider innovation as part of the strategic plan.

The word "innovation" is widely used, and it means different things to different people. A working definition of innovation is provided by Veralon, a healthcare management consulting firm:

The creation, development, and implementation of a new product, process, or service, with the aim of improving value for customers and/or stakeholders

This chapter discusses the importance of innovation in healthcare and considers ways to address innovation in each phase of the strategic planning process.

Innovations can be developed internally by clinicians, administrative team members, or employees or externally, for example, by "disruptors" who seek to transform healthcare and tap private equity or venture capital funds. Innovations can take a variety of forms, including the following:

- Patient access to care and patient engagement
- Clinical diagnostics, therapeutics, and workflow
- Alignment among physicians and between physicians and systems
- Care management and payment models
- Data management and administrative workflow

Three factors make innovation a strategic priority for hospitals and systems. The first is the need to adjust organizational culture to support innovation. Although healthcare has a long history of scientific discovery and clinical evolution (e.g., diagnostic and therapeutic devices and tools, pharmaceuticals, genomics), the culture of healthcare organizations has traditionally been cautious and slow to change. This caution is understandable—and even desirable—when consistency is part of quality control for patient care (e.g., operating room safety procedures), but caution is less desirable when it stymies improvements. Innovation requires systemic changes in culture, which may be reflected in the organization's mission, vision, and values and in its resource allocation decisions. Determining how these key elements of culture should evolve to facilitate innovation is crucial to the strategic planning process.

The second factor that makes innovation an essential part of strategic planning is the need for healthcare organizations to address competition more effectively. Many trustees of hospitals and health systems experience competition resulting from innovation within their own businesses, and therefore they press for more consideration of innovation in strategic planning. Hospitals and health systems face an increasing number of competitors and greater intensity of competition from both traditional providers and new market entrants. These new entrants (described in detail in chapter 15) include mega systems, niche organizations, private equity–backed physician practices, retail corporations, primary care aggregators, "payviders," and digital disruptors.

To proactively manage competitive challenges and enhance long-term viability, healthcare organizations must have a thorough understanding of their environment and devise fresh ways of differentiating and positioning themselves. Innovation in competitive positioning can include working individually or in collaboration with other providers to enhance existing services or develop new ones (e.g., teleneurology, hospital at home), creating new products, or designing new processes (e.g., remote monitoring of patients with chronic illnesses). Competitive positioning can also be strengthened by identifying a new target market (e.g., geographic, demographic, psychographic) or partnering with new competitors—sometimes called "co-opetition."

The third factor that ties innovation to strategic planning is the need to prioritize capital investments across a range of strategic opportunities. For example, an organization must decide whether to allocate funds for an innovation, for information system upgrades, or for routine capital needs such as facility updates. Balancing these priorities is a critical component of the organization's strategic plan. Decisions should be based also on the outcome of the strategic financial plan, which is discussed in chapter 13.

THE STRATEGIC PLANNING CONTEXT FOR INNOVATION

The analysis needed to support innovative approaches, and the actions needed to implement those approaches, is best set out in the strategic plan. Implementation of service, product, and process innovations frequently requires significant investments in resources, such as people, facilities, clinical equipment, and IT.

Because most hospitals and health systems have constraints on their capital availability (i.e., funds available and accessible through reserves, debt, grants, and philanthropy), investment in innovation competes with other requests for resources. Opportunities for innovation must be addressed within the broader resource and capital allocation limits established during the strategic planning process.

Not only does innovation compete with other initiatives for resources, but multiple opportunities for innovation may also be in competition with each other. Amid funding constraints, it is critical for organizations to prioritize and select a single or limited number of innovation opportunities to pursue. Only initiatives that address one or more of the critical planning issues identified in the strategic plan should be pursued.

When an organization has identified a need for innovation but lacks the funding or chooses not to allocate capital for innovation, an alliance or partnership may be required. The decision to enter into a partnership is strategic in nature and must support the organization's vision and goals.

To successfully apply innovation, leaders must overcome a variety of barriers. Internal barriers include underestimating pressure from new competitors, a lack of familiarity with innovation trends and options, culture, different objectives or expectations, stakeholder opposition, and resource constraints. External barriers are more consistent with those that are encountered in other aspects of the strategic plan: regulations, reimbursement, and competition.

FINE-TUNING THE STRATEGIC PLANNING PROCESS TO ADDRESS INNOVATION

The strategic planning process can be modified in specific ways to address innovation. The first opportunity occurs during the internal and external analysis process. The external assessment should address the pace of clinical and technological innovation nationally and in the organization's service area. Examples of innovation that could warrant consideration in a strategic plan include the following:

- Hospital at home, as a way to reduce capacity constraints on existing facilities
- Personalized medicine/genomics, which may require a partnership with an academic center
- Artificial intelligence and digital health capabilities, which may require a partnership with a third party or a merger with a larger system
- New primary care models tailored to specific market segments (e.g., seniors, healthy adults, etc.)

While the focus should be on disruptive innovation, rather than incremental changes to clinical treatment, occasionally, more basic innovations warrant consideration in the strategic plan. For example, the ability to perform joint replacement surgery on an outpatient basis reflects incremental improvement in surgical processes. However, shifting these surgeries to outpatient settings could result in a major loss of volume and revenue for hospitals, and therefore it may be necessary to partner with physician groups to establish freestanding ambulatory surgery centers.

Assessment of potential innovations should address the extent to which specific innovations or innovators offer an opportunity to address the organization's strategic, operational, or financial needs during the immediate planning horizon (3 to 5 years) and in the longer term (10 to 20 years). Innovations may be adopted by supplementing or supporting the hospital or health system's existing capabilities and resources or by creating a partnership with an innovator.

The assessment should also identify the extent to which innovations or innovators pose a competitive threat to the organization, either directly or indirectly, as hospital or health system competitors adopt the innovations. The degree of threat may be affected by regulatory requirements and reimbursement pressures, which may restrict or enable the adoption of an innovation or collaboration with an innovator.

For each potential innovation, the internal assessment should determine the following:

- The objectives of pursuing the innovation and the opportunity cost of not doing so
- How the innovation fits within the organization's structure and culture and reflects its mission, vision, and values
- The amount of effort the hospital or health system should put into pursuing the innovation

Exhibit 14.1 offers examples of objectives that might be pursued for specific innovations.

Exhibit 14.1: Potential Objectives of Adopting Specific Innovations

- Enhance the organization's market position or differentiation (position innovation)
- Increase the organization's core revenue or diversify revenue streams—for example, establishing a new service or taking an idea to market
- Enhance, expand, or modernize clinical services service lines (product/service innovation)
- Solve unmet patient needs or enhance engagement (workflow innovation)—for example, improve access to information, physicians, or scheduling; reduce visit wait times; improve patient handoffs
- Solve unmet physician needs or enhance physician engagement (alignment innovation)
- Enhance information technology and/or data management (infrastructure innovation)
- Solve administrative or operational issues (process innovation)—for example, automation, use of artificial intelligence, protocol changes

---

Fit with organizational culture is likely to be a significant concern for healthcare organizations, where the culture usually emphasizes ensuring consistency and safety, minimizing errors, and exercising caution. Internal innovators and innovative corporate partners are likely to have quite different mindsets, as illustrated in exhibit 14.2.

Accordingly, the planning process must address the need for cultural change to enable the innovations under consideration. One determinant of that need will be the organization's historical pattern: Has it tended to be a pioneer, an early adopter, or a follower of a proven concept? In assessing innovations, the strategic planning process must assess the capabilities and resources available to the organization to support clinical and technological innovation: people, funds, IT, and other technology. Internal resources and cultural support or antipathy will determine whether the hospital or health system can support innovation internally or whether it will need to collaborate with a third party.

INNOVATION IN EACH PHASE OF THE STRATEGIC PLANNING PROCESS

Strategic Assessment

When completing the SWOT (strengths, weaknesses, opportunities, threats) analysis during the strategic assessment phase of the strategic planning process, innovation and innovators may be identified as opportunities or threats in their own right. For example, a competitor that has strong digital health offerings may be attracting commercially insured patients, threatening the organization's market share in a key demographic.

Insights from the SWOT analysis will help leaders identify the critical planning issues that the strategic plan must address. To the extent that these issues require innovative solutions, the organization may benefit from new and bolder strategies.

Exhibit 14.2: Different Perspectives of Innovators and Healthcare Management/Boards

Innovator	Healthcare Management/Board
Entrepreneurial mindset: • Curious, creative, resourceful, solution oriented; focus on individual tasks • Embrace change, adaptable • Work smart • Focus on what they do well vs. correcting weaknesses	Operational mindset: • Seek constant improvement • Emphasize efficiency, minimizing variability, and maintaining stability rather than creating opportunity (Crowley 2012) • Highly organized—"plan the work and then work the plan" (Smolinski 2017)
Approach to risk: • Recognize that some ideas will succeed and others will not; willing to take risks and pilot ideas	Approach to risk: • Deliberate, prefer stable bets, less willing to take risks
Retention: • Continue with ideas that meet objectives, terminate those that do not; "move fast and break things" and "fail quickly and exit" approach • May sell off a product or service to realize profit and move on to the next idea	Retention: • Once a product or service is launched, will find it hard to end it
Time horizon: • Play the "long game"; willing to invest in and support a product/service over an extended time to realize financial and strategic return on investment (ROI) • Alternatively, may be driven by financing cycles and short-term rapid growth	Time horizon: • Oriented to short-term ROI • Less willing to pursue initiatives that require extended time periods to realize financial and strategic ROI

© 2024 Veralon Partners Inc.

Organizational Direction

In establishing the organization's mission, vision, and values, the planning process should assess the following:

- Whether the organization's current vision allows for or encourages the pursuit of innovation
- Whether a change to the organizational culture is needed to support innovation
- How that change can be incorporated into the organization's values statement
- Whether innovation should be highlighted in the vision statement to clarify the prioritization of innovation for organizational stakeholders

Strategy Formulation

The strategy formulation phase, when goals and initiatives are developed, is the time to determine whether innovation should be a goal of its own, encompassing one or more initiatives of its own, or whether clinical and technological innovations should be treated as major supporting initiatives. In any case, the decision to pursue specific innovation initiatives should be based on a strong business case, not simply because they are the pet projects of high-level individuals within the organization.

This phase is also the time to decide what approaches are needed to incorporate specific innovations into broader initiatives:

- Do the proposed innovations require the creation of a distinct division or business unit in which they can be pursued?
- Will it be desirable to collaborate with a third-party innovator, such as an affiliate, or contract with a primary

care aggregator to supplement the hospital's physician network?
- Where will innovation be used strategically to support other initiatives (e.g., incorporate remote monitoring to support cardiovascular program growth)

Since innovations require resources (monetary and/or staff attention), it is critical to set priorities for pursuing them.

Implementation Planning

During the implementation planning phase, internally initiated innovations require added attention, especially if the concept is still being refined and is not fully ready to be applied. Implementation planning includes establishing tactics for the research, design, and packaging of the innovation. It may be appropriate to take the product or concept to an internal or external incubator or innovation center that can offer the required expertise. Having a dedicated team working on an innovation away from routine operational distractions can increase the chances of success.

If the innovation concept is ready for application (whether the source is internal or external), the planning process should establish a clear action plan, including needed resources and adjustments (if any) to organization structure. The plan should determine whether required capabilities, competencies, and resources would best be assembled by

- purchasing or contracting,
- recruiting people with the needed expertise,
- joint venturing with a partner (whether a market-based innovator/vendor, payer, or another provider), or
- forming a consortium of organizations to pool resources.

The implementation plan should include mechanisms to ensure clear accountability for each aspect of innovation development, including monitoring of progress and performance.

By their nature, innovations have the potential to fall short of their objectives. It is important that the plan include trigger points when contingency steps (e.g., move from internal to third-party implementation, terminate the initiative) should be taken.

CONCLUSION

Product, service, process, or resource innovations are important ways for an organization to adjust to the changing environment and resolve the unmet or undermet needs of patients, clinicians, payers, and employers.

Addressing innovation during the development of the strategic plan has three benefits:

1. Enhance the ability to address competition
2. Ensure that the innovations pursued are in sync with the organization's culture, supportive of its vision and mission, and integrated with its values
3. Ensure that the required investment is justified and the innovations fit within resource and capital allocation limits

Innovations and innovators are an important source of fresh solutions and positive energy in any organization. As there are well-recognized barriers to innovation and implementation is challenging and accompanied by a moderate degree of uncertainty, it is critical for innovation efforts to include contingency plans that are ready to be put in place when needed.

REFERENCES

Crowley, S. 2012. "An Operations Mindset Is at Odds with Innovation." Atomic Object. Published October 16. https://spin.atomicobject.com/2012/10/16/an-operations-mindset-is-at-odds-with-innovation.

Smolinski, J. 2017. "The Joys and Challenges of the Operational Mindset." Littelfuse. Published May 15. www.ckswitches.com/blog/posts/2017/may/the-joys-and-challenges-of-the-operational-mindset.

CHAPTER 15

Intensifying Competition

Taste the relish to be found in competition—in having put forth the best within you.

—Henry Kaiser

To develop an effective strategy, an organization must understand its competitors. In communities across the United States, traditional healthcare providers—acute care hospitals and health systems—are facing intense competition from a variety of new types of organizations. This chapter describes the types of competition that providers may face and how intensifying competition can be addressed as a critical aspect of the strategic plan.

Intensifying competition has a substantial impact on the market position of incumbent providers, their success in accomplishing their growth objectives and strategies, and their financial performance. Although it is tempting to believe that this issue applies predominantly to urban and suburban areas served by multiple hospitals, in reality, providers in rural locations and single hospitals in urban and suburban markets are increasingly being challenged by competing organizations that offer enhanced value for patients, employers, and health plans. These new competitors include entities with a physical presence in the market as well as those providing services virtually.

Five catalysts underlie the expansion and intensification of competition in the healthcare field:

1. *Consumer expectations.* Based on their experiences with other industries (e.g., banking, travel, entertainment, personal goods), consumers expect companies to provide transparent information about pricing and services and to offer customized products and services. They are comparison shoppers who have easy access through their smartphones and value convenience over loyalty to vendors. Thus, consumers now expect—indeed, they are demanding—the same from their healthcare providers.

2. *Frustration.* The current provider network is not fully delivering the value sought by patients, employers, and payers with respect to access to care, cost, and experience (e.g., coordination of care, engaging and sharing information with the patient, outcomes, satisfaction), encouraging them to look for new solutions.

3. *Technology.* A boom in clinical and information technology innovation has created opportunities to redesign diagnostic and therapeutic care models and shift care to new sites (e.g., ambulatory, retail, home, virtual). This innovation has opened the door to new organizations to become "providers" and thus competitors.

4. *Investment.* With healthcare approaching 20 percent of US gross domestic product, the fragmented nature of the healthcare industry and the gaps in services have prompted companies on the periphery (e.g., retailers, technology companies) and those with substantial access to funds (e.g., private equity, venture capital) to develop new provider networks to capture a greater share of healthcare expenditures.

5. *Windfall returns.* The evolution of the market toward value-based care provides a competitive advantage and large financial windfalls to entities that can reduce costs while maintaining quality and service.

These catalysts have prompted a shift in the healthcare sector from being relatively noncompetitive to reaching a high level of competitive intensity. Unaddressed, intensifying competition could reduce an organization's market share and revenues, threaten the viability of its service lines, and increase the cost of attracting clinical talent.

UNDERSTANDING COMPETITORS

Increased competition for hospitals, health systems, and physician organizations takes many forms. New competitors can be grouped into seven major categories, represented by the circles shown in exhibit 15.1. As we progress up the vertical axis, the size of the competitors increases. As we progress from left to right, the degree of industry disruption increases.

Competition Among Incumbent Providers

In most markets, regardless of whether new types of competitors have established a presence, hospitals and health systems likely face competition from other local independent hospitals and/or regional hospital systems in specific service lines, community-based ambulatory care, or recruitment of physicians and other clinical staff. Hospitals and health systems often compete with members of their medical staff that have established their own ambulatory care services (e.g., surgery centers, imaging centers, women's centers, cancer centers, rehabilitation programs). Competition among local

Exhibit 15.1: Provider Competitor Landscape

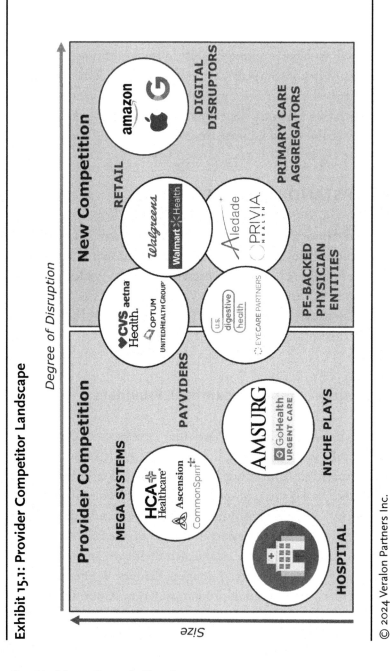

© 2024 Veralon Partners Inc.

incumbent providers is represented by the circle in the lower-left corner of exhibit 15.1.

New Categories of Competitors

In many communities across the United States, seven types of new competitors are vying to serve the same pool of patients and capture a portion of healthcare expenditures: mega systems, niche plays, private equity–backed specialty groups, corporate retail companies, primary care aggregators, payviders, and digital disruptors. It is important to understand the characteristics, strategies, and vulnerabilities of these entities when completing the strategic assessment and to establish approaches to differentiation and competitive positioning during the strategy formulation phase of the strategic planning process. A description of these categories of competitors follows.

Mega Systems
Large multistate hospitals systems—known as mega systems—are identifying attractive target markets and entering those markets using "build" or "buy" strategies. The largest and most proactive mega systems in the United States are HCA, CommonSpirit Health, Ascension, Trinity Health, Community Health Systems, Lifepoint Health, Advocate, and Christus. These organizations are able to leverage their resources (e.g., clinical, operational, information systems), purchasing power, payer contracting, and access to capital to out-position incumbent providers. Some have also leveraged their scale to invest in digital health strategies to strengthen patient access and loyalty.

Niche Plays
Increasingly, organizations focused on distinct niches—called niche plays—are entering the market to compete with hospitals and health systems and their medical staffs. This category comprises a variety of groups, such as ambulatory surgical center management firms

(e.g., Surgical Centers of America), microhospital companies (e.g., Emerus), emergency department companies (e.g., US Acute Care Solutions), and urgent care center companies (e.g., GoHealth). These entities compete with local hospitals and health systems by operating their own community-based provider sites, which are differentiated from incumbent providers by offering easier access to their services. Additionally, many niche companies form joint ventures with members of the incumbent hospital or health system's medical staff, drawing patient activity and revenue away from incumbent hospitals and health systems.

Private Equity–Backed Specialty Groups

In recent years, private equity firms have entered the healthcare field by acquiring single-specialty physician practices with a strong base of physicians, healthy financial performance, and well-regarded brand identity and then purchasing additional practices in other communities and states to establish a large geographic footprint. Private equity firms have applied this approach in specialties such as dermatology, gastroenterology, ophthalmology, orthopedics, and medical oncology. Examples include EyeCare Partners, Advanced Dermatology and Cosmetic Surgery, American Orthopedic Partners, GI Alliance, National Spine & Pain Centers, and US Digestive Health. These private equity–backed physician practices compete with local hospitals and health systems by acquiring independent groups that were once part of their medical staffs. The new groups provide as much diagnostic and therapeutic care as possible, thereby reducing patient activity and revenue associated with lab, radiology, procedures, and rehabilitation at the associated hospitals and health systems.

Corporate Retail Companies

Corporate retail companies have increasingly established their own provider networks. Most often, retailers establish clinics (e.g., urgent care, and primary care services) that compete directly with the incumbent hospital or health system's physician network on ease of access and cost. The largest retail companies that are actively competing with traditional providers are Walgreens, which offers in-store clinics and colocated freestanding clinics supported through investment in VillageMD, and Walmart, which operates in-store clinics and freestanding Walmart Health Centers. CVS Health offers similar services through its MinuteClinic and HealthHUB, and is also a major insurer (Aetna). Target, Rite Aid, and Costco are other retailers that operate in-store clinics in some states. A few large grocery store chains (e.g., Kroger, Albertson, HEB) operate clinics in selected locations.

Primary Care Aggregators

Primary care physicians employed by incumbent hospitals, affiliated medical groups, or independent physician associations are frequently targeted by entities that enter markets and establish their own primary care networks. Called primary care aggregators, these organizations often contract with Medicare Advantage and Medicare accountable care organization models that can yield better financial results for primary care practices.

Aggregators employ a variety of models and strategies to provide solutions to the unmet needs of local primary care physicians, such as lowering practice operating costs, enhancing payer contract reimbursement rates, enabling participation in financial risk arrangements, enhancing work–life balance, and supporting capital investment needs. Some companies recruit primary care physicians to join their practices (e.g., Oak Street, Cano Health, One Medical, Carbon Health, Crossover), while others proactively acquire existing practices and employ local physicians (e.g., VillageMD, Carelon, Elevance). Still others attract primary care physicians by providing management services (e.g., Evolent, Privia). A fourth group assembles primary care coalitions within clinically integrated networks and accountable care organizations (e.g., Aledade, Agilon, Vytalize).

Payviders

In the past, most payers focused on their insurance and administrative services businesses. In recent years, however, more payers have acquired and created provider divisions as well, competing directly with traditional hospitals, health systems, and physician groups. Known as "payviders," these organizations share three characteristics. First, they offer large physician networks, which they are continually expanding by acquiring independent groups or groups formerly aligned with hospitals and health systems. Second, they proactively enlarge the continuum of ambulatory care that they provide in order to increase access points for patients and to establish capacity for managing care in relatively lower-cost settings. Those new sites of care compete directly with similar services operated by incumbent hospitals and health systems. Payviders accomplish this through the acquisition of ambulatory surgical centers, urgent care centers, home health and virtual care providers. Third, payviders are building analytic platforms that support value-based care. Three payviders with significant national footprints are United Healthcare and its Optum Care division, Humana-CenterWell, and CVS Health, which offers insurance as Aetna and has a variety of provider assets.

Another type of payvider is the health system that operates a regional health plan. These provider-based payviders can compete with traditional providers by controlling and steering their health plan members to their own facilities rather than those of competitors.

Digital Disruptors

Digital disruptors such as Amazon, Apple, Google, and Microsoft are the largest in size and have the greatest potential impact on incumbent hospitals and health systems, primarily by forming their own provider networks, often by acquiring digital start-ups or other innovators. Additionally, these companies are developing diagnostic and therapeutic products, aggregating large databases, and applying artificial intelligence tools to healthcare data and challenges. As artificial intelligence takes hold, these large technology companies are likely to play a greater role in care delivery.

ADDRESSING INCREASING COMPETITIVENESS IN THE STRATEGIC PLAN

The emergence of new competitors and the increasingly competitive environment should be addressed in the first and third phases of the strategic planning process: the strategic assessment and strategy formulation.

To devise the optimal strategy, organizations should follow four steps: First, map the organization's competitive landscape by considering the types of entities presented in exhibit 15.1. Second, evaluate emerging trends in similar markets and determine each competitor's presence in the organization's market, the pace of market evolution, and the implications for the organization. Third, consider different healthcare industry scenarios and how the types and numbers of competitors may change. Finally, draw lessons by reviewing the characteristics of competition and the creative solutions applied in other industries.

During the strategic assessment phase, the following questions should be considered:

- *Threats*—What is the current prevalence in the hospital or health system's service area of national trends specific to new competitors and increasing competitiveness, the pace of evolution, and the impact of those activities in different scenarios?
- *Critical strategic issues*—What value is being sought by service area stakeholders (patients, employers, health plans, clinicians) that is not being met? Is the organization proactively handling increasing competition and resolving service gaps? Where does it have significant vulnerabilities? How are competitors positioning

themselves to address those gaps, and how will that affect the organization's options?

When setting strategy related to competitive threats, focus on addressing the most important critical threats identified in the strategic assessment.

During the strategy formulation phase, the following questions should be addressed:

- *Goals*—What goals should be set to counter competitive threats? How will success be measured?
- *Initiatives*—Which strategies or initiatives will be most effective in countering competitive threats? Are there opportunities to partner with some potential competitors to strengthen the organization's strategic position?

FINAL GUIDELINES FOR THE PLANNING PROCESS

At any given time, hospital and health system service areas will experience different forms and degrees of competition. At one extreme, providers will be temporarily sheltered from new entrants but challenged by other incumbents. At the other extreme, traditional providers will be thrust into the maelstrom created by one or more disruptors seeking to capitalize on unmet needs and service gaps.

No matter where the local market falls on the continuum between those two points, it is crucial for the organization's strategic plan to reflect a thorough understanding of competitive dynamics and for it to fine-tune its goals and strategies to proactively address competition. Doing so could entail the organization changing strategies in order to out-position competitors. Alternatively, it could mean creating a mutually beneficial partnership with one or more new market entrants.

CHAPTER 16

Partnerships, Mergers, and Acquisitions

> The best partnerships aren't dependent on a mere common goal but on a shared path of equality, desire, and no small amount of passion.
>
> —*Sarah MacLean*

Partnerships, mergers, and acquisitions (PM&A) have been occurring for many years among healthcare providers, and they continue to be common. As a healthcare organization begins its strategic planning process, it must decide whether it wishes to consider a merger or major partnership as part of that process. It is important to consider this question at the beginning of the strategic planning process because the answer may affect how the planning process unfolds, who should be involved and when, and what level of confidentiality needs to be maintained during the process. Rumors that the organization is considering a merger or major partnership could have a material impact on morale and the ability to retain staff.

This chapter outlines an approach for considering a partnership, merger, or acquisition (as either the acquirer or the seller) and discusses how that approach fits into the strategic planning process. First, however, it is important to understand recent trends in PM&A activity and what is driving the decisions of many healthcare organizations to create or become a part of a larger organization.

As exhibit 16.1 shows, PM&A activity increased following the passage of the Affordable Care Act in 2010 as hospitals and health systems became concerned about the impact of the law's requirements for value-based payment and risk management. Horizontal PM&A activity—that is, activity among hospitals and health systems—rose as organizations questioned whether their size, scale, market influence, and capabilities would be sufficient for long-term viability in a changing healthcare environment. Healthcare PM&A activity peaked in 2018 before gradually declining in each subsequent year. In 2022, the healthcare industry saw the lowest volume of PM&A activity since 2009.

The impact of prior consolidation is likely one factor driving the declining numbers of announced mergers and other material transactions—there are simply fewer small, independent hospitals and health systems than there were in the early 2010s. While the volume of hospital and health system PM&A activity has declined, the size of the transactions has increased, creating more "mega systems."

In addition to the impact of consolidation and other economic and industry factors, federal and state review of proposed healthcare mergers and acquisitions—and the high level of scrutiny for potential antitrust activity—has contributed to the slowdown in PM&A activity. Organizations are more cautious about proceeding with partnerships because of the risk of hitting a regulatory roadblock later in the process.

We have also seen the emergence of new motivations that are driving the uptick in major health system merger activity. For example, in 2022, Advocate Aurora Health of Illinois and Atrium Health of North Carolina combined to form Advocate Health, a new organization "focused on improving safety and outcomes, advancing health equity and accelerating medical breakthroughs." This merger did not provide commonly sought-after market-based advantages such as scale or negotiating power. Instead, the partnership aimed to bolster the power of collective investment in innovation and the ability to collect and analyze data to identify best practices.

Exhibit 16.1: Number of Hospital/Health System Transactions, 2007–2022

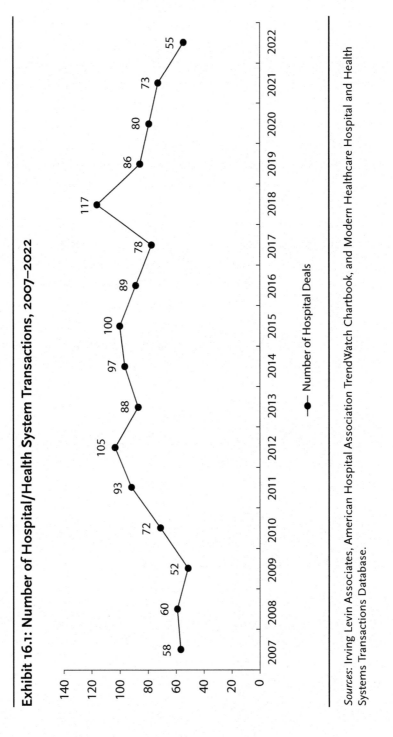

Sources: Irving Levin Associates, American Hospital Association TrendWatch Chartbook, and Modern Healthcare Hospital and Health Systems Transactions Database.

Risant Health, the entity that was created in 2023 from the partnership between Kaiser Foundation Hospitals and Geisinger Health, is another example of a partnership with a novel motivation. Kaiser, which has been highly successful within its own integrated provider/payer model, decided that it wanted to experiment with a broader market approach in which a provider network serves multiple payers. Risant is a new business model for Kaiser, and the merger is expected to be a catalyst for major business diversification, with Kaiser leveraging Geisinger as the lead health system to drive its new multipayer strategy.

In addition to horizontal PM&A deals, vertical PM&A activity has become more common across the healthcare provider landscape, with health systems using PM&A strategies to build their outpatient, physician, post-acute care, managed care, and other offerings. These vertical mergers support providers as they continue to develop value-based care capabilities. Health plans are also pursuing vertical integration by acquiring physician practices and other healthcare delivery assets. Private equity organizations and large, vertically integrated retailers (e.g., Amazon, CVS, Walgreens, Walmart) are also playing an important role in shaping the vertical PM&A landscape.

While PM&A activity has been occurring in all areas of the healthcare industry, this chapter focuses primarily on horizontal PM&A activity among hospitals and health systems.

WHAT DRIVES PARTNERSHIPS, MERGERS, AND ACQUISITIONS?

Healthcare organizations seek to achieve financial, strategic, and operational benefits from PM&A activity. Later in this chapter, we explore the decision points for an independent hospital or health system considering whether it should become a part of a larger system.

Financial Benefits

From a financial viewpoint, the combined market share resulting from a merger can support more specialized care programs than individual organizations. Merged organizations may be able to achieve economies of scale, particularly in their negotiations with vendors and suppliers. PM&A can also improve leverage when negotiating with payers, though regulators will be unlikely to approve a merger if this is its main goal.

Access to capital is another major financial motivation for partnering. This is especially true given the financial state of hospitals and health systems, many of which struggled through the COVID-19 pandemic and the economic downturn and labor crisis that followed, resulting in depressed balance sheets and an expectation of continued operating margin pressure for some time to come. Credit rating agencies typically give better ratings to larger health systems.

Strategic Benefits

There are a number of strategic reasons for healthcare organizations to merge. These are a few motivating factors:

- To expand their geographic footprint by serving additional communities or neighborhoods
- To expand or diversify their service lines to achieve a stronger mix of locations, physicians, and services; to improve quality of care; or to optimize market share
- To improve positioning for value-based care, by increasing covered lives and moving into risk-based contracts, by assimilating new or better capabilities (in population health management or risk contracting), or by acquiring a health system or large group that provides patient data needed for successful value-based payments

- To build capacity for physician recruitment by enhancing recruitment, staffing, and infrastructure; by offering more attractive and flexible pay and benefit packages to physicians; and by scaling up to support specific physician specialties.
- To achieve a scale that supports greater management expertise to address the complexities faced by healthcare organizations

Operational Benefits

The "nitty-gritty" operational benefits typically require a high degree of integration between the merged entities. A merger may offer access to technology that an organization lacks the scale or assets to support, whether it is a type of clinical technology or information technology. A merger could offer connection to a broader range of clinical capabilities and competencies.

DETERMINING WHETHER TO PARTNER

Entering into a merger or another material partnership can be one of the most significant events in an organization's history. For independent hospitals or small health systems, a merger or partnership can have a tremendous impact on the organization's strategic direction. The strategic planning process can help establish whether merger is a good idea. Since not every organization is open to the possibility, organizations initiating a strategic planning process must initially establish whether affiliation of some type will be considered if the analytic results indicate that it could be a good opportunity.

Assuming there is no deep-seated antipathy toward considering a merger or affiliation, a key question for independent hospitals and smaller health systems is whether they can or should continue to go it alone. If they cannot, what do they need to look for to ensure that a specific partnership—whether in the form of a merger, acquisition, or affiliation—is the right fit?

The stakes are high. Larger organizations may have a path to get performance back on track, but smaller, weaker organizations may not. Smaller organizations must assess their ability to remain independent by considering a number of factors, as described in exhibit 16.2. This assessment contains many of the elements that are analyzed as part of the strategic assessment phase of the strategic planning process; in this case, the assessment focuses on what could be achieved alone or through a partnership.

An independence assessment provides an objective evaluation of the feasibility of continuing to go it alone. While many quantitative indicators can be used to assess an independent hospital's current and likely future position, using a limited set of indicators across several key categories—a dashboard—balances brevity and comprehensibility (particularly for lay board members) with the requisite depth. For example, indicators of clinical and service quality might include outcome data (readmissions, mortality, hospital-acquired conditions), patient experience data from surveys, and performance on the quality aspects of value-based contracts. The dashboard allows decision makers to have a meaningful discussion and reach a consensus on the hospital's future viability as an independent entity.

Organizations that have the capacity to acquire another hospital or health system must be rigorous in evaluating potential partners. The type of partnership model selected could significantly impact success. A looser affiliation may leave a formerly independent entity happier but offer more limited financial benefits. In addition, success involves important intangible factors: it is highly dependent on cultural fit.

In assessing the potential for partnership, it is also important to consider possible impacts on organizational relationships. For example, how might payers respond? Will competitors adjust their strategies during the merger process? How will the community

Exhibit 16.2: Independence Assessment for Healthcare Organizations

	Not well positioned: short-term	Adequately positioned: short-term	Well positioned: short-term	Well positioned: long-term
	Pursue affiliation immediately	Trending unfavorably; pursue affiliation within 12 months	Address current gaps; pursue affiliation in 1–2 years	Remain Independent
COMMUNITY NEED	Underserved			Well Served
CLINICAL & SERVICE QUALITY	Worse than Benchmarks		Better than Benchmarks	
POPULATION DEMOGRAPHICS	Unfavorable			Favorable
MARKET POSITION	Weak			Strong
PHYSICIAN SUPPLY	Inadequate			Sufficient
FACILITIES & TECHNOLOGY	Needs Investment			Adequate
PROFITABILITY	Unfavorable			Favorable
FINANCIAL POSITION	Weak			Strong
VBP PREPAREDNESS	Low			High
LEADERSHIP	Limited Breadth/Depth		Significant Breadth/Depth	

INDICATES POSITION OF SUCCESSFUL COMMUNITY HOSPITAL

© 2024 Veralon Partners, Inc.

respond? What is the likelihood of staff and physician attrition before and during the partnership process, and how can it be controlled?

If the organization determines that it cannot or does not want to remain independent, that decision will have a significant impact on the rest of the strategic planning process. The focus may shift to address the following:

- Shorter-term initiatives that will improve the organization's attractiveness and leverage in a deal negotiation
- Critical strategic projects for which the organization will seek funding as part of a negotiation with a prospective partner

In any case, it will no longer be "planning as usual."

PARTNERSHIP AND AFFILIATION MODELS

Affiliations come in a variety of forms, each of which has distinct advantages, disadvantages, and special considerations. It's important to consider the implications of each model to identify which forms are optimal and—just as important—to rule out any model that the healthcare organization is not willing to consider.

The board and leadership team need to understand the full range of transactions that are possible, beyond traditional full-asset mergers or acquisitions. This is vital for organizations that want to achieve partnership synergies while retaining a degree of independence.

Non-merger affiliation options include service line joint ventures, joint operating agreements covering entire health systems, and network models. Each model may offer substantial strategic, financial, and operational benefits to both partners. The options require careful evaluation prior to execution.

Determining the Right Model Depends on the Goals of the Affiliation

The organization may have specific goals for the affiliation that are essential to achieve. For example, if an organization is highly leveraged, access to capital may be an essential outcome of any partnership. Alternatively, an organization may need an enterprise-wide electronic medical records system. Must-haves do not always take the form of concrete benefits; they may also include cultural compatibility, assurances that current clinical services are maintained for the local community, or a guaranteed level of autonomy, among many others.

When an independent hospital or small health system needs to achieve significant financial goals, it is crucial for the partnership to function as a single entity and for the partner organization to bear a greater share of the financial risk—which may entail a greater loss of control for the smaller organization. Identifying the right balance of financial benefit and control is one of the key decisions that an organization must make when seeking and evaluating potential partnerships.

Exhibit 16.3 presents a range of partnership models. The models in the lower-left quadrant are looser and have a smaller impact, while the models in the upper-right quadrant are tighter and have a greater financial impact.

Strategic Arrangements

In strategic arrangements, organizations work together to achieve a business or clinical goal while remaining independent; they may even continue to compete. For example, a community hospital may develop a clinical affiliation with a regional academic medical center. This arrangement may offer benefits to quality of care and physician retention, while financial benefits will typically be limited.

Network Models

Network models involve the creation of a separate organization to centralize corporate services such as purchasing, data management, or specialty laboratory services between organizations, usually within a given market area. This approach offers the benefits of centralization and economies of scale without requiring a change in ownership or governance.

Another form of network model entails joint pursuit of population health and value- or risk-based reimbursement strategies. Examples of this model are accountable care organizations and clinically integrated networks. This approach to partnership offers the possibility of greater financial benefit, but because the organizations remain independent, they cannot achieve the maximum advantage that a more interdependent partnership could provide.

Outsourced Management/Operations

Outsourced contractual management arrangements occur when a healthcare provider organization agrees to manage another hospital without any change of legal control. This form of partnership can be a springboard for tighter affiliation.

Long-Term Lease

When there are legal barriers to the transfer of ownership that prevent a more complete integration—in the case of district or municipally owned organizations, for instance—the initiating facility may be leased to another provider organization.

Exhibit 16.3: Understanding the Implications of Affiliation Models

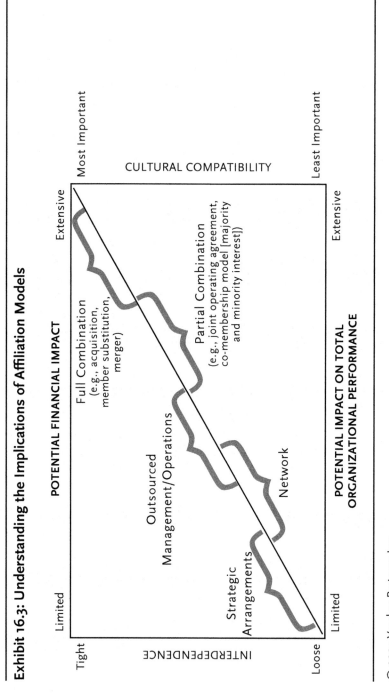

© 2024 Veralon Partners Inc.

Partial Combination

Partial combination models differ in the degree of independence that is retained and extent of the financial impact.

- *Joint ventures* are shared equity ownership arrangements that are relevant to for-profit organizations and subsidiaries. Therefore, this model is not common in horizontal hospital or health system PM&A activity. However, hospitals and health systems often pursue joint ventures for vertical advantage. For example, a hospital might share ownership in for-profit ambulatory surgery centers with a group of surgeons.
- *Co-membership arrangements* are joint ventures between not-for-profit organizations, with customized governance provisions that are unique to each transaction. This type of arrangement was created when Atlantic Health System of New Jersey became the majority (51 percent) member of CentraState Healthcare System in the same state through a co-membership agreement.
- *Joint operating agreements* are also known as "virtual mergers." Under this type of arrangement, only the profit-and-loss statements of the two entities are merged, while balance sheets remain separate. This separation can create difficulties in coordinating, managing, and establishing priorities for governance, strategy, and capital finances. This model has achieved mixed results.

Full Combination

Full combination models offer the largest potential financial impact. When organizations operate as a single entity, they gain access to the full benefits of affiliation. Combination models come in several forms:

- *Corporate member substitution.* In this approach, one hospital or health system—typically the larger one—assumes responsibility for the smaller hospital's balance sheet and becomes its sole corporate member. That corporate member (the system) can then appoint board members for the previously independent hospital and has certain key reserved powers. Negotiation can ensure that local board representation remains intact.
- The corporate member does not pay a "purchase price" in this type of arrangement, but financial commitments are often made (e.g., provision of funds to upgrade clinical technology, build or renovate facilities, or provide new IT capabilities), leading to strategic and operational integration. This option may appeal to boards that are committed to retaining their not-for-profit status for philosophical reasons and wish to keep an active hand in the governance of the institution.
- *Merger.* A merger occurs when two organizations combine to form a new, third organization. That new legal entity replaces the previously separate entities. In the not-for-profit setting, the new entity becomes the sole corporate member of both consolidating organizations.
- *Acquisition.* In an acquisition, one entity fully takes over the other party. The other party no longer retains a separate identity and becomes fully consolidated into the acquiring organization. Usually, the acquirer pays the seller. This model is commonly used when the selling entity is a for-profit organization.

An organization's ability to influence the choice of model depends on how attractive it is to potential suitors. This is especially true at a time when dealmakers are likely to apply more rigorous scrutiny in evaluating candidates for partnership.

DECISION-MAKING CONSIDERATIONS

Decisions about mergers and acquisitions involve a broad spectrum of stakeholders. The organization's board, executive leadership, key directors, and physician leaders should all be in the first circle of decision makers, followed by members of the community. Regulators may become involved soon after, depending on whether, for example, the organization is a Critical Access Hospital, there are concerns about antitrust violations, or the PM&A strategy envisioned requires a regulatory exception.

If the decision is made to seek a partnership of some kind, a formal process should be initiated to identify and select a partner (or partners). The merger and acquisition process is conceptually straightforward, but it demands substantial time and attention. The organization should leverage outside advisers, both in preparing to seek a partner and in evaluating potential partners. The goal is to establish strategic priorities for the partnership, obtain multiple partnership offers, and make the best choice of partner for the organization. In some states, the process used to evaluate options and choose a partner is subject to review to ensure that the not-for-profit community asset has appropriately considered the community's interests.

Once the decision to seek a partner is made, a board-led process should be initiated. This process is distinct from the strategic planning process. The process for seeking a partner can be handled by the executive committee or by a separate partnership task force. A more detailed discussion of how to handle partnerships within the strategic planning process is provided at the end of this chapter.

The preparatory phase of the process starts by establishing a common base of knowledge among the participants and reaching agreement about the qualities that the organization is seeking in a partner. It concludes by making a recommendation to the board and taking a vote on whether to proceed.

The partner selection phase may begin with a widely distributed, formal request for proposal (RFP). The RFP addresses governance and control issues, concerns about cultural fit, financial requirements, and regulatory concerns. It should be tailored to the deal structure that the organization is seeking.

A formal RFP process typically takes 18 to 24 months from initiation to completion of an agreement, not including the time involved in the regulatory process (which is considerable and sometimes unpredictable). Organizations that cannot or do not want to work with such an extended time frame may take an abbreviated approach; if there is some clarity on likely partners, the RFP may be targeted to a limited number of prospective partners.

Once the RFP responses have been evaluated, the agreement to proceed with a specific partner is formalized with a letter of intent. The parties then conduct full due diligence while simultaneously negotiating definitive affiliation agreements.

At appropriate milestones, key stakeholders—the board, management, and medical staff—need to be engaged and appropriate approvals obtained. Outside advisers—legal, business, and deal structure—should be engaged early in the process to ensure the best outcomes, avoid roadblocks, and guarantee that all parties are aware of and prepared to manage the required approval processes.

STRATEGIC PLANNING AND MAJOR PARTNERSHIPS

Decisions about major partnerships, including mergers and acquisitions, would seem to be strategic and therefore part of the strategic planning process. However, the complexity and sensitivity of such decisions means that they require special treatment in the strategic planning process.

One approach is for the strategic planning steering committee to determine early in the process whether a major partnership should be considered during the current planning cycle. If so, a special

Exhibit 16.4: PM&A Process Steps

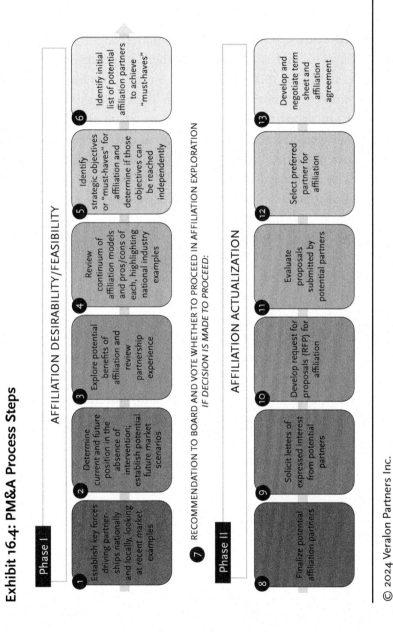

Phase I

AFFILIATION DESIRABILITY/FEASIBILITY

1 Establish key forces driving partnerships nationally and locally, looking at recent market examples

2 Determine current and future position in the absence of intervention; establish potential future market scenarios

3 Explore potential benefits of affiliation and review partnership experience

4 Review continuum of affiliation models and pros/cons of each, highlighting national industry examples

5 Identify strategic objectives or "must-haves" for affiliation and determine if those objectives can be reached independently

6 Identify initial list of potential affiliation partners to achieve "must-haves"

7 RECOMMENDATION TO BOARD AND VOTE WHETHER TO PROCEED IN AFFILIATION EXPLORATION *IF DECISION IS MADE TO PROCEED:*

Phase II

AFFILIATION ACTUALIZATION

8 Finalize potential affiliation partners

9 Solicit letters of expressed interest from potential partners

10 Develop request for proposals (RFP) for affiliation

11 Evaluate proposals submitted by potential partners

12 Select preferred partner for affiliation

13 Develop and negotiate term sheet and affiliation agreement

© 2024 Veralon Partners Inc.

task force can be assigned to consider this option and report their findings. In some cases, the existence of such a task force is kept confidential, to avoid sparking rumors or undermining confidence in the organization. In other cases, the prospect of a partnership is perceived as a positive step, in which case the existence of the task force would be known, but its proceedings would remain confidential.

In other situations, organizations may recognize an overriding need to partner and follow a partnership process like the one depicted in exhibit 16.4. However, in this circumstance, it is helpful to complete a strategic plan as well. The strategic plan becomes a useful tool in partnership negotiations, as it can articulate the opportunity associated with the market and the organization and how funds or partner resources would be invested (e.g., for facility renovations or information technology). The completion of the plan also demonstrates the competence of management and the board in guiding the organization.

CONCLUSION

Merging or entering into a major partnership is one of the most important strategic decisions that an organization can make. The considerations and processes described in this chapter provide guidance on how to make this decision. Because of the need for confidentiality, special attention must be paid to addressing partnership decisions within or alongside the strategic planning process.

CHAPTER 17

Value-Based Care

The way to transform health care is to realign competition
with value for patients. . . . If all system participants have to
compete on value, value will improve dramatically.

—*Michael E. Porter*

Since 2010, the shift to value-based care has been a critical strategic
issue for most hospitals and health systems. Despite the ubiquity of
value-based care, organizations progress at their own pace because
of factors such as health plan preferences, competition, medical
staff alignment, and organizational culture. To address value-based
care in the strategic plan, hospitals and health systems must assess
their internal capabilities and market dynamics as part of the strategic assessment phase of the strategic planning process and define
appropriate goals and major initiatives during the strategy formulation phase. Some organizations may need to revise their mission
and vision statements to reflect their commitment to the shift to
value-based care.

Many organizations refer to their "journey" to address value-based
care. Given the long-term nature of this journey, the commitment
of resources, and the cultural changes required, it is an appropriate
topic for strategic planning. This chapter explains the key concepts
of value-based care and the factors that organizations should consider
when addressing value-based care in the strategic plan.

BACKGROUND

The days of near-universal and exclusive use of the fee-for-service payment model, under which each individual healthcare service earns revenue, are over. From 2015 to 2022, fee-for-service payments decreased from 62 to 41 percent of all healthcare payments (HCP-LAN 2016, 2023). While this decrease does not represent the rapid evolution of the revenue model that some observers predicted, it does represent a steady march toward payment models that include value. Notably, the balance has begun to shift: More than half of all healthcare payments in the United States in 2022 included a value component, and 25 percent included a risk component for the provider (HCP-LAN 2023).

The evolution toward value began in earnest with the passage of the Affordable Care Act (ACA) in 2010. In addition to provisions to increase the public's access to health insurance, the ACA created the Center for Medicare & Medicaid Innovation (CMMI), which develops and tests value-based payment programs for Medicare beneficiaries. Leading the market in the shift to value, Medicare and Medicare Advantage had 30 percent and 39 percent of payments, respectively, in models that involved risk in 2022, while the commercial market had just 17 percent of payments in models with risk (HCP-LAN 2023).

Although certain aspects of the ACA were controversial when the law was passed and have been challenged since then, the work of the CMMI and the push toward value are not. These efforts have enjoyed broad bipartisan support and are seen as vital to protecting the solvency of Medicare.

The catalysts for the shift to value are many, and the urgency for change is accelerating. Healthcare leaders agree broadly that the fee-for-service model is inherently flawed. The revenue model that works in most industries does not lead to desired health outcomes. Delivering positive health outcomes requires a coordinated system in which all the components work together to serve patients, not one in which each player creates its own individual "widget," whether it is a surgery, lab test, or office visit.

The fee-for-service model has led to suboptimal results, and at an extremely high cost. The United States spent 17.8 percent of its gross domestic product on healthcare in 2021—nearly double the average of its peer countries. On a per capita basis, the United States spends two to four times more on healthcare than peer countries. Despite this high level of spending, the United States has lower life expectancy, higher avoidable deaths, and higher infant and maternal death rates than peer countries (Commonwealth Fund 2023).

There is broad consensus that healthcare spending under the fee-for-service approach has become unsustainable. A shift is necessary, and that shift must be toward a model that produces health instead of paying for healthcare widgets. Under the employer-based system of health insurance, companies, from multinational firms down to small businesses, are demanding better value for the health dollars they spend. And so is the federal government, through Medicare and Medicaid. Individual consumers, who are often shielded from healthcare costs by their insurers, have also joined the chorus of voices calling for better value as they face soaring health insurance premiums.

Hospital and health system boards have a responsibility to their communities to provide high-quality and cost-effective care. Some have extended this commitment by embracing a broader view of their role in delivering optimal health outcomes. Therefore, the push toward value is also coming from within healthcare, as providers pursue their ideals and mission—and seek competitive advantage.

Success in value-based arrangements provides new revenue streams, in the form of shared savings and quality bonuses. Additionally, value-based payment contracts can provide a more stable and predictable revenue stream. This fact became evident during the COVID-19 shutdowns in the spring of 2020. Organizations that used population-based payment models continued to receive regular monthly payments, while the revenue streams of providers that depended on fee-for-service evaporated.

Creating the system of care and networks of providers that are necessary to succeed in value-based payment arrangements may also provide an opportunity to shift market share from competitors. The strategy of developing accountable care organizations and clinically integrated networks as a means to align with physicians is discussed later in this chapter.

Lastly, pursuing value-based care can lead to a halo effect for hospitals and health systems. The ideal of value-based care—better outcomes at a lower price—is undoubtedly the right thing to do for the community. Value-based care advances the mission of healthcare organizations and allows them to live their ideals and elevate their standing in the community for doing so. Even bond rating agencies recognize the importance of an effective value-based care strategy, and they assess hospitals and health systems on their value-based care capabilities.

The transformation from a fee-for-service approach to a value-based care model is a long-term strategic endeavor. This shift will not be achieved in a single strategic planning cycle. It is a transformation that must be carefully considered, prepared for, and then staged over several years.

While in some cases, the change in the revenue model may happen quickly, building the foundation for success will take much longer. If hospitals and health systems have not started to develop a value-based care strategy, the time is now.

WHAT IS VALUE-BASED CARE?

A variety of labels have been used to describe value-based care: population health management, shift from volume to value, risk sharing, value-based contracting, and accountable care. At their core, these models seek to align providers and payers by delivering value to consumers/patients and payers.

What is value? As expressed in the following equation, value accounts for the quality of care delivered for a given cost, where quality includes patient experience (e.g., access, care coordination, satisfaction), clinical outcomes, and safety (Chambers, Benz, and Boat 2016):

$$\text{Value} = \text{Quality (Experience + Clinical Outcomes + Safety) / Cost}$$

Value-based payment models reward providers for high-quality, cost-effective care. This approach marks a shift away from paying providers for what they do—the focus of the fee-for-service model—to paying providers for what they deliver, in the form of outcomes and patient experience.

VALUE-BASED CARE PAYMENT MODELS

Value-based payment models, sometimes referred to as alternative payment models, range from those that include bonuses for achieving a few quality metrics to those that completely shift risk to providers through prospective population-based payments, also called capitation or global capitation.

The Health Care Payment Learning and Action Network (HCP-LAN) has developed a framework that describes and classifies the wide variety of value-based contract arrangements. Each category of the HCP-LAN framework represents more advanced value-based payment models with greater risks and rewards for providers.

- *Category 1: Fee-for-service—No link to quality or value.* These payer contracts are not based on value.
- *Category 2: Fee-for-service—Link to quality and value.* These contracts have a link to value in the form of bonuses for achievement in either data reporting or quality performance. Category 2 contracts may also include payments to support population health infrastructure, such as health IT or care coordination.

- *Category 3: Alternative payment models built on fee-for-service architecture.* Contracts in this category are typically shared savings contracts. In these arrangements, base fee schedules are left intact and providers are paid a fee-for-service for each unit of service provided over the course of the year. At the end of the year, total expenditures for the attributed population are tallied and compared with expected or benchmark expenditures for that population. If spending is lower than expected, savings were achieved. These savings are then shared between the payer and providers; the portion earned by each varies by agreement and may depend on the provider's quality performance.

    Shared savings arrangements may be applied to an entire attributed population, as described here, or to certain types of episodes or procedures, more commonly known as bundled payment arrangements.

    Category 3 arrangements may also include "downside risk": If expenditures exceed the benchmark, the provider owes a portion of the difference to the payer.

- *Category 4: Population-based payments.* Population-based payments represent a complete shift away from the traditional fee-for-service revenue model. Global budgets for all healthcare expenditures or "percent of premium" models are the most common approaches in this category. Under these models, a provider system is not compensated for each unit of service or care delivered to a patient, but rather receives a prospective payment for each attributed patient. The prospective payment is often risk adjusted, reflecting the aggregate impact of the health conditions of each patient in the patient population. Alternatively, the prospective payment can be based on historical costs for the patient population trended forward.

    Category 4 payment arrangements and arrangements in Category 3 that include downside risk are considered advanced alternative payment models, as providers bear risk and truly have "skin in the game."

THE SHIFT TO VALUE

While some markets in the country remain firmly in traditional fee-for-service payment models, other markets have largely shifted to being paid based on value. Experts agree that the shift to value is not a fad but rather a steady evolution, rolling out across the country on different time horizons. Value-based care will come to most markets eventually. That said, this shift is not inevitable for all markets. For example, rural areas, including those with critical access hospitals, may continue to rely on fee-for-service payment models well into the future.

The strategic issue for hospitals and health systems is, at a minimum, to be prepared for the time when their local market starts to shift to payment models that include value. This shift can happen quickly, but it can take years to build the foundation to succeed with value-based models. Therefore, hospital and health system leaders should plan and prepare in advance.

What the Shift Means for Health Systems

Shifting to a value-based approach to care and payer contracts that reward value can be scary for health system leadership, particularly chief financial officers. Success in value-based care typically reduces utilization and admissions through population health management. In a fee-for-service world, reduced utilization means reduced revenue. Value-based care provides an opportunity to capture more of the volume of the attributed population through improved care coordination, both delivering a more seamless care experience to patients and backfilling lost cases.

While the overall payment model will shift, value-based care models also offer new revenue opportunities. These income streams depend on the types of value-based contracts in place and include the following:

- Payments for building population health infrastructure, such as care management programs and health IT (HCP-LAN Category 2)
- Incentives for quality performance and/or data reporting (HCP-LAN Category 2)
- Shared saving payments (HCP-LAN Category 3)
- Proceeds from prospective population-based payments (HCP-LAN Category 4)

As health systems shift the way they receive payment for their services, they enter a new and different relationship with insurers and other payers. Traditionally, payer–health system negotiations involved squabbling over rates for different services—for example, taking a cut on inpatient admission payments to get a boost in rates for physician services. In this system, health systems are focused on how much they receive for every service provided and what they must do to get those payments.

Under value-based contracting, this negotiation can be more collaborative as each party determines how to best address the attributed population's health needs while reducing cost. As health systems take greater responsibility for the care of patients, payers often relent on insurance processes that restrain utilization, such as prior authorization and referral requirements. Health systems and their physicians are free to be creative in meeting the health needs of their patients—and not how to get paid for each unit of service that gets counted.

Though value-based care is not a panacea for all conflict between providers and payers, successful value-based providers can obtain additional revenue, improve their market position, and backfill utilization management efforts that reduce volume by increasing market share.

A Change for Providers

The shift to value-based care entails a change in providers' roles and responsibilities. They are no longer providing isolated widgets of care to patients, but rather functioning as part of a network that is, holistically, the provider of all care to a patient. The role of primary care physicians (PCPs) in this model cannot be overstated. In addition to providing longitudinal care, like PCPs in all environments, PCPs and their practice staff become the coordinators of their patients' care, ensuring that they receive the services they need when they need them. This work includes wellness, prevention, managing specialty care and ancillary services, and overseeing transitions across settings of care, such as inpatient and nursing home stays.

This expansion of the PCP's role comes with a financial upside: receiving a slice of the incentive in a value-based payer contract when targets are met and payment is earned. Hospitals and health systems that use value-based contracting must develop incentive distribution and/or compensation models that reward providers for their contribution to the overall contract results. These incentives engage the providers who are largely responsible for generating those results and can lead to larger rewards from payers overall. Traditionally, value-based contract rewards are focused on primary care providers, though increasingly, a portion of the incentives are distributed to specialists to direct their attention to relevant contract measures and overall performance.

Engaging physicians in value-based care can be an effective way for hospitals and health systems to align with independent community physicians without employing them. The benefits of this kind of alignment are many, the first being avoidance of the steep costs of employing physicians. Another key benefit is attracting specialist and hospital referrals from more PCPs, which can help with the backfill of cases.

Clinically Integrated Networks and Accountable Care Organizations

Some hospitals and health systems choose to create a formal structure for alignment in the form of a clinically integrated network (CIN) or an accountable care organization (ACO). CINs and ACOs can be wholly owned by a hospital or health system, jointly owned by physicians and a hospital or health system, wholly owned by physicians, or owned in whole or part by third-party, value-based care enablers. Such a structure is not a requirement for participation in value-based contracts, but many health systems chose to establish a CIN for a variety of reasons.

A CIN simplifies payer contracting if there will be more than one value-based contract for the health system and independent providers participating together. The contract can run through the CIN, rather than a series of agreements between the parties. A CIN also can be a platform for advancing population health initiatives to succeed overall in contracts with value-based incentives and risk. Initiatives may include shared data infrastructure, case management programs, deployment and adoption of clinical guidelines, and incentive arrangements for providers.

Having a CIN can often better achieve the physician alignment goals of health systems. Providers engaged in CIN activities, including care management programs and readmission reduction efforts, can simplify their practice and improve patient care by making more of their referrals to the CIN's aligned facilities.

More advanced CINs may meet requirements of the Federal Trade Commission to allow health systems and independent physician practices to negotiate certain elements of payer contracts. Without the advanced features of these CINs, such negotiations would be antitrust violations.

The Risk of Inaction

Many hospitals and health systems are reluctant to make any move toward developing population health capabilities and entering into payer contracts that include value components. However, there are risks to inaction. Physician groups that pursue value-based arrangements may become competitors of health systems. At a minimum, health systems must be an attractive place for these groups' inpatient work, offering an efficient and low-cost system of care. Absent that, physician groups may shift their volume to facilities that are working toward value and can offer an efficient and low-cost setting that supports the physicians' performance in value-based contracts. It is not just inpatient care that may shift in such a situation. Physician groups focused on value may also shift specialty referrals and outpatient volume, threatening a health system's core business.

ADDRESSING VALUE-BASED CARE IN THE STRATEGIC PLAN

A shift toward value-based care, which upends health systems' traditional focus on "heads in beds," requires a sustained effort through successive strategic planning cycles and collaboration across all areas of a health system. Making the first move toward value can be unnerving, considering the impending reduction in utilization. The board and health system leadership must plan the transition thoughtfully and be committed to the strategy and the reasons for pursuing it.

Another group that must be aligned with the strategy is a health system's affiliated CIN, if it has one. Since CINs typically engage independent physicians in their governance, it is important not to assume that the hospital or health system's strategic plan can simply be applied to the CIN. Health system leaders must coordinate the development of their value strategy with this key stakeholder. Affiliated CINs empower both employed and independent physicians and their voice must be heard to achieve a successful value-based care strategy.

This collaboration with the CIN presents an opportunity to ensure alignment with the constituency of the CIN, namely, the health system's aligned providers, both employed and independent.

Another challenge of addressing value-based care in the strategic plan is the array of expertise needed. Typical hospital management experience is less helpful than a deep understanding of insurance and value contracts. This possible misalignment in board and leadership experience may trigger considerations around board composition. In the least, boards should consider providing training by outside experts to ensure that members are equipped to address this unique area of oversight.

The shift to value must be addressed during all phases of the strategic planning process.

The strategic assessment must evaluate the organization's progression to value as well as the market's shift to value and competitors. Health system readiness and capabilities to manage value-based payer contracts are central to the internal assessment of the hospital or health system. The internal assessment should review the organization's performance on value-based contracts; existing value-based care and population health infrastructure, including care management initiatives and adoption of information technology tools; and physician practice culture and focus on value-based care.

One key goal of a value-based care strategy is alignment with independent providers. Therefore, the strategic assessment should consider the depth and breadth of providers' alignment with the health system, especially independent primary care providers. A CIN or similar entity is often the vehicle for achieving this alignment.

Competitors, which can be other hospitals or health systems, CINs, or investor-backed disruptors, may be aligning with independent primary care groups and peeling them away from hospitals and health systems. The strategic assessment should consider this competitive threat and determine whether the organization's response to these competitors is sufficient.

The last component of the strategic assessment for value-based care is payer interest and the prevalence of value-based contracts. The more interested payers are in value-based arrangements, the more likely they are to be good partners who are willing to contract on cooperative terms and have the infrastructure to effectively support value-based or risk contracts.

At the end of the strategic assessment process, critical planning issues can be identified. Specifically, the process should note gaps between where the market is headed on value and how fast and how prepared the hospital or health system is for that future.

During the organizational direction phase of the strategic planning process, the mission may need to be updated to reflect the health system's journey toward value-based care and the shift from treating the sick and injured to improving population health. The extent to which the health system is a pioneer or early adopter of value-based care may be reflected in its vision and values statements.

Strategy formulation will depend on the findings of the strategic assessment and the critical planning issues that are identified. Critical questions include the speed of the transition to value and how the system will make the necessary transition. Importantly, these value-based care and contracting strategies must be connected to goals related to physician alignment and the broader strategic plan.

Implementation planning and the actual work of shifting toward value require a multidisciplinary approach and, quite often, significant cultural change. This shift and the strategies and tactics developed in the strategic plan will touch on virtually all areas of the health system, and therefore they cannot be siloed in one group or department. Everyone in the organization must be involved in this work, and leaders at the highest levels must be its champions.

CONCLUSION

Value-based payment is not a fad. In most markets, this shift is inevitable, and health systems must be prepared for a time when payers force these models on providers.

In addressing value-based care, health systems can tackle other key strategic issues. Collaborating with physicians in a CIN to participate in value arrangements can be a powerful tool for aligning providers. Value-based payment models can focus care improvements, leading to better health of the communities served by health systems, which are in turn rewarded financially.

The shift toward value is a philosophical change that will touch on every part of the health system. This transformation requires ongoing strategic focus and investment, and therefore it will find its way into most hospital and health system strategic plans.

REFERENCES

Chambers, P., L. Benz, and A. Boat. 2016. "Patient and Family Experience in the Healthcare Value Equation." *Current Treatment Options in Pediatrics* 2: 267–79.

Commonwealth Fund. 2023. "U.S. Health Care from a Global Perspective, 2022: Accelerating Spending, Worsening Outcomes." Issue Brief. Published January 31. www.commonwealthfund .org/publications/issue-briefs/2023/jan/us-health-care-global -perspective-2022.

Health Care Payment Learning and Action Network (HCP-LAN). 2023. *2023 Methodology and Results Report.* Published October 30, 2023. https://hcp-lan.org/workproducts/apm-methodology-2023 .pdf.

———. 2016. *Measuring Progress: Adoption of Alternative Payment Models in Commercial, Medicare Advantage, and State Medicaid Programs.* Published October 25. http://hcp-lan.org/workproducts /apm-measurement-final.pdf.

CHAPTER 18

Physician Enterprise

A doctor gave a man six months to live. The man couldn't
pay his bill, so he gave him another six months.

—Henny Youngman

The success of any hospital or health system depends significantly
on its physicians. Approaches to engaging physicians vary. Most
hospitals and health systems employ physicians to ensure that they
maintain some control over the flow of patients to their facilities and
the way that care is provided. Other organizations seek to attract
private practice physicians. Most pursue a blended approach, com-
bining direct employment of physicians with some alignment with
private practices. Whichever approach is preferred, the physician
enterprise is so central to the success of hospitals and health systems,
and so challenging to optimize, that it is often a key element of the
strategic plan.

The physician enterprise is an important strategic consideration
for several reasons. Physicians have a significant impact on the quality and efficiency of care, and the strength of a hospital or health
system's relationships with physicians determines its strategic position relative to competitors and payers. However, physicians can also
compete with hospitals and health systems—for example, by owning

ambulatory surgery centers. In addition, employed networks of physicians often lose money, at least on paper. This chapter explains key features of the physician enterprise that should be considered when setting strategy.

ASSESSING THE PHYSICIAN ENTERPRISE

When completing the strategic assessment as part of the strategic planning process, several factors related to the physician enterprise should be considered, including employed physician network losses, value-based care, physician supply, and competitors for employing and aligning with physicians.

Employed Physician Network Losses

Physicians control, to a great extent, where patients go for specialist care, testing, and elective admissions. As a result, hospitals that employ physicians may be willing to subsidize employment costs using the profit margins earned from downstream services. For hospital-owned entities, median subsidies (losses) per physician are approximately $200,000 for primary care, $400,000 for specialty care, and $250,000 for hospital-based specialties (KaufmanHall 2023). Thus, a health system comprising 200 physicians (many systems have more) would incur an annual subsidy of tens of millions of dollars—a tough pill to swallow in the current financial environment. Health systems are increasingly targeting these losses and seeking improvement.

Given the scale hospital subsidies for employed physicians, it is reasonable to ask how private physician practices are able to succeed financially without hospital subsidies. Several factors drive the need for subsidies when hospitals employ physicians. In addition, hospitals must contend with some significant accounting issues that do not burden private practices. Typical differences include the following:

- Physicians often increase their compensation when they move from private practice to hospital employment.
- Billable ancillary services that are provided (and make a profit) in the private practice are separated in hospital employment, appearing elsewhere on the hospital's ledger.
- Payer mix often shifts under hospital employment and may include less favorable payers (particularly government payers).
- Hospitals often allocate hospital overhead to the physician enterprise, typically using a standardized institutional rate, regardless of the degree to which the physician enterprise actually draws on hospital resources (compared with other hospital divisions).

While breaking even is a high bar for an employed physician network in the current financial environment, it is reasonable to strive for an "appropriate" loss, which can be determined based on benchmarks, market conditions, and best practices. The financial loss of an employed physician network is not a useful performance measure. Other measures relevant to the cost structure and productivity of the physician practice are more instructive than gross losses. Given the positive impact that employed physicians can have on downstream revenue, when considering the financial performance of the employed physician network, it is essential to focus on the overall financial performance of the health system.

Value-Based Care

As discussed in chapter 17, value-based care is increasingly a focus of both hospitals and physicians. This shift affects the physician enterprise strategy in several ways. Private practices, operating as members in accountable care organizations (ACOs) or clinically integrated networks (CINs), are able to receive rewards from payers for effectively managing the cost of care of their patients. In some cases, hospitals or health systems create ACOs and CINs that include both employed physicians and private practices, to strengthen relations with physicians, achieve better clinical quality and efficiency, and obtain financial rewards from payers.

The hospital or health system model of an ACO or CIN focuses on providing effective, comprehensive, and coordinated care. Some of that care may be provided in a hospital in order to improve coordination even when a freestanding provider is available. In contrast, when physicians create ACOs or CINs without hospitals, they often cast the hospital as the enemy and seek to drive as much care as possible to low-cost, freestanding outpatient providers rather than hospital-based outpatient services.

Physician Supply

The United States is facing a projected shortage of 39,000 to 124,000 physicians by 2034 (AAMC 2021, 3). As a result, hospitals and health systems may not be able to find enough physicians to employ or attract to their local community to meet the population's needs. The shortage is being driven, in part, by patients' increasing life expectancy and high healthcare utilization of the aging baby boom generation. Other key factors include burnout and early retirements prompted by the COVID-19 pandemic. Several factors will determine whether the physician shortage is better or worse than expected.

New Entrants Competing to Employ Physicians

Until recently, physicians had two primary choices for employment: private practice or health system employment. New competitors are now employing physicians and competing for an increasingly limited pool of physicians. These competitors include retail stores with health clinics, telehealth companies, value-based innovators

Exhibit 18.1: Factors Affecting the Physician Shortage

Factors That Could Exacerbate the Shortage	Factors That Could Ease the Shortage
• Greater than expected physician retirement as a result of burnout • Shift toward concierge practices, reducing physician's patient panels • Increased access to care, for example, if the number of uninsured patients decreases • Greater than expected patient longevity and illness burden	• Increased presence and role of nurse practitioners and physicians assistants • Improvements in electronic medical records technology that reduce documentation time and improve physician productivity • Artificial intelligence that can meet some patient needs or streamline visit times • Increased international pipeline of physicians • Population health and value-based care efforts that reduce care utilization rates • Pharmaceutical or clinical advances that improve health

offering new models of care delivery, investor-backed "roll-ups" of previously private practices, and technology companies offering technology-enabled care models. (For a discussion of these competitors, see chapter 15.) As a result, hospitals are competing with more employers for a physician pool that is too small to meet all the needs of a growing and aging population.

Alternatives to Employment

Most medical staffs include a combination of hospital-employed and private practice physicians. This chapter focuses on the opportunities and challenges associated with the employed physician network. From a strategic point of view, it is equally important to consider the variety of approaches to engaging and aligning with private practice physicians. These may include the following:

- *Joint ventures* can provide an opportunity for hospitals to partner with entrepreneurially minded physicians typically in the development of ambulatory surgery centers and other ambulatory procedure facilities. This arrangement could provide a vehicle for health systems to participate in rather than compete with physician initiatives.

- *Professional leases* are exclusive, practice-specific arrangements whereby the hospital leases professional services from a private practice, thereby allowing the practice to remain independent yet financially affiliated. Professional leases typically relieve the practice of payer relationships, and the hospital becomes a "single payer" to the practice. Installation of the hospital's ambulatory electronic medical records system is often a condition.

- *Management services organizations* (MSOs) provide a way for hospitals to align with independent practices by offering low-cost practice services (e.g., billing, supply chain), thereby reducing practice costs and offering an attractive option for hospitals and health systems to promote practice development and relationships. MSOs may also provide for a mix of ownership and engagement options for physicians and hospitals.

- *Practice subsidies* are generally provided to independent practices when financing to sustain or expand necessary services is unavailable from the usual nonhospital sources. This arrangement is often applied to independent anesthesia groups, and sometimes it is used to encourage independent groups to recruit additional physicians. Practice subsidies and other subsidy arrangements are subject to important compliance considerations—for example, the hospital must demonstrate that losses routinely exist under typical market conditions or that there is a shortage of physicians required to meet community need.

- *Clinical affiliations* sometimes involve financial consideration, but they may also be nonfinancial services agreements, such as exclusive provider contracts in exchange for agreed-upon clinical access to a range of services. Co-management arrangements are a type of affiliation in which a hospital pays an independent group to manage the physician practice side of the service line as well as the hospital facility aspects. Determination of appropriate payment is critical when a hospital uses its revenues to pay physicians for the hospital's needs.
- *CIN/ACOs*, as described earlier, capitalize on value-based payment opportunities to strengthen relations with private practice physicians, aligning them with hospital-employed physicians.

These approaches to aligning with private practices provide a range of approaches to meet physician preferences.

The effectiveness of these approaches in engaging private practice physicians should be evaluated during the strategic assessment phase of the strategic planning process and provide an overall assessment of the organization's physician alignment and engagement needs. Initiatives to engage private practice physicians using these approaches may comprise some of the goals and strategies included in the strategic plan.

LEGAL AND REGULATORY CONSIDERATIONS

Several key features of employed physician networks and alignment approaches for private practices must be considered when evaluating strategic options.

The federal and state governments (through Medicare and Medicaid) are the largest buyers of healthcare services. As a result, the federal government imposes regulatory constraints on the flow of funds in the industry, some of which are detailed in this section.

Physicians serve a dual role as both experts who are responsible for determining the care that patients need and economic actors who potentially benefit financially from those decisions. Therefore, a dizzying array of externally imposed regulations are in place to protect patients and society from any conflicts between those roles.

Corporate Practice of Medicine

Corporate practice of medicine laws in some states restrict ownership and the practice of medicine to medical entities and those with medical licenses. These laws, which typically vary by state, constrain who can control and own medical practices, who can employ physicians, who can interfere in medical decision-making, and how fees can be shared with nonmedical entities. These laws constrain the arrangements that hospitals and health systems make with physicians. In states with corporate practice of medicine laws, hospitals and other corporate employers of physicians often apply workarounds to achieve a result that is similar to employment but has some complications and limitations.

Stark Law and Anti-Kickback Statute

The Stark Law and the Anti-Kickback Statute are federal laws intended to prevent fraud and abuse and to protect patient care decisions from financial considerations. Understanding that there are limits on the way that physicians are paid is essential when identifying strategic initiatives that change how physicians are paid or what they are paid for. Hospitals and health systems risk their not-for-profit status if they generate unreasonable profits for individuals.

When working with physicians who are not employed by the hospital, a hospital can pay physicians for personally performed services (typically professional clinical duties and administrative time), but not for referrals. That means that hospitals cannot pay physicians for the portion of hospital services that physicians generate. Physicians understand this restriction but are frustrated by it.

To define what hospitals can pay for direct physician services, the fair market value (FMV) standard is applied. This payment standard, which is based on judgment as well as data, places limits on what hospitals can pay physicians to avoid any appearance that physicians are receiving payment for the volume or value of referrals.

However, many non–health system physician entities (described in chapter 15) do not receive such hospital referrals, and thereby may avoid the FMV constraint to some extent. Without this constraint, competitors could pay physicians more than what the FMV standard would indicate. As a result, it can be difficult for health systems to pay physicians enough to counter offers from nonhospital competitors. These new entrants can pay more to attract physicians, and health systems are hard-pressed to respond competitively.

STRATEGY FORMULATION

During the strategy formulation phase of the strategic planning process, physicians are key drivers of success. Growth strategies often depend on physician recruitment. The financial performance of the hospital or health system may depend on the financial and operational performance of the employed physician network. Similarly, the success of value-based care strategies depends on physician engagement.

Growth

Most strategic plans include goals for growth in specific geographies or service lines. These growth goals are often pursued by recruiting physicians for employment or by aligning with private physician practices through one of the approaches described earlier in this chapter. Recruitment of physicians is expensive, and the time needed to reach anticipated volume has a significant financial cost.

Alignment with existing physician groups is usually preferred, but even that choice can involve costs to achieve the transition. These costs include referral reductions to specialists from former colleagues, payer credentialing delays, and reduced throughput—typically permanent—as a result of switching to or adopting an electronic medical records system. Increasingly, physician retention is an important focus in addition to growth.

Employed Physician Network Performance Improvement

Many hospitals and health systems, frustrated by the performance of their employed physician network, set a goal to improve the network's financial and operational performance in their strategic plan. While financial losses can be addressed through benchmarking and operational improvements, many hospitals and health systems underestimate the importance of creating a positive practice environment for physicians. Improvements in these "softer" features require taking a thoughtful approach to practice governance and engaging physicians in shared problem-solving and performance improvement.

The following criteria define a high-performing employed physician enterprise:

- Physician governance and leadership structures and expectations
- Engagement with IT and advanced analytics
- Culture and measurement of continuous operational and clinical improvement
- Patient-centric approach to referrals and access
- Measured and enforced clinical pathways and outcomes
- Effective and continuous improvements in cost management, professional revenue cycle, and physician compensation.

Addressing the performance of your employed physician enterprise on these factors can have a material impact on achieving the organization's strategic goals.

Value-Based Care

Value-based care strategies are often included in hospital and health system strategic plans. The role of physicians in these efforts is increasingly important to address as well. Whether the focus is the employed physician network or a combination of employed and private practice physicians, physician engagement is central to the success of value-based care initiatives.

CONCLUSION

Physicians are central to improvements in patient access, clinical care, quality improvement, and growth. For that reason, achievement of strategic goals requires buy-in and ongoing physician engagement.

REFERENCES

Association of American Medical Colleges (AAMC). 2021. *The Complexities of Physician Supply and Demand: Projections from 2019 to 2034*. Published June. www.aamc.org/data-reports/workforce /data/complexities-physician-supply-and-demand-projections -2019-2034.

Kaufman Hall. 2023. *Physician Flash Report*. Published October. www.kaufmanhall.com/sites/default/files/2023-11/KH_PFR%20 _2023-10.pdf.

CHAPTER 19

Governance

We cannot be mere consumers of good governance, we
must be participants; we must be co-creators.

—*Rohini Nilekani*

Effective governance is central to high-performing organizations
and critical in the strategic planning process. The board oversees
the development of the strategic plan and monitors its implementation on a regular basis. This requires a strong and clearly defined
relationship with the management team and an understanding of
the major issues that impact the organization.

Over the past few decades, health system governance has become
increasingly complex, mirroring the evolution of the healthcare field
itself. Catalysts of this change include the following:

- Increasing partnership, merger, and affiliation activity
  that has significantly increased the size of healthcare
  organizations—many organizations now involve more
  than one board (e.g., system and local boards), each of
  which has different responsibilities
- Continued scrutiny of board oversight, policies, and
  procedures, which hold individual board members more
  accountable than in the past.

- The shift to value-based care and the implications of those changes on the organization's infrastructure and financial position.

All these changes necessitate a board and a governance structure that meet the needs of these dynamic times. Board members must be more than generally knowledgeable—they must have specialized expertise. They must have their finger on the pulse of the organization and the industry, and they must be continuously learning about new topics to ensure continued organizational success and to mitigate risks, both known and unknown. This chapter describes successful governance and discusses how governance issues can be addressed in the strategic planning process.

WHAT DOES SUCCESSFUL GOVERNANCE LOOK LIKE?

Governance is defined as "the structures and processes by which the health system is regulated, directed and controlled" (Chanturidze and Obermann 2016, 508). But if a hospital is, as Peter Drucker described it, "the most complex human organization ever devised," where does the board even begin to try to govern a hospital or health system? And how should the board react to the continual interplay of government regulation, case law, and tradition that influences what we view as the role of governance? While there is no magical solution to the challenge of governing a health system, following a number of recognized principles can lead to better results in the boardroom.

CEO and Management Relationship

At the most basic level, successful governance depends on collaboration between the board and the CEO. One of the board's most important responsibilities is to provide management oversight for the organization. This responsibility includes selecting, empowering, monitoring, and evaluating the CEO. The relationship must strike a balance as the board is both the CEO's boss and the CEO's partner. The board can facilitate an effective partnership by engaging in regular executive sessions—both with and without the CEO—conducting robust CEO performance evaluations, connecting a portion of the CEO's compensation to their performance, and ensuring that the organization has a formal succession plan in place.

Role clarity is also paramount in the board–CEO partnership. The board and the CEO must have mutual understanding and respect and, ultimately, stay out of one another's work. When the board hovers too closely, it ends up taking on management work that the CEO and other executives have already done, while neglecting its major roles (oversight and vision development). On the other hand, if the board is too hands-off, it may fail to adequately oversee performance and hold management accountable for results. Conversely, if the CEO does not respect the board's role and either is too controlling or keeps the board in the dark, the organization will miss out on the opportunity to leverage the unique strengths that board members bring. Either way, when the board and CEO are not clear on their own and each other's roles, the organization suffers.

When the board of a not-for-profit organization remains focused on its work, it is uniquely positioned to guide the organization with its vision and perspective. The board has a fiduciary responsibility—a legal obligation—to act in the best interests of the organization's mission. So, although frontline staff answer to middle managers, and senior executives answer to the CEO, the board answers only to the mission (and, of course, regulators such as the Internal Revenue Service and state attorneys general, whose job it is to ensure that the board remains focused on the organization's charitable mission). Ideally, being immediately "mission-adjacent" should inspire the board to think big about the issues facing the organization and how to support management in achieving the organization's mission.

A constant challenge for boards is to flex between different modes of governing (Chait 2006). These modes include the following:

- *Fiduciary*—To perform legally required responsibilities (such as approving the Form 990)
- *Strategic*—Charting a course for the future of the organization
- *Generative*—Making sense of the issues and framing them for the rest of the organization

Understanding these modes and how to be effective in each mode is crucial when selecting new board members.

Composition

Having an effective board begins with having the right people on the board. The board needs to have the right mix of characteristics, competencies, and perspectives to carry out its responsibilities. Many boards have recognized that they need to become more diverse to perform their role most effectively. One component of diversity is the demographic makeup of the board (e.g., race, gender, age), which can enhance or limit the board's ability to understand the populations that the organization serves. But diversity also includes the professions, life experiences, and ways of thinking that board members bring with them. As the delivery of healthcare evolves, boards may need to consider adding expertise in areas such as actuarial risk, cybersecurity, and artificial intelligence.

"Refreshing" the board with new people and new ideas can help ensure that it evolves to meet new challenges rather than remaining static and complacent. Most boards employ term limits for this reason; the most common practice is to limit board members to three three-year terms. Some hospitals and health systems are adding board members from outside their area to provide additional perspective and expertise.

Boards are well served by developing rigorous processes for evaluating and reappointing board members. Board members should not be reappointed automatically; rather, a board member's attendance, preparation, participation, and ability to contribute to current challenges should all be factors in determining whether the individual will serve multiple terms. Whether board members are paid for their service and expertise is another consideration. There are certainly benefits and drawbacks to having paid board members; a major drawback is the financial impact on the organization. However, a major benefit of paying board members is that it allows the organization to obtain greater expertise, set higher expectations, and apply performance, engagement, and accountability metrics that may be difficult to apply to a volunteer position.

Publicly elected or appointed hospital boards may not have full control over the composition of their board. In this case, it is particularly important to establish clear expectations and provide guidance outlining board members' roles and responsibilities. In addition, establishing a program for ongoing board member education can help ensure that board members are as competent as possible to take on their role.

Structure

Having the right people and skills on the board is an important start, but the structure of the board, including its size, committees, and approach to meetings, plays a major role in maximizing the contributions of each board member.

The board needs to be big enough to include a wide variety of backgrounds and perspectives so that board members can look at issues from different perspectives and expand the views of their peers and management. But it also needs to be small enough that it can reach consensus and engage all board members. Boards that are too large often take so long to come to agreement that they inhibit the organization's ability to be nimble and act quickly, or they do not permit all board members to participate fully and share their views. As a result, needed perspectives may not be fully considered, and board members may become disengaged.

Committees are another important structural component of effective governance. When used well, committees enable the board to assign a group of individuals to dive deeply into issues, make low-level decisions, and highlight important focal points for the board. In a healthy committee report to the board, board members respect and appreciate the work of the committee members and ask questions for clarification. Recommendations of the committee are generally accepted, though in some instances, the board may make adjustments to recommendations or request further consideration by the committee.

Because committees require an investment of board and staff time, it is important for boards to determine whether they have the right committees. Committees should focus on governance-level topics (quality, strategy) and rarely on operational issues (facilities, human resources). The most common committees are quality, finance, executive, and governance.

Boards need to carefully consider what level of authority committees are given. A careful balance must be struck: The committee should not have so much authority that it takes decision-making power away from the board, but not so little that it is unable to move issues forward. All committees should function in accordance with charters that clearly define their roles and authority. Every few years, the board should update the committee charters and evaluate whether the overall mix of committees makes sense given the organization's current strategy and issues.

Meeting timing, frequency, and length are also important considerations. Key questions include the following:

- Are meetings long enough to allow for deep discussion of certain topics rather than merely a cursory introduction to all topics?
- Are meetings frequent enough that nothing falls between the cracks, but infrequent enough that they do not feel redundant?

- Does the timing of key board meeting agenda items (e.g., approving the audit, selecting new board members) make sense for the way the organization functions?

Culture

Culture is difficult to quantify, but it is one of the most important contributors to board effectiveness. The following are a few hallmarks of a board with a good culture:

- *Engagement*—Board members attend meetings, read materials in advance, and participate in active discussion at meetings.
- *Role clarity*—Board members and executives respect the unique roles that they play; they do not step into others' roles or pull others into their role.
- *Collaboration*—Board members respect the unique strengths that everyone brings to the table. Meetings are not dominated by a small number of board members, but allow everyone to contribute in their own way.
- *Robust dialogue*—Board members are willing to express views that differ from those of their peers and management. They are able to disagree constructively, consider opposing views, and support the final decision.

Board Leadership

Successful boards rely on strong leadership, including board officers and committee chairs, to ensure that they function effectively. Board leadership is strongest when there is an ethos of cultivating leadership qualities at all stages of a board member's tenure. For example,

- Considering leadership potential when recruiting individuals to join the board
- Providing board members with opportunities to grow and have experiences that make them effective board officers or committee chairs (rotating board members through committees, letting board members facilitate discussions, etc.)
- Providing effective education opportunities
- Evaluating board members and agreeing on personal development plans with effective education opportunities
- Defining competencies desired of board officers and committee chairs so that expectations are clear
- Implementing an orientation program specific to board leadership roles

Education and Assessment

A board cannot succeed while remaining static; it must always be evolving and developing.

A crucial ingredient for ongoing board development is education. Board members need education on their core governance functions (e.g., quality, finance, strategy) as well as "hot topics" that impact the organization's ability to deliver on its mission. In 2023, some of the hottest topics included workforce issues, artificial intelligence, and improving health equity and outcomes for all populations.

Board members can receive this education through self-study, by reading articles and white papers, going to conferences, or taking part in online learning. Many organizations also offer more structured educational opportunities to board members. The availability of online learning platforms allows board members to fill gaps in their knowledge and allows board leaders to provide education on topics that will be coming before the board. This is both a good practice and a good investment, to ensure that board members are aligned on issues that affect the healthcare industry and can connect that knowledge to their roles as board members.

Another ingredient for ongoing board development is regular assessment of the board's effectiveness. Assessing the board can help reinforce what the board is doing well, eliminate blind spots, and identify areas for improvement. The most basic way to assess the board is to use a checklist or questionnaire about board practices (a self-assessment). To make the process more robust, boards can have a third-party review of board documents, interview board members, or observe meetings. Ideally, the assessment will touch on the major areas addressed in this chapter—board composition, structure, and culture—and allow for comparison with best practices at other organizations. However, if the assessment merely provides an opportunity for the board to simply pat itself on the back without looking inward and outward, the board will not gain any benefits from it.

To ensure that education and assessment efforts are worthwhile, the board should create an ongoing development plan. Charging a committee (such as the governance committee) with reviewing assessment results and creating an ongoing education plan will help ensure that the assessment is a good use of the board's time and yields benefits down the road.

Oversight

If an understanding of roles is the foundation of good governance, then the board's composition, structure, culture, leadership, education, and assessment represent the framing that holds up the house. Upon that foundation, and supported by that framing, the board can establish the rooms of the house—the different areas where the board will provide oversight. These include quality, finance, strategy, management, and advocacy on behalf of the organization and the people it serves. It is in these "rooms" that the board's work of providing oversight meets the work of management in each area.

In collaboration with management, the board helps set the strategic plan for the organization.

ADDRESSING GOVERNANCE IN THE STRATEGIC PLAN

The board has a clear role in strategic planning—to oversee the process of strategic plan development, to approve the plan, and to monitor plan implementation—that is highlighted throughout this book. However, should governance itself be addressed directly in the strategic plan? The answer is "it depends." The issue of governance typically comes up in one of two ways: ineffective governance practices can undermine strategic planning, or governance may be flagged as an issue or weakness during the strategic assessment.

Poor governance practices can undermine the strategic planning process in a variety of ways, but the most common is a poor understanding of roles. A board may raise operational issues or seek too much involvement in implementation, or management may try to hinder the board in its important role in setting strategy. The emergence of these issues during the strategic planning process provides an opportunity to model the proper roles and clarify responsibilities by, for example, distinguishing operational issues from strategic issues and directing the board's focus away from operations.

Furthermore, achieving a shared understanding of issues is important to effective strategic planning. A lack of understanding among board members can undermine an otherwise effective strategic planning process. Some of these gaps in understanding can be addressed by reviewing the strategic assessment with the board, and this can also be an opportunity for general education of the board on key topics.

If governance practices are raised in the strategic assessment as a major weakness or barrier or competitive disadvantage, the issue should be handled like other critical planning issues. First, a goal is identified for improved governance, then initiatives and metrics are established to track progress. These initiatives then become part of the implementation plan.

CONCLUSION

The process of cultivating effective governance (in structure and practice) within the organization is a long-term, ongoing strategic issue for many hospitals and health systems, but it is worth the investment in time and resources. Effective governance can propel an organization to success; ineffective governance can stifle decision-making and inhibit long-term sustainability. Finding the right balance between oversight and a strong relationship with leadership can drive accountability and allow the organization to operate effectively, ultimately achieving its mission.

REFERENCES

Chait, R. 2006. "Governance as Leadership." *Independence* 31 (2): 4, 7–9.

Chanturidze, T., and K. Obermann. 2016. "Governance in Health: The Need for Exchange and Evidence." *International Journal of Health Policy and Management* 5 (8): 507–10.

SUGGESTED READING

American Hospital Association (AHA). 2022. *National Health Care Governance Survey Report*. Chicago: AHA. https://trustees.aha .org/aha-2022-national-health-care-governance-survey-report.

Index

Note: Italicized page locators refer to figures or tables in exhibits.

Digital disruptors, 284–85

Directional strategies, 5, 132

Disrupters, 92

Drucker, Peter, 3, 137, 332

Duncan, W. Jack, 5–6, 14, 21, 87, 132, 175

Edison, Thomas, 25

Elevance, 283

Emerus, 282

End product: of external assessment, 116; of internal assessment, 110, *111*

Environmental assessment, 101–29. *See also* Strategic assessment

Equity, health, 43, 45

Evolent, 283

Execution, 221–38; annual strategic management process components, 236, *237*; balanced scorecard and, 230–35; celebrating implementation phase, 224–25; challenges of implementation and, 221–22; communication in, 225; fostering implementation process and, 223–26; implementation subcommittees and, 225; leaders for, 224; monitoring system and, 225–26; moving from strategic planning to strategic management, 226, *235*, 235–38; preplanning stage of, 223; progress review and, ongoing, 226–30; roles and responsibilities of those involved in, 224; ten steps for successful implementation,

223–26; warning signs of execution failure, 225; while formulating strategy, 223–24

Expectations: communication and, 206; context and, 206; management and leadership and, 206; organizing and setting, 205–7

Expenses, impact of goals and initiatives on, 261

External assessment, *102*, 110–16; analyzing competitors, 113, 114, 115, *117*, *118–19*; end product of, 116; interview topic, *107*; market forecasts and implications in, 115–16; review population characteristics and, 110, 113; review state of healthcare delivery in local and regional market, 113, *114*, *115*

Facilitation, in strategic planning: facilitators for, identifying, 59; successful strategic planning process and, 69–72

Facilitators: identifying, in strategic planning, 59; skills of, 70–72, *71*

Fair market value (FMV), 327

Fee-for-service payment model: alternative payment models built on, 310; with link to quality or value, 309; with no link to quality or value, 309

Fiduciary governance, 334

Fiduciary mode of governing, 334

Financial analysis, 164–65. *See also* Strategic plan financial analysis (example)

167–71; strategic plan financial analysis (example), 173–74

Hamel, Gary, 89–91, 121, 122
HCA, 281
HCPLAN. *See* Health Care Payment Learning and Action Network
Health Care Payment Learning and Action Network (HCPLAN), 309–11, 312
Healthcare quality, 37
Healthcare strategic planning: applicability of, 19–21; evolution of, 17, 19; history of, 15–17, *18*; state of the art in, 241–44; value in, 34
Health equity, 43, 45
HealthHUB, 283
Health Resources and Services Administration (HRSA), website of, *106*
HEB, 283
Hemingway, Ernest, 175
Historical data: assembling, 61; overanalyzing, 62
Honda, vision statement of, *144*
Horizontal PM&A activity, 288–90
Hospital discharge databases, state-specific, *106*
HRSA. *See* Health Resources and Services Administration
Humana-CenterWell, 284
Human capital, 39–40

Ikea, vision statement of, *144*
Implementation planning, 8, *8*, 175–95; in annual review and update, 212–13; board review and approval of strategic plan, 184–90; detailed year 1 implementation plan, 177–84; four-step process to create plan, 180–81; innovation in, 274–275; key elements of, 176, *177*; relationship between strategy and, *179*; seven deadly sins that doom, 175–76; strategic goal with detailed objectives and year 1 implementation plan, *182–83*; strategic plan rollout and communication, 191–93; systems for monitoring and reporting progress, 194

Inamdar, Noorein, 231, 232
Initiatives: competition and, 286; financial impact from, 173, *174*; in financial-planning process, 259–61; in Regional Health System's strategic plan, 161–62, *162*

Innovation, 265–75; assessment of potential, 269–70; forms of, 266; in implementation planning, 274–75; modifying strategic planning process to address, 268–71; objectives of adopting, *270*; organizational culture and, 271, *272*; in organizational direction, 273; in strategic assessment, 271–72; strategic planning context for, 267–68; as strategic priority, factors of, 266–67; in strategy formulation, 273–74; working definition of, 265

Institute of Medicine, 37

Integrated Strategic, Operational, and Financial Plan (ISOFP), 214–15

Interconnectedness, of effective strategy, 5

Internal assessment, *102*, 107–10; Community Hospital's, *112*; end product of, 110, *111*; information summary categories, *108–09*; interview topic, *107*

Internal business processes, balanced scorecard and, 231

Interview: in internal assessment, *107*; in research approach, 77

ISOFP. *See* Integrated Strategic, Operational, and Financial Plan

Issue documentation (example), 167–71; barriers and constraints, 171; goals, 170; issue definition and situation description, 167–68; measurement criteria, 170–71; objectives, 170; options available to medical center, 169, *169*; recommendation, 170; strategies employed by others, 168; strategy proposed by medical center, 169–71

Jefferson Health, vision statement of, *144*

Jennings, Marion C., 94

Joint Commission, The, 134

Joint operating agreements, 299

Joint ventures, 299, 324

Kaiser, Henry, 277

Kaiser Family Foundation (KFF), website of, *106*

Kaiser Foundation Hospitals, 290

Kanter, Rosabeth Moss, 67

Kaplan, Robert S., 133, 230, 231, 232, 234

Kaplan, Sarah, 91

Kar, Jayanti, 92

Kay, Alan, 241

Kennedy, John F., 221

KFF. *See* Kaiser Family Foundation

Kickoff retreat, 74–75

Kim, W. Chan, 95–97

Krueger, Richard A., 78

Leaders: key contributors to success and failure for, *248*; for plan execution, 224

Leadership: asserting CEO leadership of strategic planning, 55–56; the board and, 57; facilitators, identifying, 59; in organizing for strategic planning, 55–59; oversight bodies and, 58; roles and responsibilities of, defining and formalizing, 57–58; stakeholder involvement in, 57–58

Learning and growth, balanced scorecard and, 231

Lee, Thomas H., 241

Leeds University (UK), vision statement of, 133

Legacy statements, 136, 137

decision-making considerations in, 301–2; drivers of, 290–92; entering into, 292–95; financial benefits in, 291; horizontal PM&A activity, 288–90; independence assessment for healthcare organizations, *294*; letter of intent in, 302; number of hospital/health system transactions, 2007–2022, *289*; operational benefits in, 292; partner selection phase of, 302; partnership and affiliation models and, 295–300 (*See also* Models for PM&A); preparatory phase of, 301; process steps, 301–2, *303*; request for proposal and, 302; strategic benefits in, 291–92; strategic planning and major partnerships and, 302–4, *303*; vertical PM&A activity, 290

Patient: patient-centered care delivery models, 36; satisfaction, 36–37; volume, estimates of, 257–58

Payviders, 284

PCPs. *See* Primary care physicians

Performance benefits, of effective strategy, 4

Physician enterprise, 319–29; assessment of, 320–25; employed physician network losses and, 320–21; employed physician network performance improvement and, 328–29; employment alternatives and, 323–25; growth and, 328; legal and regulatory considerations in, 325–27; new entrants competing to employ physicians and, 322, 323; overview of, 319–20; physician supply and, 322, *323*; strategy formulation and, 327–29; value-based care and, 321–22, 329

Physicians: alignment of, 30; primary care, 313–14; as stakeholders, 79–80; in strategic planning, 79–80

Planning process considerations, 67–84; for evolving and improving the process, 83–84; facilitation, 69–72; levels of inquiry and, 83; overview of, 67–69; planning retreats, 73–76; research approaches, 76–79; settings for strategic planning activities and meetings, 68, *69*; stakeholder involvement, 79–83; teamwork, 72, *73*

Planning retreats, 73–76; concluding retreat, 75–76; kickoff retreat, 74–75; midprocess retreat, 75

Planning scenarios, 254, 262

PM&A. *See* Partnerships, mergers, and acquisitions

Pollard, William, 265

Population-based payments, 309, 310–11, 312

Population health management, 43

Porter, Michael E., 3, 4, 86, 134, 149, 241, 305

Practice subsidies, 324–25

Prahalad, C. K., 89, 121, 122

Primary care aggregators, 283

Primary care physicians (PCPs), 313–14

Private equity-backed specialty groups, 282

Privia, 283

Problems, of strategic planning, 9–13; analysis paralysis, 12; critical issues overlooked, 12; environmental shifts or organizational change and, 10; failing to align those responsible for executing, 12; failing to involve stakeholders, 11; financial considerations excluded from strategic planning, 11–12; formal structures undermining strategic thinking, 10; ignoring resistance to change, 12–13; ineffectively transitioning from planning to execution and, 13; reliance on the past to predict the future, 9–10

Process options, 208–10; formal and lengthy update, 209–210; formal but somewhat abbreviated, 209; informal and very abbreviated, 208–209

Product benefits, of strategic planning, 28, 29, 31

Product scope and extent, 28

Professional leases, 324

Progress review, 226–230; example of, 229; individual performance reviews and, 228; informal, 228; interventions in, 228, 230; mechanisms used in, 227; meetings, 228; reasons for conducting, 226–227; rewards and, 230; structured approach to, 227

Quality healthcare, 37

"Question" retreat, 75

Reactor panels, 78–79

Regional Health System's strategic plan: critical issues and goals of, 157, 159; critical issues and key metrics for goals of, 157, 159, 160; current and desired future state of, 157, 158–159; environmental factors driving need for change and, 198; example prioritization of five-year initiatives of, 161–162, 162; goals for five-year planning horizon of, 199; initiatives to achieve goals, summary of, 200; metrics for measuring progress of, 201; mission, vision, and values of, 198–199; organizational direction of, 198–199; strategy recommendations of, 160, 161

Regulatory considerations: in financial-planning process, 258; in physician enterprise, 325–327

Request for proposal (RFP), 302

Research approaches, 76–79; focus groups, 78; interviews, 77; reactor panels, 78–79; surveys, 77–78

Resources: for data gathering and analysis, 103–107; lack of, in strategic execution, 222; for online healthcare data, *106*

Revenue: estimates of, 258; impact of goals and initiatives on, 260–261

RFP. *See* Request for proposal

Scenario planning, 93–94

Senior management, in strategic planning, 80–81

Sensitivity analyses, 254, 262

"Seven deadly sins . . . that doom effective strategy implementation," 175–76

Shaw, George Bernard, 249

SHSMD. *See* Society for Health Care Strategy & Market Development

Social determinants of health, 41, 43

Society for Health Care Strategy & Market Development (SHSMD), 211, 245–46

Sony, vision statement of, *144*

Stakeholders: board members, 79; failing to involve, 11; interviews, in data gathering and analysis, 105, 107; involvement of, 79–83; leadership roles, 57–58; other clinicians, 81; other management, 81; participation grid, 81–82, *82*;

physicians, 79–80; senior management, 80–81

Stanford University, vision statement of, *144*

Stark Law, 326–27

Strategic arrangements, 296

Strategic assessment, 7, *8*, 101–29; in annual review and update, 210–11; assumptions about the future and, 120, 121, 122–25, *124*, *125*; baseline scenario and, 259; competitive advantages and disadvantages and, 117–20, *121*, *122*; critical planning issues and, 125, 126–29, *127*, *128*, 151–53, *152*; data gathering for, 103–6, *104*, *106*; external assessment and, *102*, 110–16; goal of, 7; governance and, 340–41; illustrated, *102*; increasing competitiveness and, addressing, 285–86; innovation in, 271; internal assessment and, *102*, 107–10; needed services provided in, 42; the physician enterprise and, 320, 325; processes of, 7, 103; purpose of, 101–3; questions considered in, 285–86; questions examined by, 103; relevant historical data assembled for, 61; in strategic planning process, 271; value-based care and, 316–17

Strategic financial planning, 253–64; key elements of, 254–57, *255*; process of (*See* Financial-planning process)

Strategic governance, 334

Strategic mode of governing, 334

Strategic plan document: examples of, *186–87, 190*; preparing the draft, 184–85

Strategic plan financial analysis (example), 173; baseline operating income estimates, 173, *173*; financial impact from initiatives, 173, *174*

Strategic planner: areas of future emphasis for, 246; future challenges for, 241–249; key contributors to success and failure for, *248*; new, 245–49; roles of, 246–247; state of the art in healthcare strategy and, 241–44

Strategic planning: approaches to, 6–7, *8*; benefits of, 25–47; board review and approval of plan, 184–90; chief executive officers in, 55–56; communication in organizing for, 51–55, *52*; community benefits of, 41–46, *44*; competition and, intensifying, 277–86; criticisms of, 9–11; definitions of, 5–6; execution, enabling more effective, 221–38; financial benefits of, 30, 32–35, *33*; future challenges for strategic planners, 241–49; governance and, 331–41; in healthcare, 15–21, *18*; health equity and, 43, 45; innovation and, 265–275; literature

on, review of, 132–134; market benefits of, 27–28, *29*; mindset in organizing for, 62–64; moving to strategic management from, 226, *235*, 235–38; operational benefits of, 35–41, *38*; organizing for success, 51–65; partnerships, mergers, and affiliations in, 287–304; physician alignment and, 30; physician enterprise and, 319–329; planning process considerations in, 67–84; problems of, 9–13; product benefits of, 28, *29, 31*; senior management in, 80–81; stages of, 7–8; state of the art in healthcare strategy and, 241–44; strategic financial planning, 253–64; strategic thinking and (*See* Strategic thinking); value-based care in, 305–18; value of, 3–21. *See also* Healthcare strategic planning; Management, in strategic planning; Stakeholders

Strategic planning process: annual review and update in, 203–17; phase 1: analyzing the environment, 101–29; phase 2: organizational direction, 131–46; phase 3: strategy formulation, 149–65, 167–71, 173–74; phase 4: transition to implementation, 175–95, 197–201

Strategic thinking, 85–97; for avoiding mimicry, 63–64; blue ocean strategy and, *95*, 95–97,

US Department of Health and Human Services (DHHS), 43, 45
US Digestive Health, 282
University Health System (UHS), 37–38
University Hospital (New Jersey), vision statement of, *144*

Value, in healthcare strategic planning, 34
Value-based care, 305–18; accountable care organizations and, 314; background of, 306–8; clinically integrated networks and, 314; description of, 308–9; health systems and, 311–13; inaction and, 315; payment models, 309–11; physician enterprise and, 321–22, 329; providers and, 313–14; shifting to, 311–15; in strategic plan, 315–17

Values statements: development of, 139–41; examples of, *141*; organizational direction and, 134, 136–37, 139–41
Vermeulen, Freek, 85, 91–92
Vertical PM&A activity, 290
VillageMD, 283
Virtual mergers, 299
Vision statements: characteristics of, 142–45; concepts of, *143*; development of, 141–45; examples of, *144*; organizational direction and, 133, 140, 141–46; revising, 136–37
Volume, impact of goals and initiatives on, 260

Walmart Health Centers, 283
Welch, Jack, 131
World Medical Association, 43

About the Editors and Contributing Authors

John M. Harris, MBA, is managing director for strategy and planning at Veralon, a healthcare management consulting firm. He has over 35 years of healthcare experience in consulting, management, and entrepreneurship. His work focuses on strategy, the transition to value-based payment, and partnerships, mergers, and acquisitions. He has consulted to hospitals and health systems, accountable care organizations, clinically integrated networks, physician organizations, health plans, and human services organizations.

John is a faculty member of the American College of Healthcare Executives (ACHE) and regularly conducts seminars on strategic planning and the future of healthcare. He is also a frequent speaker at national conferences on the strategic issues faced by hospitals, health systems, and physicians and the future of value-based care. He is coeditor of the fifth edition of this book.

Meredith C. Inniger, MHA, FACHE, a principal with Veralon, has over 15 years of healthcare experience in consulting and healthcare operations. She advises many types of healthcare organizations nationally, including academic medical centers, large community health systems, and independent hospitals. Her work focuses on strategic planning (including service line, ambulatory care, and partnership planning), governance, and board development.

Meredith is a fellow and faculty member of the American College of Healthcare Executives, where she teaches courses on strategic planning and the future of healthcare. She currently serves on the board for the Philadelphia chapter of ACHE and has been the recipient of ACHE's Early Career Healthcare Executive Award, Administrative Achievement Award, and Service Award. In addition to serving as coeditor of the fifth edition of this book, she is a contributing author to chapter 15, "Intensifying Competition," and chapter 19, "Governance."

The following members of Veralon contributed chapters to this book:

Danielle Bangs, MHA, a director with Veralon, has more than 10 years of experience in healthcare consulting and corporate development, working with health systems, behavioral health providers, and large physician groups. Her work focuses on mergers and acquisitions, joint ventures, and other transactions, including partner selection, partnership development and deal structuring, negotiation, and process facilitation. She is a contributing author to chapter 16, "Partnerships, Mergers, and Affiliations."

Mark Dubow, MSPH, MBA, a director with Veralon, is a national expert in strategy and innovation with more than 30 years of consulting experience. In addition to strategy, he focuses on enhancing the effectiveness of clinical service lines and ambulatory and post–acute care development. Mark has taught courses for ACHE since 1999 and has authored more than 30 articles. He is a contributing author to chapter 14, "Innovation," and chapter 15, "Intensifying Competition."

Daniel M. Grauman, MBA, CPA/ABV, is managing director and CEO of Veralon. He has more than 40 years of experience with clients including health systems, hospitals, physician-hospital organizations, clinically integrated networks, and health plans. His current work focuses on mergers and affiliations, business valuation, due diligence, and transaction support. He frequently presents to national and regional healthcare organizations. He has published numerous articles in national publications, in addition to authoring for the Healthcare Financial Management Association. He is a contributing author to chapter 16, "Partnerships, Mergers, and Affiliations."

Molly Johnson, MHSA, a consultant with Veralon, has more than 15 years of experience in the healthcare field, with a special focus on value-based payment, including development of clinically integrated networks and development of strategy for existing networks. Molly has authored several articles and is a regular industry speaker. She is a contributing author to chapter 17, "Value-Based Care."

Karin Chernoff Kaplan, MBA, CVA, a managing director with Veralon, has more than 30 years of experience in healthcare consulting and management. Karin is an expert in physician compensation, professional service agreements, and co-management agreements, speaking nationally on these topics. Karin is a Certified Valuation Analyst of the National Association of Certified Valuators and Analysts. She is a contributing author to chapter 18, "Physician Enterprise."

Rudd Kierstead, MBA/MPP, a director with Veralon, brings 25 years of experience in a range of provider settings to his work on strategic physician initiatives. He has focused on enterprise performance improvement, medical staff planning, financial analysis, physician alignment, compensation planning, acquisition and employment analysis, and fair market value projects. He is a contributing author to chapter 18, "Physician Enterprise."

Clare O'Mara, MHA, MSG, a manager with Veralon, supports Veralon clients across a wide range of Veralon's service offerings, with a concentration in market analysis, utilization forecasts, and financial modeling. Her experience and expertise support strategic and business planning, feasibility studies, and expansion engagements.

She has worked with a wide range of healthcare entities and is a contributing author to chapter 13, "Strategic Financial Planning."

Ross Shuster, MHM, a principal with Veralon, has experience in both consulting and provider settings. He supports clients in financial and other business planning efforts including long-range financial planning, feasibility studies for hospital remodeling and expansion, and ambulatory care engagements. Ross also assists organizations with medical staff planning and demand forecasting. He is a contributing author to chapter 13, "Strategic Financial Planning."

Keith Wysocki, a manager with Veralon, has almost 15 years of experience advising and educating healthcare organizations on governance issues, including board structure and effectiveness, organizational alignment, governance efficiency, and the role of the board in meeting new challenges. He is a contributing author to chapter 19, "Governance."